Sutra of the Wise and the Foolish

(mdo mdzangs blun)

or

Ocean of Narratives

(üliger-ün dalai)

Translated from the Mongolian

by

Stanley Frye

LIBRARY OF TIBETAN WORKS & ARCHIVES

First Published in 1981
Second Edition: 2000

ISBN: 81-85102-15-5

Published by the Library of Tibetan Works & Archives, Dharamsala, H.P. 176215 India, and printed at the Indraprastha Press, CBT, 4, Bahadurshah Zafar Marg, New Delhi-110002.

Publisher's Note

The *Sutra of the Wise and the Foolish* (mdo mdzangs blun) also known as *Ocean of Narratives* (üliger-ün dalai) is one of the most popular Buddhist scriptures concerning the previous lives of the Buddha. Translated widely into Chinese, Tibetan, Mongolian and Oirat etc., these tales have been widely read in every Buddhist country for its universal appeal in explaining the *Karmic* relationship of human tragedy and triumph, happiness and sorrow.

This is the first translation from Mongolian that the Library of Tibetan Works & Archives is publishing. As a mine of Buddhist and specifically Tibetan Buddhist literature is available in Mongolian, we hope that this Library would be able to cooperate in further translation and publication of similar works. We also congratulate Dr. Stanley Frye for his excellent translation of the *Sutra of the Wise and the Foolish* and hope that all readers of this work will earn much merit and benefit from reading this.

Publication Department
Library of Tibetan Works & Archives
July 2000

Contents

❦

Foreword

❦

One of the great treasures of Buddhist literature which have come down to us in Tibetan translation is the Do-dzang-lün (*mDo-mdzangs-blun*) or the *Sutra of the Wise and the Foolish*, known to the Mongols, into whose language it was translated from Tibetan, as the *Uliger-un dalai* or *Ocean of Narratives*. The history of this unusual scripture is still uncertain, e.g. we are not sure whether there ever was a Sanskrit or Prakrit original (none has yet been found), though legend telling us that the tales were heard in Khotan by Chinese monks who translated them (but from what language?) into Chinese from which language it was translated into Tibetan, thence into Mongolian and Oirat. Whatever the history of the Sutra may be, it is one of the most interesting, enjoyable and readable of Buddhist scriptures and has for centuries been an inexhaustible source of inspiration, instruction and pleasure for all who have been able to read it.

The narratives (of which the Tibetan version has fifty-one, the Mongolian fifty-two) are Jātakas or rebirth stories whose purpose is to trace the causes of present tragedy in human lives to events which took place in former lifetimes. The theme of each Narrative is the same: the tragedy of the human condition, the reason for this tragedy and the possibility of transcending it. It might be of interest to point out here that unlike Greek tragedy, Buddhist tragedy is never an end in itself, i.e. a catharsis, but a call to transcend that which can be transcended and need not be endlessly endured.

The people we meet in the Narratives, although supposedly living in the India of the Buddha's time, might also be living at present in New York City, a small midwestern town or Leningrad and the problems they face are the same problems that men have had to face always and everywhere. We see two thieves on their way to receive punishment for their misdeeds, a clergyman wavering in his faith and vows, an agriculturalist who has lost his neighbor's property, orphans deprived of their inheritance, a man in so deep a depression that he considers suicide, unjust confiscation of property by the state—the entire human tragedy. But whereas we of today would be likely to turn for relief to a psycho-analyst or the law, the people in the Narratives seek the Buddha or one of his disciples who, through wisdom and compassion, show that a change of thought-processes can bring about a change in circumstances, i.e. when the eye of prajna is opened and insight into the true nature of things are seen, things themselves change and are not what they seem. This is certainly the underlying message of the Sutra and the reason why generations of Tibetans and Mongols have read and re-read it.

But the Sutra contains much more, and great adventure awaits the reader, adventure no less amazing than that which we read in modern science fiction. We travel through outer space at a speed faster than light, visit other worlds and realms of the universe where there are beings of a quite different order than humans, see shining beings descend to our earth and converse with man, meet sub-human species of beings and other unusual creatures. Amazing illumination appears and astonishing sounds become audible. Matter changes its form before our very eyes and time, as we know it, ceases to exist and loses all meaning: at one moment we are standing on the banks of an Indian river, in a second we have travelled back countless kotis of kalpas of time and are watching events take place in worlds of which we have no record or name. One is tempted to wonder whether the compilers of the Narratives were writing science fiction two thousand years in advance, or whether it might not be possible that the science fiction writers of today are catching glimpses, albeit faint ones, of a different order of reality, one which the Buddhist have always claimed (and still claim) is there "for those who have eyes to see."

Not the least of the charms of the Narratives is the gentle humor which occasionally peeps out from between the lines. Somehow one cannot help but feel that when the monk Majestic Being, after going through a shattering psychic experience which shook him to his very foundations and transformed him from a self-pitying old man into an Arhat, comes before the Buddha and the Buddha asks him: "Well, Majestic Being, have you been to the seashore? and the monk replies: "Yes, Lord, I have indeed been to the seashore"—that the Buddha's eyes twinkled and that Majestic Being came close to a chuckle which the other monks would hardly have understood. The ghastly scene in which a wealthy society matron, shrieking in uncontrolled rage, orders the corpse of her pilfering old maid-servant (because the latter had deceived her, even in death) dragged out of her apartment with a rope, would certainly provide high comedy if seen on the stage. The Narratives are not funny stories any more than the other scriptures, but the element of humor is unquestionably there.

Whenever we read the Narratives to gain instruction, knowledge and enlightenment (which it is the function of the scriptures to give), or whether we read them for other reasons, it must always be remembered that the compilation is a do (*mdo*) or Sutra in the original meaning of a cord or thread upon which are strung the precious jewels of the Enlightened One's teaching. Like the fool (lun, *blun*), we may miss what is important if we become infatuated with the unimportant. This, ofcourse, the dzang-pa (*mdzangs-pa*) or intellectual man will not do.

The *Ocean of Narratives* has long been known to Western scholars. The Dutch-Russian scholar, I.J. Schmidt translated the entire Sutra into German in the 19th century. Jāschke was thoroughly acquainted with its contents and used its vocabulary extensively for his Tibetan-German, then Tibetan-English dictionary and Das, in his dictionary, repeats these entries. It has been mentioned by almost all Mongolists and is found in all the great Western collections and catalogues. From time to time fragments of translation have appeared in English (e.g. by Professor John R. Krueger in *The Mongolia Society Occasional Papers*, No. 4, Bloomington, 1967 and by Geshe Wangyal in his *Door of Liberation*, New York, 1967), but a complete English translation of this unusual scripture has long been overdue.

The present translation of the Do-dzang-lun was made from the Mongolian translation of the Tibetan, which differs from the original in only a few minor details. The translation is, admittedly, tentative as there exists as yet no good dictionary of Mongolian Buddhist terminology. Most of the proper names, it is believed, have been correctly returned to Sanskrit, although the name of the custodian monk, Paladi, transliterated straight from the Mongolian *galik* letters, is doubtful. The xylograph used is the Peking edition of 1714 which was graciously sent to the translator several years ago by Professor Luvsanvandan of the State University, Ulan Bator, Mongolian People's Republic.

Stanley Frye

1

The Beginning of the Narratives

Thus have I heard at one time: when the Victorious, Perfectly-Departed Enlightened One had entered the great realm of victory and had achieved Supreme Enlightenment, he dwelt in the land of Magadha. And the thought came to him: "Of what benefit can I be to the beings of this world who have long been blinded by false views which are difficult to correct? It would be better to attain final Nirvana."

The deities of the realm of Brahmā, perceiving the thoughts of the Blessed One, descended from their realm, prostrated themselves at his feet, folded their palms in devotion, and pleaded with him to turn the Wheel of the Law.

The Blessed One spoke to them: "Deities of the Brahmā realm, these beings are obstructed by burrowing in the defilements. They are given to the pleasures of the world. As they have no perfect thought of wisdom, while they are in this world there is no help for them. For this reason I shall enter final Nirvana."

Again the deities of the Brahmā realm pleaded: "Lord, the Ocean of the Law has been filled. The Banner of the Law has been furled. The time has come to make known the Law. Now that there are many beings to be saved, what is the reason that the Lord refuses to do this and wishes to enter final Nirvana? Have compassion on these beings who are blinded by great ignorance and become a refuge to them, we beseech you.

"Countless aeons ago, Lord, you were born on this earth as an emperor by the name of Kaśapala. This emperor had subject to him many kings, wives, princes, eighty-four thousand cities, and twenty thousand palaces. Because of his loving compassion the emperor was revered as a father by all his subjects.

"One day the emperor thought: 'Because I am the leader of all these people who love and trust me, I shall benefit them with the precious jewel of the Divine Law.'

"He then issued a proclamation, saying: 'To whomever can instruct me in the Divine Law I shall give whatever he asks.'

"At that time a Brahmin teacher by the name of Liu Ciunche came to the palace gate and said: 'If the Divine Law is required, I possess it.'

"When the emperor heard this, he and all his retinue went out to greet the Brahmin. They placed him on a dais, bowed, folded their palms in reverence, and said: 'Great teacher, you have come to teach us, who are blinded by ignorance, the Divine Law.'

"The Brahmin said: 'Your Majesty, the Law which I teach is not easy to learn, nor can it be cheaply obtained.'

"The emperor replied: 'Teacher, only speak, and whatever it is that you wish I shall command to be given you.'

"The Brahmin said: 'Your Majesty, if you sufficiently desire the Law to offer your own body as a sacrifice, to have it pierced with a thousand shafts and burnt with torches, I shall consent to teach the Law.'

"The emperor accepted with joy and sent a courier with a mighty voice to all the lands of the continent of Jambudvīpa to proclaim to the princes and the people that within seven days he would make a sacrifice of his body for the sake of the Divine Law, that it would be pierced with a thousand shafts and burnt with torches.

"Hearing this proclamation, the princes and people were overcome with grief. Coming before the emperor, they knelt and pleaded:

" 'Your Majesty, just as the blind depend upon those who can see, as infants depend upon their mothers, so do we depend upon you. Your Majesty, if you die we shall have no one on whom to depend. If your body is burnt with a thousand torches, you will certainly be separated from life. Will you abandon all these beings in the world for the sake of a single Brahmin?' And with folded palms, the emperor's wives, his five-hundred children, and a thousand of the nobles besought him to renounce the sacrifice.

"Then the emperor spoke with firm resolution: 'People, do not obstruct me! When Perfect Enlightenment has been obtained, I shall, without fail, deliver you.' Hearing the emperor's resolve, the people fell to the ground in great grief, sobbing.

"The emperor then said to the Brahmin: 'I am ready to have my body pierced and burnt with a thousand torches.' When he said: 'Pierce my body,' the Brahmin pierced the emperor's body and plunged the torches into the oil. When the people saw this, they fell to the ground like a great mountain when it collapses.

"The emperor then spoke to the Brahmin: 'Teacher, first teach me the Law, then burn me with the torches. Otherwise I shall be unable to hear the Law.'

"The Brahmin then spoke the following verses:

> 'All component things disintegrate.
> What rises must fall.
> All meetings end in separation.
> What is born must die.'

"The emperor rejoiced, and without a single thought of regret said: 'This is the Law which I have sought, the Perfect Enlightenment which I would have made known. I vow that when I shall have attained to Perfect Enlightenment I will, with the Light of Transcendental Wisdom, give light to all those who are blinded by ignorance.'

"When he had uttered these words, the heavens trembled and the palaces of the divinities in the pure lands shook. The divinities descended, and seeing the broken body of the bodhisattva-king, wept a rain of tears and made offerings of showers of flowers.

"Then Indra, the ruler of the gods, approached the emperor, lauded him in many ways, and said:

" 'Great Emperor,—these terrible sufferings! Do you have no thought of regret?'

"The Emperor replied: 'There is no regret.'

"Again Indra spoke: 'Your Majesty, when one sees your body thus trembling in agony, it is difficult to believe that you have no thought of regret.'

"The emperor replied: 'There is no regret.'

"Again Indra spoke: 'Your Majesty, when one sees your body thus trembling in agony, it is difficult to believe that you have no thought of regret.'

"The emperor said: 'If there is not one single thought of regret within my entire body, may these wounds be healed.'

"And immediately the emperor's body became whole.

"Lord, at that time it was you who was that emperor. Long ago, Lord, you experienced limitless suffering in order to obtain the Divine Law for all beings. Why is it that you now abandon them to obtain final Nirvana?

"Again, Lord, long, long ago you were born in this Jambudvīpa as a great king called Byin-ling-kar-li. This king had subject to him many princes, eighty-four thousand cities, many wives, and twenty thousand palaces. He had five-hundred sons and ten thousand ministers. In his great compassion, he looked upon each of his subjects as an only son.

"At one time this great king, believing in and desiring the Divine Law, made the proclamation: 'Whoever will deign to instruct me in the Divine Law, to him I shall gladly grant whatsoever he desires.'

"One day a Brahmin named Leu Du Ci appeared at the palace gate and said: 'If there is someone here who wishes to hear the Divine Law, I will teach it.'

"When the king heard this, he went out to meet the Brahmin with great joy and devotion. He bowed at his feet, praised him with kind words, invited him into the palace, prepared a dais for him to sit on, folded his palms in reverence, and said: 'I beseech the great teacher to teach the Divine Law.'

"The Brahmin said: 'I have had to endure great sufferings in order to learn the Law. If you, Your Majesty, wish to learn it, the cost will be great.'

"Pressing his palms together in reverence, the king replied: 'Teacher, whatever you command shall be done.'

"The Brahmin said: 'If this be so, Your Majesty, then only after a thousand iron spikes have been driven into your body shall I teach the Law.'

"For seven days the king issued a proclamation and sent out a messenger with a mighty voice riding an elephant and announcing to all Jambudvīpa that within seven days the king's body would be pierced with a thousand iron spikes.

"When the people heard this, they all came to the king and said: 'Oh, King, we who come from the four directions have been greatly happy, each in his own land, because of your wisdom and kindness. We now beseech you to have pity on us and to renounce this evil deed of allowing your body to be pierced with a thousand iron spikes.'

"Then the queens and the princes and all the ministers said: 'Your Majesty, what is this lack of compassion? Why, for the sake of one man do you allow your body to be broken? Why do you abandon your people?'

"The king replied: 'Through passion, anger, and ignorance in former cycles of birth I created sins without number with this body. My bones from former deaths are piled higher than Mt. Sumeru. I have shed more blood than the five great rivers can hold by having mens' head cut off. I have shed more tears than the four great oceans can contain. In various ways I have created great demerit with this body. Now, by my body being pierced with spikes, may Supreme Enlightenment be realized. When I shall have attained to Perfect Supreme Enlightenment, I shall cut away all the ills of your defilements with the sword of wisdom. Then you will ask why you tried to obstruct me.'

"When all the people remained silent, the king said to the Brahmin: 'Great Teacher, first compassionately teach me the Law, then pierce me with the spikes. If I do not hear the Law, I shall die.'

"The Brahmin then recited this verse:

'All compounded things are impermanent.
All that is born is subject to suffering.
All the elements of becoming are empty and without self.
What is called the self does not exist.'

"Having said this, he drove a thousand spikes into the body of the king. When the princes and nobles and all the people saw this, they fell to earth moaning like a great mountain when it collapses.

"At that moment the heavens shook in six ways and the divinities in the realm of desire and those in the realm of form marvelled greatly. They descended to the bodhisattva-king and seeing his body, wept a rain of tears in great pity and made offerings of flowers.

"Then Indra, lord of the gods, approached the king and said: 'Great King, in order to achieve what end are you undergoing this terrible suffering? Is this for the sake of the Law, or do you wish to become endowed with the might of an Indra, of a universal monarch, a Māra-king, a Brahmā-king, or a Maheśvara!'

"The king answered: 'This deed of mine has not been done to obtain happiness in the three worlds. It has been done to attain Supreme Enlightenment.'

"Indra asked: 'Your Majesty, while your body is suffering thus, have you no feeling of regret?'

"The king replied: 'There is no thought of regret.'

"Indra said: 'Seeing your body trembling thus, who could believe that you have no regrets?'

"The king replied: 'If what I have just said is true, and if I truly have no thoughts of regret, may my body again become whole as it was before.'

"And immediately the king's body became whole and the divinities and men believed and rejoiced.

And again they said to the Buddha: "Lord, you have filled the Ocean of the Law with countless virtues. Why do you now totally abandon all beings and enter final Nirvana without teaching the Law?

"Again, Lord, inconceivable, countless aeons ago you were born in this Jambudvīpa as the son of an emperor called Brahmādeva. This prince, desiring the Divine Law, sought it in all directions, but being unable to obtain it, became depressed and despondent. The lord of the gods, Indra, knowing the mind of the prince, transformed himself into a Brahmin, and coming to the gates of the palace, spoke thus: 'I have the Divine Law. If it is required, I will teach it.'

"The prince, hearing these words, bowed at the teacher's feet, invited him into the palace, placed him on a dais, folded his palms in reverence, and said: 'Great teacher, compassionately teach me the Divine Law, I beseech you.'

"The Brahmin said: 'This teaching is exceedingly difficult to learn. Even though one strives, it is hard to find a teacher. You cannot learn it cheaply. If you truly wish to hear the Law, know that it can be done only with great difficulty.'

"The prince replied: 'Great teacher, whatever thing you desire I shall gladly give you, even my own body, my wife, my sons and daughters. Only consent to teach the Law.'

"The Brahmin said: 'If you are able to prepare a pit of fire ten cubits deep and burn yourself in it, I shall teach the Law.'

"In accordance with the Brahmin's words, the prince had the fire pit prepared. The emperor, the empress, and all the nobles, realizing what was going to take place, were grief-stricken. Going to the prince's palace, they circumambulated him and the Brahmin and begged: 'Oh, divine teacher, have compassion on us all. We beseech you not to burn our prince. In his place we offer you our lands, our wives, our children, even our own bodies.'

"The Brahmin said: 'I have no need of such things. If the prince can do as I have said, I will teach the Law. If he cannot, then I will not.'

"The Brahmin then remained silent and all those who were gathered there knew that he had sworn an irrevocable oath.

"Then the emperor sent out a mighty-voiced courier to all the continent of Jambudvīpa who announced that within several days the prince, desiring the Law, would sacrifice his body in a pit of fire. All were to present themselves immediately.

"Then the princes and all the people, even the old and the weak, sadly came, one by one, to the prince, kneeled, pressed their palms together, and in one voice pleaded: 'Oh, Prince, we all rely upon you. You are father and mother to us. If you are burnt in this pit of fire, who will then be our protector and refuge? Why do you abandon your people for the sake of a single person?'

"The prince answered: 'Listen to me. During countless former births, while circling in the round of birth and death, born as a human-being, I did great evil by angrily participating in killing. When I obtained birth among the gods, I experienced the sufferings of death and was deprived of happiness. When born in the hells, I underwent suffering by being burnt in fire, boiled in a cauldron, cut and chopped with swords and sabres. I was made to climb mountains of sharp knives, to swim in poisonous waters, and more, too. I have undergone limitless suffering. I have experienced sickness which reduces one to bones. Born as a hungry ghost, I suffered beyond belief. Born as an animal, I was forced to carry burdens until I was exhausted, nor could I find remedies to heal my wounds. Times without number have I suffered torture and death. Evil was done with this body. I have done nothing with thoughts of virtue for the sake of the Divine Law. Do not, now, obstruct me in establishing a thought of Supreme Enlightenment. In order to realize Buddhahood I shall make a perfect offering of this body. When I shall have attained Supreme Enlightenment, I shall give you gifts with the Dharma-Body.'

"The people remained silent and the prince approached the pit of fire and stood at its edge. He then said to the Brahmin: 'Great Teacher, first teach me the Law, I beseech you. If I die in the fire I shall be unable to hear it.'

The Brahmin then spoke the following verses:

'Meditate on thoughts of love.
Cut off thoughts of anger and hatred.
In great compassion, aid beings.
Mercifully forgive all.

Meditate on the Great Joy.
Be in harmony with others.
When with the Mind of Enlightenment one teaches the
    Dharma,
The bodhisattva course is realized.'

"When these words had been spoken and the prince was about to leap into the fiery pit, Brahmā and Indra, ashamed, held him back and said: 'By your merits all the beings in Jambudvīpa have been made happy. If you are now burned in the fire, all the common people will be deprived of their father and mother. Why do you enter the fire and bereave these beings?'

"Seeing the lords of the gods and all the people, the prince answered: 'While I am bringing forth the thought of Supreme Enlightenment, do not obstruct me.'

"When the prince entered the pit of fire, the firmament trembled greatly and the gods in the heavens wept and sent down showers of tears. The pit of fire was transformed into a palace of flowers and the prince was seen sitting on a lotus. The gods sent down a rain of flowers that reached the people's knees.

"At that time King Śuddhodana was that King Brahmadeva, and you, Lord, were that prince. Oh, Enlightened One and Teacher, at that time you, out of compassion for all beings, sought the Law. Now having attained Supreme Enlightenment, why do you say that it would be better if you entered final Nirvana without enlightening all the beings who are blinded by ignorance?

"Again, Lord countless aeons ago, there lived in Benares five-hundred sages with their teacher, Udpala. Udpala wandered here and there in search of the Divine Law to learn and meditate upon and at one time proclaimed: 'If anyone can teach me the Divine Law, I shall become his slave.'

"A Brahmin teacher, hearing these words, said: 'I have the Divine Law. If you require it, I will teach it to you.'

"The sage bowed low before the Brahmin, pressed his palms together in reverence, and said: 'Great Teacher, have compassion on me and teach me the Law.'

"The Brahmin answered: 'It is exceedingly difficult to learn the Divine Law. I have learned it only by enduring great sufferings. If you wish to learn the True Law, will you do as I command?'

"When the sage answered: 'Great Teacher, command, and I shall obey,' the Brahmin said: 'Cut off your skin and make paper. Make ink of your blood, and write the Law. Then I shall teach it to you.'

"With great joy and devotion the sage, in reverence for the Law of the Enlightened Ones, flayed his skin, made a pen from his bones, and mixed his blood into ink. Then he said: 'The time has come, Teacher, quickly teach me the Law and I shall write it.'

"The Brahmin teacher then spoke these two verses:

'Control the acts of the body.
Do not passionately desire the thief who destroys the mind.
Do not speak false, harsh, or thoughtless words.
Do not abandon yourself to desire.

Cut off thoughts of anger.
When all wrong views are cut off...
This is the Supreme.
This is the course of the bodhisattvas.'

"When the sage had written these verses, he was glorified throughout all Jambudvīpa and men endeavored with great zeal to learn
what he had taught and to cut off evil deeds. It was you, Lord, who
at that time, with no thoughts of regret, underwent great suffering
to find the Law for the sake of many beings. What now is the
reason that, abandoning all beings, the Lord refuses to teach the
Law and says that it would be better to enter final Nirvana?

"Again, Lord countless, numberless aeons ago you were born
in this Jambudvīpa as a king called Sibsen. This king had a palace
called Pardi and countless possessions. He was the master of all
Jambudvīpa and had subject to him eighty-four thousand princes,
sixty-thousand nobles, eighty-thousand cities and towns, and sixty-
thousand palaces. He had five-hundred sons and a thousand great
ministers. Now, while this king was reigning with great compassion and benevolence, Indra, the lord of the gods, was losing the
five virtues of his body, was drawing nigh to death, and suffered
greatly. Viśvakarman, the craftsman of the gods, seeing his great
suffering, asked him the cause. Indra said: 'I am approaching death.
The signs of death have become manifest. The Law of the Enlightened Ones has disappeared. The bodhisattvas do not reside in the
world and because there is no one in whom to seek refuge, I suffer
and am tormented.'

"Viśvakarman said: 'Oh, Indra, at present there dwells in the
world a man who follows the bodhisattva path whose name is King
Sibsen. This king is unshakable and through great endeavor is indeed realizing Supreme Enlightenment. Should you seek refuge in
him, he will certainly save you from death and you will attain
peace.'

"Indra said: 'This may be true, but first we must ascertain
whether or not the king is really a bodhisattva. In order to do this,
you, Viśvakarman, transform yourself into a dove. I shall change
myself into a falcon and pursue you. When we enter the king's
palace we will know the true nature of the king.'

"Viśvakarman said: 'Indra, even with the cleverest of ruses it will be impossible to deceive the bodhisattva-king.' Thereupon he changed himself into a dove and Indra, transforming himself into a falcon, pursued him. In great terror the dove flew into the king's palace and hid himself under the king's arm, crying: 'Oh, King, save my life!'

"The falcon flew into the palace and addressed the king: 'Your Majesty, this dove is mine. It is my food. I request you to return it to me immediately, for I am perishing with hunger.'

"The king said: 'I have pledged to save the life of all who take refuge with me. I cannot give you the dove.'

"The falcon said: Your Majesty, if you save every living thing from death, you will take all my food from me. I shall become helpless and die.'

"The king said: 'If I give you other meat to eat, will you eat it?'

"The falcon answered: 'I require freshly-killed meat.'

"The king thought to himself: 'If I were to give the falcon freshly-killed meat I should have to take life and this would create sin. How many living beings would have to sacrifice their lives! I can only give him the flesh from my own body.'

"Then, with a sharp knife, he cut flesh from his own thigh and gave it to the falcon. When he had thus saved the life of the dove, the falcon said: 'Oh, King, you are indeed the master of charity, but the flesh you have given me is not equal to the dove. Weigh the dove and more of your flesh on a pair of scales and give me that flesh, I beg you.'

"The king commanded that scales be brought and on one pan he placed the dove and on the other he put more flesh which he cut from his thigh. As this did not balance with the dove, he cut flesh from his shoulders, from his ribs, and finally from his entire body, but even this did not balance with the dove.

"As he was preparing to put his entire body on the scales, he began to faint and lose consciousness. Then, suddenly taking thought, his mind reproached itself: 'Oh mind, since beginningless time while wandering in the three worlds I have undergone every kind of suffering and no merit has been achieved. Now, mind, your hour has come! This is not the time for shirking!'

"Saying this, he reproached his mind in many ways and, with great effort, arose and place his body on the scales. Then, in great joy, he realized that his mind was at peace.

"The heavens trembled and shook in six different ways. The palaces of the gods trembled and shook. The gods in the realm of form and all the divinities went to the highest heaven and watched. Seeing the bodhisattva-king give his body for the Law, they wept and sent down showers of tears and flowers as offerings.

"Then Indra, lord of the gods, assumed his own form and said to the king: 'Your Majesty, what birth is it you wish to obtain by undergoing this agony? Do you wish to become a universal monarch, an Indra, a Māra-king? Do you desire the powers of the three worlds? What is it you wish?'

"The king answered: 'My desire has nothing to do with the pleasures of the three worlds. I seek Supreme Enlightenment.'

"Indra said: 'With your body and bones thus trembling in agony, certainly you must have some thought of regret.'

"The king replied: 'There are no thoughts of regret.'

"Indra said: 'Seeing your body trembling and unable to return to life, who could believe what you say?'

"The king said: 'Within my entire body, from head to foot, there is no single thought of regret so large as a hair. My desire certainly will be fulfilled. And if my words are true, may these wounds on my body be healed.'

"And immediately the king's wounds were healed and his body became more lovely than before. And all the beings in the realms of the gods were astonished and rejoiced and worshipped.

You, Lord, were that king by the name of Sibsen. It was you, Lord, who in aeons long past offered your body for the welfare of all sentient beings. Now, Lord, you have filled the Ocean of the Law, have furled the Banner of the Law, have beaten the Drum of the Law, have lighted the Lamp of the Law. Now that the time to help living beings has come, why does the Lord refuse to teach the Dharma, abandoning all creatures, and saying that it would be better if he entered final Nirvana?

"Then Brahmā, coming before the Enlightened One and folding his palms in reverence, lauded and praised him, saying:

"'Lord, as in times long past you gave your head a thousand times for the sake of beings and sought the Law, I implore you to turn the Wheel of the Law for the sake of all beings.'"

Then the Victorious Buddha proceeded to Benares, and at a place called the Deer Park turned the Wheel of the Law.

And thus with the Turning of the Wheel of the Law, the Three Precious Treasures became manifest in the world. And when the Law was taught, the gods, men, nāgas, yakśas, asuras, and all the eight classes of living beings rejoiced, believed, applauded, and approved.

2

Prince Mahāsattva Gives his Body to the Tigress

❦

Thus have I heard at one time: The Enlightened One was residing in the city of Śrāvastī at the Jetavana monastery in Anāthapiṇḍika's park. At the time of the alms-round he put on his upper and lower robes, took his alms bowl, and went with Ānanda to seek alms.

At that time there was an old woman in the city who had two sons who were thieves. A property owner had apprehended them and at that moment was taking them to the magistrate for punishment. On the way to the place of execution the thieves' mother saw the Buddha from a distance, prostrated herself in his direction, and cried out: "Oh Lord, god of gods, in great compassion save, I beseech you, the lives of my two sons!" Hearing her cry from afar, the Buddha had pity and in order to save boys' lives, said to Ānanda: "Ānanda, go to the king and beg for the lives of these boys." Ānanda went to the king, made his request, and the king freed them both. Greatly rejoicing that they had been spared by the compassion of the Buddha, they went to him, bowed their heads at his feet, folded their palms in reverence, and said: "Lord, thanks to your great compassion, our lives have been spared. You who are supreme among gods and men, allow us, in great compassion, to become monks." When the Buddha had approved their request by saying "Welcome," their hair and beards fell away and they became monks clad in the red robe. Attaining to great faith, the dust and defilements were removed through their questioning of the Buddha, and they become arhats. The old mother of the thieves, hearing the Dharma, became a once-returner.

When Ānanda had seen these marvels take place, he lauded the timeless merits of the Enlightened One, but also thought to himself: "By doing what former deeds have this old woman and her sons been able to meet the Buddha, become freed from great sin, and attain to the bliss of Nirvana? Marvelous indeed is this, that in one single lifetime they have been able to attain this great blessing."

The Buddha, knowing Ānanda's thoughts, said to him: "Ānanda, this is by no means the first time that I have saved this woman and her sons. In times long past I also protected and saved them.'

Ānanda said: "I beseech the Lord to relate how in times long past he saved this woman and her sons."

The Buddha said: "Ānanda, in aeons long past, aeons beyond recall, there was an emperor in this world by the name of Mahāyāna who had a thousand kings subject to him. He had three sons: the eldest, Mahānada, the middle son Mahādeva, and the youngest, Mahāsattva. From childhood the youngest son was of a loving and compassionate nature and thought of all beings as his only sons.

"Upon a certain occasion the emperor, his ministers, and his wives and sons went to the forests and mountains to divert themselves. The princes went into the woods to explore and saw there a mother tiger who had given birth to cubs and was so exhausted with hunger that she was on the point of eating her young. The younger brother said to the others: 'Brothers, this mother tiger is starving and going to eat her own offspring.' When the elder brothers agreed that this was so, the younger brother asked: 'What would the tigress eat?' The elder brothers said: 'She eats freshly-killed meat and drinks blood.' The younger brother said: 'Who could give his own flesh and blood in order to save her life? To which the brothers replied: 'Who, indeed, could do so difficult a thing!'

"The younger brother thought: 'For long I have been wandering in the round of birth and death wasting life and limb, and through attachment, anger, and ignorance have brought forth no merits. For the sake of the Dharma I should have entered the field of virtue. Now, in order to bring about merit, I shall give my body to the tigress.'

"As they were returning, he said to the two elder brothers: 'You two go on ahead. I have something private I want to do in the woods. I'll come back to you in just a moment.' Going back to the tigress, he lay down in front of her, but the tigress was unable to open her mouth to eat. The prince then took a sharp stick and pierced his body. When the blood flowed the tigress licked it, was then able to open her mouth, and ate the prince's body.

"Soon the two elder brothers began to wonder what had happened to their brother and returned, fearing that he had given his body to the tigress. Coming to where the tigress lay and seeing the bones, they knew that he had been eaten and fell to the ground in a faint. Regaining consciousness, they screamed and again fainted.

"At that moment the empress-mother dreamed that three doves were flying and frolicking and that a hawk had caught the youngest. Awaking in terror, she told the emperor: 'Sire, there is an old proverb that says that a boy's soul has the form of a dove. Just now I dreamed that three doves were playing and that a hawk caught the youngest and carried it away. Surely something has befallen my youngest son.'

"Instantly all were sent out in search of the boys, but just then the two elder brothers appeared without the younger, and when asked what had happened to Mahāsattva, they reported that he had been eaten by a tiger. Hearing these dreadful words, the empress fainted. When she regained consciousness, she and the entire entourage proceeded to the place where her son had died. Seeing the blood and bones on the ground where the tigress had eaten, the empress held her head and the emperor, supporting her, wept aloud and fainted.

"When Mahāsattva died he was reborn in the Realm of Perfect Joy. Finding himself there, he thought: 'By what good deed have I been born here?' and with his deva eye he searched the five realms of being. Seeing his own bones in a forest and his father and mother and their entourage all gathered together and weeping and wailing loudly, he thought: 'I have caused my parents great distress and this will shorten their lives. I shall go and comfort them.' Appearing before them in the sky, he comforted them with loving words. Looking up, they asked: 'Who are you, devaputra?' He told that he was their son, Mahāsattva and said: 'It was by virtue of giving my body to the tigress that I was reborn in the Realm of Perfect Joy.

Father and mother, listen! The end of all that is created is, without question, destruction. Where there is birth, death is certain. When one commits sins, one falls into hell. When one creates virtue, one attains a higher birth. Since all experience birth and death, do not be distressed because of me. Rejoice that I have attained a good birth and strive for virtue. There is no cause for bitter suffering.'

"The father and mother said: 'Son, it was with a mind of great compassion that you gave your body to the tigress. Since you are compassionate to all, do not leave us now. When we think of you it is as though our flesh were being cut. Greatly-compassionate one, why do you abandon us?'

"And again the devaputra comforted his father and mother with loving words. And they, taking comfort, made a casket of the seven precious jewels and placed his bones in it. Burying it in the ground, they erected a stupa over them. The devaputra returned to his own realm and the emperor and his entourage returned to the palace."

The Buddha then said to Ānanda: "Ānanda, what do you think? At that time and under those circumstances my father, Śuddhodana, was that emperor Mahāyāna. My mother, Mahāmāyā, was the empress. Maitreya was the elder brother Mahānada. Vasumitra was the brother Mahādeva. I myself was the younger brother Mahāsattva. These two men were the tiger cubs. In times long past I saved them from the obstacles, saved their lives, and gave them joy. Now that I have attained Buddhahood, I have delivered them from the obstacles and rescued them from the terrible sufferings of the Round."

When the Buddha had thus spoken, Ānanda and the assembly lauded what the Lord had taught, rejoiced, and had faith.

3

The Mendicant Keeps the Precepts

ॐ❦ॐ

Thus have I heard at one time: the Enlightened One was residing in the city of Śrāvastī at the Jetavana monastery in the Anāthapiṇḍika's park. Upon a certain occasion, during the first watch of the night, two devas came to the Enlightened One and the brilliance of their bodies illuminated the entire park with a golden light. When the Buddha had taught them the Divine Law, their minds were liberated and they both attained to the fruit of Enlightenment. They then bowed their heads at the Buddha's feet and returned to the realm of the gods.

At dawn Ānanda said to the Enlightened One: "Lord, last night two devas came and honored the Enlightened One and their light beautifully illuminated the park. What former deeds did the two devas perform that this should have happened?"

The Buddha said to Ānanda: "In former times, when the Buddha Kāśyapa had attained Nirvana and when the Dharma was nearing its end, two Brahmins took upon themselves the vow of the Eight Daily Precepts. The one did this in order to be reborn as a deva, the other in order to be reborn as a king. Upon a certain occasion when a woman offered the evening meal to one of the mendicants, he told her: 'I have taken the Buddhist vow not to eat the evening meal.' The woman replied: 'You are a Brahmin monk! We have our own religious vows. Why, then, do you take vows from another teacher? If you refuse to eat with me, I shall report what you have said to the other Brahmin mendicants and they will refuse to have anything to do with you.' Hearing this, the Brahmin was alarmed and ate the forbidden food.

"When the time came for the Brahmins to die, each went to his own realm. He who had taken his vow in order to become a king was born as a king. But the one who had taken the vow to be born as a deva was born as a nāga because of breaking his vow.

"At that time there was a gardener who cared for the king's orchard and daily took fruit and vegetables to the palace. Upon a certain occasion he found a fragrant, beautiful apple in a spring and thinking: 'I have to run here and there with fruit and vegetables and always have trouble with the gatekeeper,' gave the apple to him. The gatekeeper took the apple and thought: 'I have to go here and there on errands and always have trouble with the inner gatekeeper,' and gave the apple to him. The inner gatekeeper gave the apple to his wife who, in turn, gave it to the king. When the king ate the apple he found it more fragrant and delicious than any he had ever eaten, and learning where it had come from, ordered the gardener to appear before him. The king said: 'Since such delicious fruit grows in my own orchards, I would like to know the reason why it is given to others and not to me.' The gardener explained what had taken place, but the king commanded: 'In the future, bring me only superior apples of this kind.' The gardener was terrified and told the king: 'But, your Majesty, there are no more apples of that kind in your orchards. I found the apple in a spring and there are no more.' The king replied: 'If you can bring me no more, I'll have your body chopped into mincemeat!'

"In great fear, the man went home, sat down, and began to wail loudly in bitter travail. A nāga heard him, and transforming himself into the form of a man, approached the gardener and asked him the cause of his sorrow and wailing. When the gardener explained what had taken place, the nāga disappeared and returned in a few minutes with a golden tray filled with fruit which he gave to the gardener and told him: 'Take this to the king. Give it to him and repeat these words: 'Your Majesty, you and I are related. In a former lifetime we were Brahmin mendicants who took the vow of the Eight Daily Precepts, each for his own purpose. Because you, your Majesty, kept your vow, you were re-born as a king. I was unable to keep my vow and have been re-born as a nāga. Now I wish to observe the vow and be delivered from this body. Obtain the ritual of this vow and give it to me. If you do not deign to do this, I shall cause your lands to be flooded by the sea.'

"The gardener quickly took the fruit to the king and repeated the nāga's words. The king became frightened and said: 'At present there is no Buddha residing in the world and the Divine Law has come to an end. Where, then, shall I obtain the ritual of the Eight Daily Precepts? If I do not obtain it, the sea will most certainly flood my lands.' In great agitation, he called his chief minister and told him: 'Ah, minister, a nāga has demanded from me the scripture called the Ritual of the Eight Daily Precepts. Try to find it for me. 'The minister replied: 'Since the Dharma is absent from the world, where shall I find it?' The king told the minister that if he did not find it he would be executed.

"In great fear the minister went to his home and sat down in deep despair. Now this minister had an aged father who, seeing his son thus, thought: 'Usually my son is of good countenance, but today his mien is sad and extremely troubled. I wonder what the trouble could be?' When he asked, the son told him of the king's command. The old man said: 'Son, in our house there is a pillar which constantly emits light. Go see what is inside of it.' When the minister broke open the pillar he found in it the Sutra of the Twelve Links of Interdependent Causation and the scripture entitled the Ritual of the Eight Daily Precepts. In great joy he took these to the king, and the king, placing them in a golden casket, sent them to the nāga. When the nāga received these he rejoiced and offered many precious jewels to king. The nāga then kept the vow of the Eight Daily Precepts and caused others to observe it. When he died he was re-born as a devaputra. Because the king observed the Precepts in accordance with the Dharma, he was re-born with the nāga in the realm of the devas.

"Ānanda, the two devaputras who came to me during the first watch of the night and to whom I expounded the Dharma, have attained the fruits of streamwinners and have been delivered from the three evil states of birth. They now enjoy the things of gods and men and I shall finally lead them to Nirvana."

When the Buddha had thus spoken, the assembly believed and rejoiced.

4

The Boy Who Sold Himself to Make an Offering

~~~

Thus have I heard at one time: the Enlightened One was residing in the city of Śrāvastī at the Jetavana monastery in Anāthapiṇḍika's park. At that time, in that country, a handsome, comely son was born to a householder. This boy began to speak at an early age and upon a certain occasion asked his parents if the Buddha was at that time residing in the world. When told that he was, the boy asked: "Are Śāriputra, Ānanda, and the others alive?" His parents told him that they were and thought: "Since our son has been able to speak from birth, he must not be just a boy." Puzzled, they one day went to the Enlightened One and asked concerning this. When told that the boy was normal with the usual male signs, they trusted the Buddha's word and were happy. When they arrived home the son said: "Father and mother, we must invite the Buddha and the Sangha." The parents replied: "Son, we have nothing with which to prepare food and the other necessities, how can we invite the Buddha and the Sangha?" The boy said: You clean the house and sprinkle it with water and prepare high seats. The food will take care of itself. My mother from a former life is now living in Benaras and she, too, must be invited." In accordance with the boy's wishes, the parents sent a messenger to Benaras to invite the former mother. The boy said: "The Buddha is to sit on one of the high seats, my mother from a former life on another, and the mother who bore me in this lifetime on the third."

When the Buddha and the Sangha had arrived and the Lord was seated on a high seat and food had been offered and the Buddha and all had eaten, the Buddha instructed the boy in the Dharma and he, his father and two mothers rejoiced greatly and all attained the fruit of streamwinners. When the boy came of age he was ordained a monk and exerting himself in the Dharma, became an arhat.

Ānanda asked the Enlightened One: "Lord by reason of what former good deeds was this monk born into a good family, was able to speak from an early age, and, becoming a monk, was quickly able to master the miraculous powers?"

The Lord said: "Ānanda, in a previous lifetime this man was the son of a prince of Benares who had become impoverished. Meeting the Buddha who was then residing in the world and having nothing with which to make an offering, he became despondent and, although a member of a high caste, hired himself out as a laborer and within a year accumulated a thousand measures of gold. A prince of the upper caste asked him: 'Son, are you preparing for marriage?" When the boy told him that he was not, the prince asked: "Then what are you going to do with all that gold?" The boy said: "I intend to prepare almsfood and invite the Buddha and the Sangha." To this the prince replied: "If you wish to invite the Buddha and the Sangha, I myself shall furnish the gold for the food and other essentials and you may invite them to my home." To this the boy agreed. Thereupon the prince prepared food and the other requisites and invited the Buddha and the Sangha, honored them, and made offerings to them. When he died he was re-born as the son of a prince, invited the Buddha and the Sangha, and having heard the Dharma, has attained release. The poor boy, Ānanda, is now this monk, the son of the householder."

When the Buddha had thus spoken, the assembly believed and rejoiced.

5

The Sea-God Asks Questions

⮜⮞

Thus have I heard at one time: the Enlightened One was residing in the city of Śrāvastī at the Jetavana monastery in Anāthapiṇḍika's park. There were at that time five-hundred merchants of that country who wished to embark upon a sea voyage to search for precious gems. They hired the services of a lay-disciple who was a guide and put to sea. When they arrived at the very middle of the sea, the sea-god, transforming himself into a rakśa and showing his hideous, frightful, black fangs, his head blazing with fire, approached the merchants and cried out: "Men, give me your boat!" Then he asked: "In your country is there anyone as terrible as I?"

The lay-disciple said: "Yes, in our country there are many people more terrible than you."

The sea-god asked: "Is that so? Who are they?"

The lay-disciple said: "In our country there are those who wilfully do stupid, ignorant, sinful acts, those who take life, take what is not given, those who are attached to wrong desires, tell lies, speak false words, bear false witness, speak harshly, are attached to great anger, and have erroneous views. When such people die they will be re-born in hell and will be bound by the keepers of hell. Some will be cut to pieces with knives, some tied to a carriage and constantly beaten, some will be held in steam until they perish, some will be ground in a mill, some will be made to climb a mountain of swords, some will be burned in pits of fire, some will be cooked in a copper kettle together with ice and putrid filth. Undergoing these various kinds of suffering for a hundred-thousand years, these people are much more terrible than you."

When the sea-god heard this, he disappeared. As the merchants sailed on, he changed his appearance into that of a dried-up, bony, emaciated old man and again appeared to the merchants. Shouting:

"Men, give me your boat," he again asked: "Men, in your country is there anyone as dried-up, bony, and terrible as I?"

The lay-disciple said: "In our country there are many who are more emaciated and dried-up than you."

"Is that so?" asked the sea-god, "who are they?"

The lay-disciple replied: "In our country there are those who have ignorant, stupid, greedy and malevolent minds. There are people who have no charity. When these people die they are re-born as pretas. Their bodies are as big as mountains and their throats are as small as the eye of a needle. Their hair is tangled and matted and they are emaciated and dried-up. For hundreds of thousands of years they never even hear the word "water". Such people are much worse than you."

Again the sea-god disappeared and the merchants continued their journey.

Then the sea-god transformed himself into a handsome, comely youth and again appeared, saying: "Men, give me your boat!" Then he asked: "Is there anyone in your country as handsome and comely as I?" The lay-disciple replied: "In our country there are a hundred thousand much more handsome and comely than you."

The sea-god cried: "Who is more handsome and comely than I?"

The lay-disciple answered: "In our country there are those the minds of perfect wisdom, those who perform virtuous acts, those who are completely pure in speech, thought, and deed, and have faith in and are devoted to the Three Precious Things. With whatever property they have they make offerings. When such people die, they attain a good birth as devas, are exceedingly beautiful and comely and have bodies that are a hundred thousand times more lovely than yours. To compare you with them would be like comparing a silly monkey with a lion."

Then the sea-god filled his palm with water and said: "Lay-disciple, tell me, which is greater, the water in my palm or the water in the sea?"

The lay-disciple answered: "The water in your palm is greater."

The sea-god said: "This time, lay-disciple, you err."

The lay-disciple answered: "What I say is true and I do not err. Listen carefully, and I shall tell you why. It is true, as you say, that the water in the sea is greater. But the time will unquestionably come when it will evaporate. At the time of the destruction of the aeon, a second sun will appear and the springs and brooks will evaporate. When a third sun appears, the streams will evaporate and dry up. When a fourth sun appears, the great flowing rivers will evaporate. When a fifth sun appears, the water of the great ocean will dry up and Mount Meru will ignite and burn from the first dhyana. Whoever makes an offering of even a palmful of water to the Buddha, to the Honorable Sangha, to father or mother, to the poor, or to animals, will, because of this, have indestructible virtue throughout the aeon. It is for this reason that the water in your palm is greater than all the water in the sea."

When the sea-god heard this he was delighted and offered many jewels to the lay-disciple the most perfect of which he sent to the Buddha and the Sangha. The lay-disciple and the merchants were satisfied with a few of the jewels and joyfully returned to their own country where they went to the Buddha, bowed their heads at his feet, and offered the jewels which the sea-god had sent. Kneeling, they spoke to the Enlightened One: "Lord, we desire to become monks in your Teaching."

When the Buddha said: "Welcome, lay-disciples," their hair and beards fell away and they were dressed in the robes of the monk. When the Lord had explained the Dharma, their outflows were stopped and they became arhats. All the assembly approved what the Buddha had said, rejoiced, and had faith.

6

The Devaputra Gaṅgadhāra

⊙⊱∿⊰⊙

Thus have I heard at one time: the Enlightened One was residing in the Bamboo Grove of the Kalandaka bird. At that time there lived a wealthy prince in that country who had no son. There was a deva shrine on the banks of the Ganges which was called Manibhadra and in order to obtain a son people went there, prayed, and made offerings. The prince went to this shrine and prayed: "Oh, deva, I have heard that you have limitless powers. Deva, you who protect all, I am without a son and beg you to give me one. If you can fulfil the desires of others, fulfil mine, I beseech you. Should you deign to grant me a son, I shall cover your image with gold and silver and perfume your dwelling with incense and fragrances, but if you refuse, I shall wreck your shrine, burn your image, and cover it with filth."

When the deva heard this, he thought: "This prince is wealthy and powerful and it would not do for him to have an inferior son from one of the lower castes. My powers are too feeble to fulfil his wish, but if I fail, evil will certainly befall." Going to Vaiśravaṇa, the guardian of the north, he related what had taken place. Vaiśravaṇa thought: "I cannot produce a son either," and proceeded to Indra and said: "Oh, Indra, my representative Manibhadra has told me that in the city of Rājagṛha there is a prince who demands a son. If he fulfil the prince's wish he will honor him, but if he does not, the prince will destroy his shrine, —which he will most certainly do. Do you, Indra, King of the Gods, deign to give him a son?"

Indra replied: "These things are difficult. There is at the moment, however, a possibility." At that very moment a devaputra was being separated from the desires and joys of the gods and was approaching death. Indra said to him: "Son, you are to be re-born in Rājagṛha as the son of a prince."

The devaputra said: "I wish to become a monk and to follow the Divine Law. If I am re-born in a high caste this will be hard to do. It would be easier if I were to be born in a low caste."

Indra said: "You have no choice, you must be born as the prince's son. But if you wish to become a monk, I will befriend you."

The devaputra died and entered the womb of the prince's wife. When her days were fulfilled, a handsome comely son was born and was immediately taken to a soothsayer who asked: "What were the circumstances of the child's birth?" The father explained that he had petitioned the deva on the banks of the Ganges, and the soothsayer said: "The child's name will be Gaṅgadhāra."

When the boy had come of age he requested his parents' permission to become a monk. They told him: "We are extremely wealthy and our clan is a large one and you are our only son. If you leave us, what will we do?"

Depressed by his parents' refusal, the boy thought: "If I destroy this worthless body and am re-born in a low caste, it will be easy to become a monk." Leaving home secretly, he climbed a high cliff and threw himself down, but was not harmed in any way. He then went to the banks of a great river and jumped into the stream, but did not drown and floated back to the shore. He took poison, but did not die. Then he reasoned: "If I violate the king's law, the king will certainly execute me." Waiting until the queen and the princes went to their park to bathe, he entered the park, and when they had removed their clothing and jewels and hung them on a tree, stole them. The gatekeeper apprehended him and took him to king Ajātaśatru, and when he had explained what had happened, the king became infuriated, took his bow and arrows and shot at the boy, but the arrows missed and returned to the king. When this had happened three times, the king became frightened, threw down his arrows, and asked: "Boy, what are you, —a deva, a nāga, a preta, a yakśa, a rakśa, or what? Who are you?"

The boy replied: "Your Majesty, I have a request. Should you deign to hear, I shall tell you." The king said: "Tell me your request."

The boy said: "Your Majesty, I am not a deva or a nāga. I am the son of a great prince of Rājagṛha. When I told my parents that

I wished to become a monk, they disapproved, and I am trying to destroy the body and attain another birth. I jumped off a cliff, tried to drown myself, and took poison, but did not die. Thinking that if I broke the king's law I would be executed, I stole the queen's ornaments and was caught by the gatekeeper, but when Your Majesty shot at me I still did not die. Oh. King, in great compassion, allow me to become a monk."

The king approved, took the boy to the Buddha, and explained what had happened. The Lord allowed the boy to become a monk, he donned the religious robes, and was ordained. When the Buddha taught the Dharma to him, his mind became liberated and he became an arhat endowed with the three sciences, the six powers, and the eight liberations.

Thereupon King Ajātaśatru asked the Buddha: "Lord, what former good deeds did this young man perform that, although he threw himself down from a cliff, he was not killed, when he jumped into a river, he was not drowned, when he took poison he did not die, and when shot at he was not hit. Now, having met the Buddha, he has been liberated from the Round. What is the reason for this?"

The Buddha said: "Countless aeons ago in the country of Benares there was a king by the name of Brahmadatta. Upon a certain occasion this king, his queen, and their entourage went to a park, and while amusing themselves someone outside the park began to shout in a loud, unpleasant voice. When the king heard this he became enraged and ordered the man executed. While the man was being bound, a minister came, and seeing him being fettered, asked what crime he had committed, and when told, said he would speak to the king. Coming before the king, he said: 'Your Majesty, this man has committed no great crime. There are worse offences than shouting in a loud voice. Spare his life and let me have him.' The king ordered the executioners to spare the man's life and to free him. Thereupon the man became the slave of the minister.

"Many years later the thought came to that man: 'Long ago, because I became excited and shouted, this evil befell me, but it is an error to be attached to it.' He then requested the minister to permit him to become a monk and to tread the Path of Liberation.

The minister told him: 'If you truly wish to enter the Path of Liberation, I shall not hinder you. When you have become a monk, let me hear from you.'

"The man retired to a remote hermitage and by dint of right thinking and effort became a Pratyekabuddha. He returned to the city and went to visit the minister who, upon seeing him, rejoiced greatly, offered him alms-food and the four necessities. Immediately the Pratyekabuddha soared into the firmament, remained suspended there, and exhibited the eighteen kinds of miraculous powers such as making water flow, flames to burst forth, and great lights to appear. Seeing this, the minister was delighted and thought: 'Because of my virtuous deed, my servant has come to this. Hereafter, where I am re-born may there be virtue. May I be born in a noble caste and have long life, and may my virtue and wisdom be equal to those of this man.'"

The Buddha then said to the king: "Your Majesty, this boy was that minister who at that time saved that man's life and attained merit. Because of that merit, wherever he is re-born he will be without the obstacles, and now he has met me."

When the Enlightened One had thus spoken, the entire assembly rejoiced greatly and had faith.

7

Prince Swasti

❧❦❧

Thus have I heard at one time: upon a certain occasion when the Enlightened One was residing in the Bamboo Grove of the Kalandaka bird, he put on his upper and lower robes and taking his alms-bowl went with Ānanda to seek alms. At that time, in that city there lived under a gatehouse belonging to a certain householder a blind old couple who had no dwelling place, no property, and no food. This couple had a seven-year old son who begged food, took it to the old man and woman, and thus fed them. The best of the food he gave to his parents, the scraps he ate himself. When Ānanda saw how this boy honored and cared for his parents, he was pleased and praised him.

When the Buddha had returned from the alms-round and had eaten, he taught the Dharma to the assembly. Then Ānanda, kneeling and folding his palms in reverence, said to the Buddha:

"Lord, during the alms-round we saw a little boy who honored and cared for his parents by begging. When he received food or fruit or whatever was given him, he gave the best to them and ate the scraps himself. Nor does he do this for one day only, but all the time. And it would seem that this makes the boy happy.'

The Buddha said: "Ānanda, whenever anyone, whether a monk or a married person, or whoever it may be, honors his parents and makes sacrifices for them, it is exceedingly difficult to calculate the merits that he gains. Why is this? I recall that in aeons long past, in a former birth I honored my parents with loving thoughts and even sacrificed my own flesh for them. Because of this I was liberated from the obstacles and by the power of that root of virtue I passed beyond a universal monarch's birth and an Indra's birth and became the Supreme of the Three Worlds and attained Buddhahood."

Ānanda said: "Lord, I beseech you to tell how in time long past, in order to honor your parents, you sacrificed your own life and gave your own flesh and delivered them from the bonds of death."

The Buddha said: "Ānanda, listen well and bear it in mind, and I shall tell you."

Ānanda said: "Lord, so be it."

The Buddha said: "Ānanda, in aeons long past, aeons beyond recall, beyond conception, there was an emperor in this Jambudvīpa by the name of Deva who lived in the country called Śribhadra. This emperor had a thousand sons whom he established as kings in the ten directions. The youngest son was named Virtuous and was made king of the land of the large-bodied people. He was devote and honored and made offerings to the gods.

"The emperor had a great minister called Rāhula who, because of his poisonous mind, murdered the emperor and usurped the throne and sent his soldiers in all directions to spy and to assassinate the kings. One day, when King Virtuous had gone to the park to rest, a yakśa appeared to him from an opening in the ground and, kneeling, spoke: 'King, the minister Rāhula, because of his poisonous mind, has murdered your father, the emperor, and your elder brothers, and now the soldiers are approaching to murder you, too. You must find some means of escape.'

"The king was exceedingly worried and began to make plans to escape that very night. Now this king had a son called Swasti whom, because he was handsome and comely, he was going to take with him. Seeing them making haste, the queen said: 'My Lord, what is the cause of your odd behavior and your hasty departure?' The king replied" 'This is not for you to know.' The queen said: 'My Lord, for the sake of my peace of mind, whatever works are afoot, do not, I beg you, conceal them from me.' The king replied: 'while I was in the park a yakśa appeared to me and told me that the minister Rāhula has killed my father and my elder brothers and that his soldiers are now coming to kill me and that I must find some means of escape.' The queen knelt and said: 'Lord, I shall accompany you, do not abandon me.'

"The king took provisions for a week, loaded them on his back, took the queen and his son and set out. They travelled for twelve days, but in their great haste lost their way and the provisions ran out. Thereupon the king thought: 'There is no other way, I shall have to kill the queen and eat her flesh.' Sending the queen on ahead, he put the boy on his back, followed her, drew is sword, and as he was about to stab her, the son pressed his palms together and pleaded: 'Father, I beseech you, do not kill the queen, my mother.' Repeating this again and again, he sought to save his mother's life. Then he said: 'Father, without killing me, cut off my flesh bit by bit and feed the three of us. If you kill me, the flesh will become wormy and spoil.' The king then cut off bits of the boy's flesh which nourished them each day, and when the flesh had been eaten, sucked the marrow from the bones. As they were about to abandon the boy, he said: 'Father and mother, my body has become weakened. Give me a little of the flesh, then go on, I beg you.' The father and mother divided the flesh into three parts, each took one part and gave one part to the boy, then went on.

"The son then made the following wish-prayer: 'By the merit of having offered the flesh of my own body to my father and mother, may I attain Enlightenment and deliver all beings in the ten directions from their many sufferings and lead them to Nirvana!'

"Immediately all the realms of the three great chiliocosms trembled in six ways. All the gods, from their palaces in the realm of desire to the realm of form, asked what such a sign portended. Looking with their divine eye, they saw that the earth and firmament trembled because, on earth, a bodhisattva had cut the flesh from his own body and sacrificed it to his parents, and offered this sacrifice to attain perfect Buddhahood and to deliver all living beings. Then the gods descended from the firmament and let fall a shower of tears.

"Thereupon Indra, the lord of the gods, in order to test the boy, transformed himself into a beggar, took the boy's hand, and begged for its flesh. The boy gave it to him. Then, transforming himself into a tiger and a lion, Indra came to devour the boy. The boy thought: 'Since these beasts of prey desire to eat me, I shall give them what flesh and bones and marrow are still left in my body.' With this thought he became joyful and every thought of regret left him. When Indra saw that the boy's mind was irreversible and firm, he changed himself back into his own form and spoke to him: 'Son, do you desire to attain the birth of an Indra, lord of the gods, that you have so devotedly sacrificed your own flesh for your parents? If not, do you wish to become a Māra-king, or a Brahmā-king?'

"The boy replied: 'Indra, I have no desire for the pleasures of the three worlds. I wish to attain Buddhahood and to deliver countless beings.'

"Indra said: 'Surely, you regret having sacrificed the flesh from your own body for the sake of your parents!'

"The boy replied: 'I feel no regret, not even so much as the tip of a hair.'

"Indra said: 'Seeing your body without flesh, who could believe that you experience no regrets?'

"The boy replied: 'If, in truth, I have no regrets, and if I am to attain perfect Buddhahood, may my body become as it was before!' When he said this, his body became as it had formerly been. Thereupon Indra and the other gods lauded him and all exclaimed in one voice: 'Excellent! Excellent!'

"Then the boy's father and mother and all the people of that land came to where the boy was, and were astonished. The king of that country, seeing this amazing feat of the boy-prince, rejoiced greatly and believed, and taking the boy and his parents to his palace, showered them with countless honors. In compassion, he sent an army, together with the king and the prince, to their own country, deposed the minister Rāhula and made the king emperor. When he had ascended the throne agriculture flourished and the land enjoyed peace."

The Buddha then said to Ānanda: "Ānanda, he who is now my father, Śuddhodana, was the emperor. She who is now my mother Mahāmāya, was the queen, and I was the prince. Ānanda, through the virtue of compassionately sacrificing my own flesh for my father and mother and saving them from disaster in times long past, wherever I was re-born, among the gods or among men, I was born in the supreme, excellent lineage and became endowed with countless virtues. By the power of those virtues I have attained perfect Enlightenment."

Those who had listened to the Lord tell one of his former birth-stories,—of how he had sacrificed himself for his father and mother, —were astonished. Some became streamwinners, some became never-returners, and all had faith and rejoiced greatly.

8

Vajra, the Daughter of King Prasenajit

❦

Thus have I heard at one time: the Enlightened One was residing in the city of Śrāvastī at the Jetavana monastery in Anāthapiṇḍika's park. At that time there was born to the first wife of King Prasenajit a daughter who was named Vajra. The child's features and complexion were exceedingly ugly and her flesh was as rough as the hide of a horse. Her hair was as coarse as a wild horse's mane, and the king and queen regarded her with horror, kept her hidden away in the palace, and allowed no one to see her. Ugly as she was, however, she was cared for tenderly because the queen was her mother.

When the girl had come of age and it was time for her to be given in marriage, the king, in great sorrow, spoke to one of his ministers: "Minister, find for me an impoverished noble who is unmarried." The minister searched and found a man who had formerly been a prince but had become impoverished and was reduced to begging. When he brought this man to the king, the king took him to a private room and told him: "Poor son who is a beggar, I have a daughter who is ugly and unmarried. You are of the caste of nobles but are impoverished, and I intend to give my daughter to you." The noble knelt, pressed his palms together, and said: "Your Majesty, your will be done! If your Majesty were to give me a bitch from one of his kennels, I would accept it. Since the king gives me his daughter, it is impossible to refuse and I conform with the king's command."

Thereupon the king married his daughter to the beggar-noble and put the couple in a seven-storied, gated castle, saying to his son-in-law: "Son, whenever you go out, lock the gates and take the key with you. See to it that all the gates are secured so that no stranger may see my ugly daughter." Giving him all that was required in goods and supplies, he established him as a prince with great wealth.

Some time later, the prince was invited to the wedding festivities of another prince to which all the wives and children were also invited. When he arrived without his wife, all wondered about this and said to each other: "His wife must be either exceedingly beautiful or very ugly since he didn't bring her. We'll employ a ruse and find out which. We'll make him drunk on wine, steal his key, and send five men to look at the princess."

At that moment the princess was thinking: "Because of what former sinful deeds have I been born so ugly and am obliged to live in this dark house, never seeing the sun or man, never meeting other people, and subjected to such suffering? The Enlightened One is now residing in the world and he delivers suffering beings from their misery." Bowing to the Buddha from afar, she prayed mentally: "Lord, compassionately show me my former existences, I beseech you."

The Buddha immediately knew her ardent desire and appeared to her, showing only his flame-like tuft of hair or uṣṇīṣa. When the princess saw this she rejoiced greatly, had faith, and her mind became totally pure. Because her mind had become pure, her hair became soft and black.

Then the Enlightened One manifested his face to her. When the princess saw this she rejoiced greatly and because of her faith her face became beautiful and lovely and its coarseness and ugliness disappeared.

Then the Enlightened One manifested to her the upper part of his body, radiant with golden light. When the princess saw this she had deep faith in the Buddha and her ugly complexion disappeared and she became more beautiful than a daughter of the gods.

Then, in his great compassion, the Buddha manifested to the girl his entire body, and the girl, attaining to even greater faith, became without blemish, her body endowed with all the signs and in its beauty incomparable in the world. When the Lord had explained the Dharma to her, her sins were purified and she attained the fruit of a streamwinner. Thereupon the Buddha returned to where he was residing.

At that moment five men unlocked the gate and entered the palace. Seeing this incomparable loveliness, they said to each other: "It is because she is so beautiful that the prince keeps her hidden away and shows her to no one." Going out, and again locking the gate, they returned to the festivities and returned the key to the prince.

When the prince had become sober and awakened, the festival was over and everyone had gone home. When he returned to the palace and saw an exquisitely beautiful woman, he was astonished, rejoiced, and asked the woman who she was. When she told him that she was his wife, he exclaimed: "But you were ugly! What is the cause of your having become so lovely?"

The princess replied: "It is because I have seen the Buddha that I have become beautiful." Then she explained what had taken place and expressed the wish to see her father, the king.

When the prince went to the king and reported what the princess had said, the king interrupted and told him: "Go back immediately and guard the door and don't let her out!" The son-in-law cried: "But, Your Majesty, through the compassionate blessing of the Buddha, your daughter has become beautiful and as lovely as one of the daughters of the gods!" The king said: "If this is actually true, go as quickly as possible and bring my daughter to me."

The prince returned to the palace, took his wife and placed her in a beautifully decorated carriage and brought her to the king who, seeing that she had truly become beautiful, rejoiced.

Thereupon the king, the queen, the daughter and the son-in-law all went to the Buddha, bowed at his feet, sat at one side, and king Prasenajit, kneeling with his right knee and folding his palms in reverence, spoke to the Buddha:

"Lord, by virtue of what former good deeds was this daughter of mine born in a high caste and with great wealth, and by reason of what sinful deeds was she born ugly, her hair and skin like those of an animal? What were the causes of this?"

The Buddha replied: "Your Majesty, it is because of both virtuous and evil deeds done in the past that she was taken on both these forms. Your Majesty, in times long past there was a householder in the land of Benares who was wealthy beyond compare.

All his property he place at the disposal of a Pratyekabuddha. This Pratyekabuddha's body was rough and ugly and his complexion was very bad. Every day when he came to the householder's home, the householder's little daughter would insult him and ask her father what he was doing with such an ugly person. Upon a certain occasion, the Pratyekabuddha came to the house, accepted offerings, and prayed that he might obtain Nirvana. Then, for the benefit of the master of offerings, he soared up into the sky, shot flames and made water flow from his body, sat and lay down in the sky, and appeared in the different quarters of the firmament. These and other wonders he performed for the householder and his friends. Descending from the sky, he entered the householder's house and the householder was delighted. The little girl, seeing all this, regretted having insulted the Pratyekabuddha and asked for his forgiveness: 'Noble One, I confess my sin of insulting you with silly, bad words. May I be forgiven.' The Pratyekabuddha told her: 'You are forgiven.'

"Your Majesty, this daughter of yours was that girl. At that time, because she insulted the noble Pratyekabuddha with a sinful mind, she has suffered from ugliness. When she saw his wonders, repented and confessed and made offerings, she became beautiful and endowed with a good mind. It is because she made offerings to a Pratyekabuddha that in whatever place she is re-born she will be born in a high caste with wealth and in the end will be perfectly liberated. Thus it is, Your Majesty, that one should not despise or insult others, regardless of their station in life, but guard oneself from the sins of body and speech."

Having heard the Enlightened One teach the law of the maturation of actions, through attaining a mind of faith, King Prasenajit and those with him attained the fruits, some as streamwinners, some as arhats. Some brought forth a mind of Perfect Enlightenment, some entered the realm of no-return. The king and all those present approved and lauded what the Buddha had taught.

9

Golden Gem

❦

Thus have I heard at one time: the Enlightened One was residing in the city of Śrāvastī at the Jetavana monastery in Anāthapiṇḍika's park together with a great assembly of one thousand, two-hundred and fifty monks. At that time in that city there was born to the wife of a householder a son who was so handsome and comely that one never tired of looking at him, and who, through the power of former virtues and to the astonishment and delight of his parents, produced two golden coins each time he clenched his fists together and opened them. When the parents took the coins, two more would appear and soon the house was filled to overflowing with golden coins. The child was given the name of 'Golden Gem.'

When the boy came of age, he begged his parents to allow him to become a monk, and attaining their consent, went to the Buddha, bowed his head at his feet, and requested ordination. When the Buddha consented, his hair and beard were shaven, he donned the religious garb, and became a monk. Later, when he was twenty years old and the time had come for him to take the arhat's vow and become fully ordained, he bowed with faith and devotion to the Sangha according to rank and wherever he placed his hands gold coins appeared. After being fully ordained, he applied himself and through meditation became an arhat.

Ānanda asked the Buddha: "Lord, this monk by the name of Golden Gem,—what former good deeds did he do that form the time of his birth until now gold coins appear inexhaustibly in his hands? I request the Lord to explain the cause of this."

The Buddha said: "Listen well, Ānanda, and bear it well in mind, and I shall explain it to you."

"Ānanda replied: "I beg the Lord to speak. I shall listen."

Thereupon the Enlightened One said: "in times long past, sixty-one aeons ago, when the Buddha Kāśyapa had come into the world, he taught the Divine Law, and the aid which he brought to living beings was beyond conception. While the Buddha and his Sangha were traveling through the various countries, a wealthy householder of the upper caste prepared different kinds of food, invited the Buddha Kāśyapa and his disciples, and offered it to them. At that time there was a poor man who made his living by bringing wood down from the mountains and selling it to those who had saved two coins. Seeing the Buddha and his disciples invited and going to the noble's palace, he had faith and rejoiced, and offered his two coins to the Buddha. In compassion, the Buddha said: 'I accept the two coins.'"

The Lord then said to Ānanda: "Ānanda through the power of the virtue of that poor man's offering those two coins to the Buddha and his disciples, gold coins have appeared in his hands without interruption for sixty great aeons and that man has had an abundance of property, jewels, and the necessities. Ānanda, this monk Golden Gem was that poor man who lived at that time and under those circumstances. Soon he will attain the highest fruit and his future fruits will be inconceivable when they are matured. Thus it is, Ānanda, that every living being should strive to perform the act of giving."

Thereupon Ānanda and many of the assembly, hearing the Buddha's words, had faith and believed. Some became stream winners, some once-returners, some never-returners. Some became arhats, and some brought forth a mind of Supreme Enlightenment. Some entered the realm of no-return, and when the Lord had thus taught, all rejoiced greatly.

10

Flower of the Gods

❧❧❧

Thus have I heard at one time: the Enlightened One was residing in the city of Śrāvastī at the Jetavana monastery in Anāthapiṇḍika's park together with an assembly of one-thousand two-hundred and fifty monks. At that time, in that country, when a handsome and comely son was born to the wife of a householder of the highest caste, a shower of flowers of the gods fell from the sky and filled the house, and the boy was named Flower of the Gods. When he had come of age, he went to the Buddha, and seeing the Lord's body endowed with the incomparable signs, rejoiced greatly and thought: "I have been born into this world where I have met the Supreme Among the Noble Ones. I shall invite the Lord and his assembly," and said: "Lord, tomorrow I shall prepare alms-food in my home. In order to lay the foundation for Enlightenment, I beseech the Lord and the Sangha to deign to come." The Buddha, seeing the boy's pure and firm intention, said: "We accept your invitation."

Thereupon the boy called Flower of the Gods returned to his home and in his mansion caused a great throne of jewels to magically appear along with many other seats, and adorned the dwelling with various kinds of decorations.

Upon the morrow the Enlightened One and his Sangha came, and when each had taken his seat according to seniority, the boy thought: "Now I shall offer various kinds of food," and, because of his virtue many different kinds of food appeared by themselves and these he offered to the Lord and the Sangha.

When the Buddha had taught the boy the Dharma, the house became filled with flowers of the gods and the boy requested permission of his parents to become a monk. When his parents consented, he went to the Buddha, bowed his head at his feet, and said: "Lord, I request ordination," and when the Buddha said:

"Welcome, monk," his hair and beard fell away by themselves and he was dressed in the red robes. Exerting himself in the word of the Buddha, he became an arhat.

When Ānanda saw what had taken place, he knelt and said: "Lord, this monk Flower of the Gods,—by reason of performing what former good deeds did a shower of flowers descend and jeweled thrones and various kinds of good appear? I beg the Lord to explain the reason for this."

The Buddha said: "Ānanda, if you wish to hear this, listen carefully. In aeons long past, when the Buddha Kāśyapa was in the world and was visiting the cities for the wealth of beings, a householder of the highest caste honored and made offerings to the Sangha. When a poverty-stricken beggar saw the Noble Sangha, great faith was born in him and he thought: 'I have nothing with which to make an offering to the Sangha.' He gathered various kinds of grasses and flowers and with a mind of faith showered them on the monks, bowed, and venerated the Sangha. Ānanda, this monk Flower of the Gods was that beggar who at that time made an offering of flowers. Because he sought Enlightenment with a mind of firm faith and gathered flowers and showered the Sangha with them, for sixty aeons, wherever he was born he was always handsome and comely and endowed with whatever he wished to eat and drink. As a result of that merit he has attained bliss. Therefore, Ānanda, one must not think that there is no merit when one gives, even if it is very little. As was the case with the boy Flower of the Gods, the fruits will come by themselves."

Thereupon Ānanda and the assembly believed what the Lord had taught and rejoiced.

11

Jewel of the Gods

❧❧❧

Thus have I heard at one time: the Enlightened One was residing in the city of Śrāvastī at the Jetavana monastery in Anāthapiṇḍika's park. At that time, when a son was born to the wife of a householder, there fell from the sky a shower of the seven jewels which filled the entire house. The parents invited a soothsayer who examined the boy and pronounced his signs to be good. The father was delighted and asked him to name the boy, and when he asked whether there had been any omens at the boy's birth and told that a shower of the seven jewels had fallen and filled the house, he called him "Jewel of the Gods." When the boy grew up he studied many sciences and grew to be of great strength and asked his parents' permission to become a monk. When they approved, he went to the Buddha, bowed his head at his feet, and requested ordination. When the Lord said: "Welcome, monk," his hair and beard fell away and he was dressed in the religious robes. After the Buddha had explained the Dharma to him, he became an arhat.

Thereupon Ānanda asked the Buddha: "Lord, this monk by the name of Jewel of the Gods—what good deeds did he do in a former lifetime that showers of jewels fell from heaven when he was born and everything he requires appears by itself,—what is the reason for this?"

The Enlightened One said: "Ānanda, in times long past, when the Buddha Kāśyapa had come to this world, he aided all beings beyond conception. At that time when many of the Sangha were going through the cities, householders invited them and made various kinds of offerings. There was a beggar who, seeing this, rejoiced and believed and a mind of faith was born in him. As he had nothing of value to offer, he filled his palms with ornaments made of white pebbles and offering them to the Sangha, sought Supreme Enlightenment. Ānanda, this monk, Jewel of the Gods, was that beggar who offered pebbles to the Sangha. The fruit of that offering is that he has been endowed with jewels for sixty-one aeons and that everything he has needed has appeared by itself. Because of his mind of firm faith at that time, the fruit of that faith is that he has now met me and attained Liberation."

Having heard the Buddha's teaching, a mind of faith was born in the assembly. Some became streamwinners, some became arhats. Some brought forth a mind that resided in the realm of no-return. All had perfect faith in what the Lord had taught and rejoiced greatly.

12

Kṣāntivādin, or the Patient Rishi

❦

Thus have I heard at one time: the Enlightened One was residing in the Bamboo Grove of the Kalandaka bird in the city of Rājagṛha. At that time, soon after he had attained Supreme Enlightenment, the Buddha ordained the Five headed by Kaundinya and thereafter Nadī Kāśyapa and the thousand brethren. After he had ordained many others and many were endeavoring in the Dharma, all the people of the city of Rājagṛha rejoiced with exceedingly great joy and lauded the Enlightened One thus: "Ah, the Buddha, the Tathāgata, has come to this world and this is greatly marvelous as he aids all peoples and nations." And they also said: "The first monk was Kaundinya, and he and Nadī Kāśyapa, because they were the first to meet the Buddha, are now the first to taste the nectar of the Dharma." When the monks heard this, they reported it in detail to the Buddha. The Lord then said to them:

"In times long past, with a firm mind I made the vow that when I attained Enlightenment I would aid them before all others.

Hearing the Buddha's words, the monks asked: "Lord, we beg you to relate how in times long past you made a mighty vow with a mind of compassion."

The Buddha said: "Listen well, monks, and bear it in mind and I shall tell you. Long aeons ago, monks, aeons past counting, past reckoning, past conceiving, beyond telling, there lived a king of Benares by the name of Kalinga. At that time, in the mountains of that country there dwelt a rishi by the name of Kṣāntivādin who lived together with five-hundred disciples and applied himself to meditation on patience. Upon a certain occasion the king, together with his queen, ministers, and entourage, went to the mountains to enjoy the scenery and amuse themselves. The king became weary and fell asleep and the queen and her entourage went into the forest to admire the flowers, where they saw the rishi Kṣāntivādin, his body unmoving, sitting in serene majesty. A mind of faith was born in the queen and her attendants and they made offerings of various kinds of flowers, and, sitting down before the rishi, listened to the Dharma.

When the king awoke, he looked about, and seeing that the queen was absent, went into the forest in search of her. When he spied her and her attendants seated before the rishi, he addressed him: 'Have you attained the four stages of ecstasy?' The rishi replied that he had not. The King then asked him if he had attained the Four Stations of Brahmā. The rishi said that he had not. The king then asked him if he had attained the four dhyānas, and when the rishi said that he had not attained to dhyana, the king became angry and said: 'Since you have no attainments, you are a scoundrel. Who would trust you here in this deserted place with these women? What do you have to say for yourself, living here in this place? The rishi said: 'Here in the mountains I meditate on patience.'

The king quickly drew his sword and said: "So, you meditate on patience, do you? Well, I'm going to kill you. We'll see about this patience of yours,' and cut off the rishi's two hands. "Now who are you?" asked the king. The rishi replied: "I am Kṣāntivādin." Then the king cut off the rishi's two feet and asked: "Who are you now?" Again the rishi replied: "I am Kṣāntivādin." At that moment the heavens and earth trembled in six ways and the rishi's five-hundred disciples came flying through the air to where he was. Seeing him, they asked: 'Ah, teacher, while undergoing these unbearable sufferings, have you not lost the thought of patience?" The rishi answered: "My mind has not been separated from patience in the least."

"Thereupon the king became terrified and said to the rishi: 'Ah, rishi, when you said that you were Kṣāntivādin, who would have believed it?' The rishi said: 'My words are not false. If they are, indeed, true, may my blood become milk and my limbs which were severed become as they were formerly! When the rishi had thus spoken, his blood became milk and his limbs appeared as before. Seeing this, the king was even more frightened and said: 'Great rishi, I have harmed you because of ignorance and sin. I confess these sins to you, do you have compassion on me.' The rishi said: 'It was because of the women that you cut off my limbs with a sword. This did not harm me because my patience is like the earth. When I shall have attained the Enlightenment of a Buddha, I shall cut away your three poisons with the sword of wisdom.'

"When the gods and nāgas of that mountain saw that the king had harmed the rishi, they were enraged and stirred up the clouds and brought them together. The nāgas roared and sent down thunderbolts from the sky and the king and those with him, about to be killed, became terrified and cried: 'Great rishi, have compassion and save us!' When the rishi commanded the gods and nāgas not to harm living beings for his sake, they became calm and disappeared.

"The king, having confessed his sins, invited the rishi to his palace and honored him with various kinds of offerings. When a thousand mendicants who followed other teachers saw the king and his entourage honoring the rishi Kṣāntivādin and believing in him, they became envious and threw filth on the rishi.

"The mendicants who at that time threw filth on me are now Nadī Kāśyapa and his thousand monks. My meditation on patience at that time was a vow that when I should have attained Supreme Enlightenment I would cleanse their impurities with the waters of amṛta and would totally purify their attachments.

"Oh, monks, do not think that at that time and under those circumstances the rishi Kṣāntivādin was anyone else but me. Kaundinya and the four were King Kalinga and his four ministers. When at that time I meditated on patience, I vowed that when I attained supreme Enlightenment I would first liberate them from suffering and now that I have attained Buddhahood I have indeed liberated them first."

The monks had faith in the Buddha's word and greatly rejoiced.

13

King Maitrabala Makes a Gift

❧

Thus have I heard at one time: the Enlightened One was residing in the city of Śrāvastī at the Jetavana monastery in Anāthapiṇḍika's park. Upon a certain occasion when Ānanda was going on the alms-round, he sat down in a deserted garden and the thought came to him: "Marvelous it is that the Perfectly Enlightened One has come to this world and has brought joy to many beings and that because the Five headed by Kaundinya created former virtues, the door of the Dharma has been opened and they have entered. The drum of the Dharma has been sounded and they were the first to hear. They, too, were the first to taste the nectar of the Dharma."

Arising, he went to the Buddha and told him of what he had been thinking. The Buddha said: "Ānanda, in times long past when the Five headed by Kaundinya were starving and dying of thirst, I fed them with my own body and gave them my own blood to drink and caused them to rejoice. Now that I have attained Supreme Enlightenment, I have set them on the Path of Liberation. This is not without its causes and reasons."

Thereupon the Noble Ānanda said to the Buddha: "Lord, I beg you to recount how in times long past you satisfied their hunger and thirst and caused them joy. If those present hear this, they will understand."

The Enlightened One said: 'Ānanda, in aeons long past, aeons beyond recall, there was a king in this Jambudvīpa by the name of Maitrabala who had subject to him eighty-four thousand lesser kings. He had twenty-thousand queens and ten-thousand princes. This king was endowed with love and compassion, practiced the Four Immeasurables, and in his compassion for all beings ruled according to the ten virtues. All honored the king, and because of his grace there were no enemies in the land and it was a happy one.

"The lords of contagious disease, the preta-demons, who deprive men of their blood and health, were helpless, without strength and perishing in that land and at that time because all the people guarded their speech, thought, and acts and practiced the ten virtues. Upon a certain occasion five yakśas appeared before the king and said: 'Oh, King, we are starving and our lives are in danger. When we attempt to obtain human flesh and blood we cannot because all the people in your kingdom practice the ten virtues. Being without food and drink, we are going to perish. Great King, why is it that in your compassion you are so cruel?'

"The king thought: 'These beings require no other food than bloody flesh and if they do not have it they will die. I shall cut the five veins in the five members of my body and give them blood to drink.' He then cut himself, took the blood from his body, and gave it to the yakśas who were then happy and satisfied. They then said to him: 'Your Majesty, how will you now perform the ten virtues?' The king replied: 'Just as I have now taken the blood from my own body and given it to you, satisfied you and made you happy, when I shall have attained Supreme Enlightenment I shall purify your three poisons with the teachings of the Body of the Law, samādhi, and wisdom. I shall change into joy your suffering which arises from attachment, and shall cause you to enter into the bliss of Nirvana.'

"Ānanda, I was that king Maitrabala. The Five headed by Kaundinya were those yakśas, and I vowed that wherever we would be re-born they would be the first that I would deliver. It is for this reason that I have taught them the Dharma first and totally liberated them."

Thereupon the Noble Ānanda and the many people who were present had faith in the word of the Buddha and rejoiced.

14

The Taming of the Six Heretic-Teachers

ᗢᐰᕗ

Thus have I heard at one time: the Enlightened One was residing at Rājagṛha in the Bamboo Grove of the Kalandaka Bird together with an assembly of a thousand, two-hundred and fifty monks. At that time King Bimbisāra, his mind of faith and devotion having increased through hearing the Dharma, regularly supplied the Buddha and the Sangha with the four necessities. While the people were striving toward virtue a heretic-teacher by the name of Pūrṇakāśyapa who was followed by five other heretic-teachers came to that country in order to deceive beings with their evil, false views. Many accepted these views and they spread greatly.

A younger brother of King Bimbisāra believed that these false views were the Path to Liberation and made offerings to the six heretics. Although the Buddha, like the risen sun, illuminated all with his wisdom, the younger brother, obstructed by these false teachings, refused to have faith in the Lord Buddha and although the king tried various means to induce him to honor the Buddha, he refused to believe. Again and again, the king requested him to make offerings to the Buddha, but he replied that since he already had a teacher there was no need to honor Gautama.

Upon a certain occasion the younger brother prepared a feast of offerings, and setting out a great table, made known that he would give alms-food to all who came, and especially invited the six heretic-teachers who immediately appeared. The Buddha and his followers, not having been invited, did not come. An invitation was then sent to the Lord Buddha and the Sangha, and the Enlightened One, surrounded by his noble assembly, came and sat down according to seniority. Through the power of the Buddha the seats of the six heretic-teachers suddenly became the lowest. Embarrassed by this, they again resumed their high seats, but suddenly found themselves in the lower places again. Three times they returned to their high seats, but each time found themselves again in the lower seats, and giving up, they remained there, ashamed.

When the master of gifts brought water for the washing of the hands, the Buddha told him: "First offer it to your teachers." When he tried to pour it over their hands the water did not flow, but when he offered it to the Buddha it flowed and he washed everyone's hands according to rank.

When the younger brother offered the food and asked for the blessing, the Buddha told him: "Ask the blessing from your teacher." The host went before the six heretic-teachers, but they were unable to open their mouths and motioned for him to ask the Buddha. The Lord Buddha then said the blessing in a voice as sweet as the voice of Brahmā.

When the food was given, the Buddha said: "First offer it to your teachers," but when the servants tried to serve the six heretics it flew up into the sky but after the Buddha and his disciples had been served, it returned to their hands. When the offerings had been eaten, the Buddha and his followers rinsed their mouths, washed their hands, and again sat in rows according to seniority. The master of gifts then asked the Buddha to teach the Dharma, but the Buddha said: You should ask your own teachers." When he asked the six heretics, they were unable to open their mouths and by gestures indicated that he should ask the Lord Buddha. The Buddha then taught the true nature of the Dharma in a melodious voice and the people's minds were calmed, they understood it thoroughly, and impressed it upon their minds. The younger brother of King Bimbisāra attained the pure eye of the Dharma and the others attained from the first to the third fruits. Some established a mind of Supreme Enlightenment, some became streamwinners, and all comprehended the truth and honored and had faith in the Three Jewels, and no longer desired to listen to the six heretic-teachers or honor them. In anger, the six teachers retired to a solitary place and sat, brooding.

Thereupon the evil Māra thought: "It has been a long time now since I have caused trouble for the monk Gautama. There has been no opportunity, but now I think I can make some." Transforming himself into the form of a mendicant, he appeared before the six heretics, Pūrṇakāśyapa, Maskarigośāliputra, Sañ-jayivairaṭṭhiputra, Ajitakeśkambala, Kakudakātyāyana, and Nirgranthajñatiputra, and exhibited many magic powers such as making fire burst forth, making water flow, lightining flash, and so forth. They said to him: "Ah, perfect one, have you attained such great virtue?" Māra said: "I have." Thereupon each one of them thought: "Only we can perform wonders of this sort," and later, at an assembly, announced: "Formerly the king, the ministers, the brahmins and all the merchants honored us, made offerings of food, robes, beds, medicine, and all the necessities. But now they honor this monk Gautama and we no longer receive these things. We would like to test Gautama's ability in magic. If he performs one feat, we will perform two. If he performs two, then we will perform four. If he performs eight, then we will perform sixteen. If Gautama performs sixteen, then we will perform thirty-two. We will double any wonder that the monk Gautama can perform."

They then went to the king and greeted him: "May you be victorious, Your Majesty, may you have long life!," then said: "Your Majesty, we are wise and have supernatural powers. Since the monk Gautama also pretends to have wisdom and unusual powers, we would have a contest with him in magic. Your Majesty, the monk Gautama must confront us."

The king laughed and said: You idiots! How can you possibly compete with the Buddha, who is endowed with countless virtues, with countless spiritual powers, and with mighty attainments? How can a firefly compete with the sun or moon? How can the water in a cow-hoof puddle compete with the great ocean? How can the timid fox compete with the lion? How can a dung-hill compare with Mt Meru? Why do you who have wrong views vilify the supreme among the Aryans with these silly words?"

Again the six teachers spoke: "Your Majesty, you speak without knowing. When you see proof, then you will understand. We shall certainly compete with Gautama and everything will become clear after the contest."

The king said: "If you must have a contest, have it when and where you wish, but you are going to be put to shame. When you have it, inform me." The teachers said that the contest would take place within a week and that they would prepare the place for it.

The king immediately went to the Buddha and told him: "Lord, the six heretic-teachers say that they are going to compete with you in miraculous powers and it was impossible to dissuade them. I beg the Lord to manifest his own miraculous powers, turn them from their wrong views and establish them on the path of virtue. If you do exhibit miraculous powers, I also beg to be allowed to see them."

The Buddha said: "Your Majesty, it is I, not they, who shall set the time for the contest. Prepare a large area and I shall participate in the contest."

The king ordered his ministers to prepare a large, level field and in the center placed the lion's throne and adorned it with the banner of victory, the standard of the Conqueror, and many kinds of offering. But when the time had come for the contest to take place, and all the people were assembled to watch it and marvel, the Buddha and his disciples went from Rājagṛha to Vaiśālī whereupon the Licchavis and many others went out to welcome him. The six heretic teachers arrogantly announced: "You did not believe us when we said that the monk Gautama could not compete with us in magic powers," and in great pride followed him to Vaiśālī. Then King Bimbisāra made ready five hundred chariots and with a hundred and forty-thousand followers for whom he took provisions, proceeded to the place in Vaiśālī where the Buddha was.

The six heretic-teachers went to the Licchavis and told them that they had come to compete with Gautama in magic powers and that the contest would last for a week. Thereupon the Licchavis went to the Buddha and told him: "Lord, six stupid heretic teachers who pretend to have great abilities have reported that they are going to compete with you in magic powers. We beseech you to vanquish them." The Buddha replied: "So be it, but I shall set the time." Then the Licchavis and all the people prepared all the necessities, as had King Bimbisāra. But the next day, the day before the contest, the Buddha and his followers proceeded to a place called Kauśāmbhī where King Udrayana and all his ministers went out to meet him. From Kauśāmbhī the Buddha proceeded to Varaci, from Varaci to Digyaśrī, from Digyaśrī to Benares which was ruled by King Brahmadatta, from there to Kapila, the land of his own people, the Śākyas and from Kapila to Śrāvastī, the land of King Prasenajit, followed by the kings of these countries, their entourages numbering many hundreds of thousands, and the six heretic-teachers with their ninety-thousand followers.

Thereupon the six heretic-teachers went to King Prasenajit and said: "Your Majesty, the monk Gautama keeps postponing our contest of magic powers, and has finally made his way here. Many great kings and others have assembled. Do you command that the contest begin?"

King Prasenajit laughed and said: "You cannot compete with the Enlightened One who is endowed with amazing powers, whose thought is inconceivable and cannot be grasped. How can an ordinary human-being compete with the King of the Dharma?" Nevertheless, he went to the Buddha and said: "Lord for a long time now these six heretic-teachers have been insisting upon competing with you. I beseech the Lord to put them to shame with his powers." When the Buddha said: "So be it," the king ordered his ministers to prepare the place, clean it and strew it with flowers and incense, set up the lion throne and the victory banners. Calling together a great entourage, the king prepared many kinds of food and great offerings, and on the new moon of the first month of spring the Buddha and his disciples came, the Lord sat on the lion throne, offerings were made to him, and he was honored.

The Lord placed a toothpick on the ground and a tree sprang up whose branches and foliage extended for five-hundred yojanas and bore flowers as large as cart wheels. From the flowers came forth many kinds of fruit as large as gallon jars. The roots, branches and foliage of the tree were loaded with the seven kinds of jewels which shone and gleamed in many colors, more brightly than the sun and moon. When one ate of the fruit it was more delicious than ambrosia and its very aroma filled one with delight. When the leaves and branches rustled in the breeze, the true voice of the Dharma was heard. All who saw this tree attained a mind of firm faith and when the Buddha had taught them the Dharma, their minds were pacified, they obtained the fruits, and there were many who obtained birth among the gods.

The next day when King Udrayana made offerings to the Lord Buddha there appeared on each side of the Buddha two lofty jewel mountains adorned with precious gems, iridescent with sparkling colors, from which sprang exquisite trees, flowers, and fruit, and, if one listened, lovely sounds could be heard. On the summit of one mountain there appeared delicious fruits of a hundred different flavors and all the people ate them with delight. On the summit of the other mountain there grew tender, lush grass and the animals ate of it until they were satisfied. When the Lord taught the Dharma the people's minds were liberated, they established a mind of Supreme Enlightenment, and those reborn among the higher classes of the gods were beyond count.

The next day King Socinadi made offerings to the Buddha and his disciples. When the Buddha rinsed his mouth after eating and the water fell to the ground, a great jewel-lake appeared whose shores extended for two-hundred yojanas and were covered with the seven kinds of jewels which shone in various colors. The lake was covered with blue, yellow, red, white, and various colored lotuses as large as cart wheels whose brilliance extended into the firmament. All who saw the jewel-lake were amazed and delighted, and they extolled it. When the Buddha had taught the Dharma and the people had understood it, some established a mind of Supreme Enlightenment, some obtained the fruits and were reborn as gods, and those who established virtue were beyond numbering.

The next day King Indravarma made offerings. The Buddha caused eight streams to flow from the jewel-lake and return to it. From the sound of the streams flowing there came the voice of the teaching of various dharmas: the Five Powers, the seven Aspects of Bodhicitta, the Eightfold Noble Path, the Three Doors to Liberation, the Six Supernormal Abilities, the Six Pāramitās, Great Love, Great Compassion, and the Four Immeasurables. Through hearing this voice of the Dharma and understanding it, some attained the fruits of Buddhahood and many attained the desire to be reborn among the gods and established an accumulation of virtue.

The next day King Brahmadatta made offerings. The Buddha brought forth from his face a golden light which illuminated the entire Universe of the Great Thousand. This light removed the three poisons and the five obstacles of all beings and their minds and bodies became totally pacified as shown a monk attains to the third dhyāna. There were countless people who established their minds in Supreme Enlightenment when the Lord taught the Dharma and many were born among the gods and created virtue.

The next day the Licchavis made offerings and the Buddha made it possible for all to know each others' thoughts. When the people understood each others' virtues and non-virtues, all were filled with joy and approved and lauded the virtues of the Lord. When he had taught them the Supreme Law and they had understood it, countless beings desired and sought Supreme Enlightenment, attained the friends, and wished for birth among the gods.

The next day the Śākyas made offerings and the Buddha transformed all into Cakravartins, each possessing the seven precious things, a thousand sons, honored by vassal kings and all their nobles. When all were delighted and amazed, the Lord explained to them the differentiation of dharmas. The minds of all were pacified, and there were countless beings who established a mind of Supreme Enlightenment, attained the fruits, and were reborn among gods and men.

The next day Indra prepared a lion-throne and when the Buddha had seated himself upon it, Indra made offerings on his left hand and Brahmā made offerings on his right while the great assembly remained speechless. The Buddha pressed the lion throne with his right hand, and from the throne there came forth a sound like the great roar of an elephant and five rakṣas who smashed the seats of the six heretic-teachers to bits. Vajrapaṇi appeared and brandished the tip of his vajra, which was flaming with fire, at the heads of the six teachers. In utter terror, they jumped into the water and perished. Thereupon their ninety-thousand followers came to the Buddha and begged to become monks. When the Lord said: "Welcome," their hair and beards fell away and they were monks. When the Buddha had taught them the Dharma, all their outflows were stopped, they were totally liberated from the defilements, and they became arhats. Then the Buddha brought forth eighty-four thousand rays of light from the pores of his skin and these completely filled and illuminated the firmament. Upon each ray of light there appeared a lotus, and upon each lotus there appeared a Buddha and his attendants teaching the Dharma. When the great assembly saw this, they rejoiced and exclaimed: "How fortunate we are to see this great wonder which the Lord has created!" When the Buddha had taught them the Dharma, some established their minds in Supreme Enlightenment, some attained the fruits, some desired to be born as men and gods, and those who established virtue were without number.

The next day King Brahmā made offerings to the Lord and his disciples, and the Buddha projected a beam of clear light as far as the realm of Brahmā. It illuminated the entire firmament and the earth. All who saw it heard the Word of the Buddha and attained blessings as before.

The next day the Four Great Mahārājas made offerings, and the great assembly saw the Lord's body extend to the realm of the Mahārājas and fill all space as far as the extreme limits of the Samsara. From it, there streamed a great light and the people saw and heard the Dharma, rejoiced and believed, and attained blessings as before.

The next day Anāthapiṇḍika made offerings and the Lord sat on the lion throne invisible, but a great light appeared and when the Dharma was taught in sweet tones. All heard it and they attained blessings as before.

The next day Prince Canda made offerings. Upon that day the Lord was absorbed in the meditation of love. Bringing forth a great beam of golden light which illuminated the entire Universe of the Great Thousand, this beam purified the poisons of all beings. A mind of great compassion arose in them and they loved each other as fathers and mothers, as brothers and sisters, and rejoiced. When the Lord had taught them the Dharma, they attained blessings as before.

The next day King Sunjanadi made offerings. On that day the Buddha sat on the lion throne and projected from his navel two rays of light which extended into the firmament for seven fathoms. On the point of each ray was a lotus and a Buddha appeared on each lotus. From the navel of each Buddha there appeared two rays of light with lotuses and Buddhas, and this was extended until the entire great universe was filled with them. All the people were astonished when they saw this, and when the Buddha had taught them the Dharma, they attained blessings as before.

The next day King Udrayana made offerings, and when he strewed flowers before the Lord they were transformed into two-hundred and fifty jewel-vehicles which filled the entire universe of the Three Thousand Great Thousand. When the people saw this their minds became totally pure and when the Buddha had taught them the Dharma as a healing medicine which cures illness, they attained blessings as before.

The next day King Bimbisāra made offerings to the Buddha and when the Lord said: "Your Majesty, it is time to prepare food," a hundred vessels were miraculously filled with various kinds of delicious food which satisfied the minds and bodies of all. Then the Lord touched the earth with his hand and the sufferings of the countless beings in the eighteen hells became visible. These beings said to each other: "It is because of our former evil deeds that we now undergo this inconceivable misery."

When the great assembly heard this, they were so terrified that their hair stood on end and a mind of great compassion arose in them. When the Lord had taught them the Dharma, their minds were pacified and they attained blessings as before. When the beings in the hells saw the Buddha and heard the Dharma a mind of faith was born in them, and when they were reborn they took birth as gods and men.

Then King Bimbisāra knelt and spoke to the Buddha: "The Lord has the amazing thirty-two marks on his body. I beseech the Lord to show this great assembly the mark on the sole of his foot, which is the wheel with a thousand spokes." When the Buddha had shown them the wheel, they were amazed and asked: "Lord what former good deeds did you do that this came about?" The Buddha said: "It is because in times long past I practiced the ten virtues and exhorted others to practice them." The King then said: "Lord, I beg you to compassionately tell how you practiced the ten virtues and caused others to practice them." The Buddha said: "Listen well, Your Majesty, bear it well in mind, and I shall tell you.

"In ages long past, ages past recall, there lived a great king by the name of Śatanimi in this Jambudvīpa who ruled over eighty-four thousand minor kings, had a hundred-thousand ministers, a hundred-thousand wives, but no son. Being without an heir, he was miserable. He made offerings to the Three Jewels and performed various virtuous deeds in order that a son might be born to him, and his queen, Sulipala, did indeed become pregnant. When she became pregnant, her intelligence increased and she exhorted many people to do works of virtue. When the months of pregnancy were fulfilled, a son was born to her who was exceedingly handsome and comely, of good complexion, and from all the pores of his body there radiated a light. The king was overjoyed and called a soothsayer, who examined the boy and said: 'This is an extraordinary child. According to the signs, he will be a Cakravartin and rule over the Four Continents.'

Delighted, the king asked the soothsayer to name the boy. The soothsayer asked: 'Your Majesty, when the child was still in the womb were there any unusual signs?' The king said: 'Yes when the queen became pregnant her intelligence increased and she found pleasure in doing virtuous deeds.' Thereupon the soothsayer named the child Prajñāprabhā. When he grew up he was unsurpassed in wisdom and intelligence.

"When the king died, all the nobles and ministers petitioned the prince: 'Prince your father has died and there is no other son. We beg you to become king.' The prince said: 'I cannot become king. The people commit corrupt sinful acts; killing imprisoning and so on and I cannot participate in that kind of activity. If the people would perform the ten virtues then I would consent to become king.' The nobles and ministers said: 'Your Majesty, it shall be as you desire.'

"As soon as the prince became king he issued a proclamation to all the people: 'Subjects, abandon evil deeds and practice the ten works of virtue.' The people did this and they then lived in great happiness. Then the mind of jealousy arose in Māra, and in order to disturb the king's rule he issued a false proclamation in the king's name saying: 'Formerly I commanded you the people to abandon sinful acts and perform works of virtue. This has proven to be an error and has benefitted no one. You may now commit all the evil deeds you wish.' When this proclamation came to the hands of the minor kings they became worried and thought: 'This cannot be true. Why would the king encourage evil? We must ask the king himself about this.' When they reported to the king he was astonished and said that no such proclamation had been issued and he himself went to visit his various kingdoms.

"Thereupon Māra caused a great bonfire to appear along the highway, and in it a man burning and crying out in a piteous voice: 'Long ago I caused people to perform the ten virtues. That is the reason I am now undergoing this unbearable suffering. The king stopped and said: 'There is no law which says that the result of encouraging others to do good is suffering. I have no compassion for your present misery because only happiness results from virtue.' Māra and the bonfire then disappeared. The king visited all his lands and peoples and exhorted them to continue to perform the ten virtues. All made efforts to do this with body, speech, and mind. When they had praised and lauded the king's virtues, he became endowed with the golden wheel and the seven precious things, and then he went through the Four Continents exhorting all beings to enter the Dharma.

"Your Majesty, my present father, Śuddhodana, was that great king, my mother, Mahāmāya, was his queen, and I myself that king, Prajñāprabhā, who exhorted others to practice the ten virtues. Because at that time I myself practiced virtue and caused others to do so, I now have the sign of the thousand spoked wheel on the soles of my feet."

Then King Bimbisāra asked the Buddha: "Lord, why did the six heretic-teachers challenge you to a contest which they could not win, and when they were unable to compete with your miraculous deeds, ran away in fear and shame and drowned themselves?"

The Buddha said: "Your Majesty, it is not only in this lifetime that those six teachers have challenged me and lost their lives for the sake of name and fame. They also did this in ages long past and did great harm to themselves."

When King Bimbisāra knelt and begged the Buddha to relate how the six teachers had challenged him in times long past, the

Lord said: "Listen well, Your Majesty, bear it well in mind, and I shall tell you.

"In aeons long past, aeons past counting, past recall, there was a king in this Jambudvīpa by the name of Mahāśakulī who had four-hundred minor kings subject to him. Although he had five-hundred wives, no heir had been born to him and the king thought: 'Old age and death are approaching and I have no heir. When I pass on there will be dissent among the five-hundred minor kings, they will not live in peace, and there will be great destruction and suffering.' While he sat sadly thinking on these things, Indra, the lord of the gods, saw his misery and, descending from the firmament, transformed himself into a doctor, he approached the king, and asked: 'Your Majesty, what is the cause of your worry?' When the king explained to him, the doctor said: 'Your Majesty, fret no more. I shall go to the Himalayas, gather medicinal herbs, bring them and give them to your many wives who will then become pregnant.' Hearing this, the king rejoiced greatly and approved. The doctor then went to the Himalayas, gathered many varieties of herbs, brought them to the king's palace and boiled them in milk. He gave the potion to the king's first wife, but the smell nauseated her and she refused to take it. The four-hundred and ninety-nine other wives did take the potion and immediately became pregnant. Meanwhile, the doctor returned to the realm of the gods. When the first queen learned what had happened, she regretted what she had done and asked if there was any of the potion left. When told that there was not, only the dregs, she took the dregs, boiled them in milk, drank the medicine, and also became pregnant. When sons were born to all the lesser queens they were handsome and comely and the king rejoiced, but kept asking: 'When will my first queen give birth?' When the first queen's time came, she gave birth to a son whose complexion was so bad that he resembled a tree stump, and they gave him that name. When the other sons grew up, wives were found for them, but no one would marry Prince Stump because of his ugliness. Sometime later the kingdom was invaded by the army of another king, and the four-hundred and ninety-nine prince went out to do battle but were defeated and, in terror, returned to the palace. When Prince Stump came out and asked them why they were retreating, he said: 'These few enemies cannot over-come us; bring me our ancestor's bow and horn and I shall go out battle with them.' (The prince's ancestor had been a Cakravartin, and no one but a World Ruler could draw the bow or blow the horn). When the prince was given the bow and drew it, it made a sound like the roar of a dragon and could be heard for forty yojanas. Going out alone to face the enemies, he blew the horn and the sound was like a thunderbolt crashing to earth. Hearing it, the ar-mies ran away in terror. The prince returned to the palace and was honored as a hero by the king, the queen, and all the nobles, and it was decided that the time had come when he must marry. The king, hearing that a king called Lośipaca had a daughter who was rare in the world for her beauty, sent two ambassadors to him ask-ing for her hand. King Lośipaca sent word back: 'Which son are you asking her for? If it is one of your handsome sons,—good. If it is the ugly one,—the answer is no.' When the ambassadors re-turned and reported to the king, he decided upon a ruse and sent King Lośipaca one of his most handsome sons with the message: 'This is your son-in-law.' King Lośipaca was pleased and agreed to marry his daughter to him. King Mahāśakuli then sent his repre-sentatives to bring the girl, and when she arrived, arranged things so the prince and the girl never saw each other during the daytime, but slept together every night. Sometime later, when the girl was talking with the other princesses and each was praising her husband's prowess, the girl also praised her husband, Prince Stump. The other women laughed and told her: 'Your husband is so terri-bly ugly that he looks like a tree stump. Why don't you look at him in the daytime? You'll be terrified.' Wondering if this were true, that night when her husband was asleep she lit a lamp and looked at him. Seeing his ugliness, she did become terrified and ran away to her own country.

In the morning when Prince Stump found his wife gone, he searched for her and, hearing that she had returned to her own country, took the bow and horn and followed her. When he arrived at her country he found that six other princes, hearing that the princes had returned, had come with their armies to carry her off. This worried the king who called his ministers together and said to them: 'If I give my daughter to one of the princes, the others will be angry and will cause trouble. What shall I do to rid myself of these enemies?' One minister suggested cutting the girl into six pieces and giving a piece to each prince. Another of the ministers disapproved of this, and thought it would be better if the king gave his daughter to whomever could force the armies to return to their own lands. The king liked this idea and issued a proclamation to that effect. When Prince Stump knew of this he took the bow and horn, went outside the city where the armies were encamped, and blew the horn and drew the bow. When the armies heard these sounds, they were paralysed with fear. The prince went among the armies, cut off the heads of the six princes, took their crowns, and the armies surrendered. The king was delighted, returned his daughter to him, and made him ruler over the six countries belonging to the six princes. Taking his wife with him, Prince Stump returned to his own palace. One day when he asked his wife why she had left him, she said: 'When I saw how ugly you were I feared that you were not a human being, was terrified, and returned home.' The prince obtained a mirror and looked in it, and when he saw his own ugliness decided that it would be better to die than be so ugly. Going to the forest, he made preparation for death. Indra, lord of the gods, seeing him from afar, quickly came to him and asked: 'Son, why are you preparing to die?' When the prince explained to him, Indra said: 'There is no need to die, I will help you,' and gave him a magic jewel to wear in his hair. Immediately the prince became handsome, returned to the palace, and as he was taking down his bow and horn, his wife, not recognizing him, asked: 'Who are you? You must not touch these things because when my husband returns he will certainly kill you.' When the prince said: 'But I am your husband,' the princess did not believe him and told him: 'You cannot be my husband. My husband is exceedingly ugly and you are handsome.' When the prince removed the jewel from his hair and again became ugly, his wife believed him. After he had explained what happened, they both lived together in happiness and he was no longer called Prince Stump, but Sulaśan, or Most Handsome of All.

"Sometime later the prince decided to build a palace and commanded his subjects to erect one in a great plane. The king of the nāgas transformed himself into human form and coming to the prince said: 'Your Highness, you are going to build a great palace. How will you build it,—of earth, or what?' Prince Sulaśan said: 'Yes, it will be constructed of earth.' The nāga king asked: 'But why don't you build it out of jewels?' When the prince said that it would be impossible to find that many jewels, the nāga king said: 'If you wish to build your palace of jewels, we will help you.' Thereupon he magically created four springs in the four directions and told the prince: 'If you will draw water from the spring in the east, it will become lapis lazuli. If you draw from the south, it will be gold. If from the west—silver, and from the north—crystal.' The prince did as the nāga king had told him and built a jewel-palace four-hundred yojanas in circumference and like a palace of the gods. Along the highways he constructed many buildings of wood and crystal and caused clear, sparkling water to flow. When he had completed this, the seven precious possessions arrived by themselves, and the prince became a ruler over the four continents and caused all beings to perform works of virtue.

"Your Majesty, my father Śuddhodana was that King Mahāśakuli. My mother Mahāmāya was his queen. I myself was Prince Stump. Prajāpatī was his wife and Kāśyapa was her father. The six heretic teachers were the six princes who tried to obtain the princess. At that time they fought against me and, because I killed them and captured their armies, from that time until now, attached to fame and gain, they have continued to fight me. Although they have no miraculous powers, they would rather drown than correct their faults, and now their ninety-thousand disciples have become monks."

Then King Bimbisāra asked: "Lord, what had Prince Stump formerly done to become so mighty, and what had he done that he was born so ugly?"

The Buddha said: "Listen carefully, Your Majesty, and I shall tell you of the law of cause and effect. Aeons ago, aeons beyond recall, beyond counting, there lived in this Jambudvīpa, in the land of Benares, at a place called the hill of the rishis, a certain Pratyekabuddha. This Pratyekabuddha was subject to a nervous disorder and treated it with clarified butter. One day he went to the house of a buttermaker and begged for some. The man became angry, insulted the sage, and told him: 'You beggar! If you didn't beg, you wouldn't be able to eat. Your heads looks like a tree stump and your hands look like dried up bark!' Nevertheless, he gave the Pratyekabuddha the less of clarified butter. As the sage was leaving with the tiny bit of butter, the buttermaker's wife came in and only met the man and had faith in him. She asked: 'Ah, Noble One, from where do you come and what will you do with this drop of butter?' When the Pratyekabuddha explained, the woman invited him back into the house and filled his begging bowl with clarified butter. Turning to her husband, she said: 'You have given this holy man only the dregs of the butter and have insulted him. You must ask the saint's forgiveness for this offense.' A mind of repentance was born in the man and both he and his wife bowed before the Pratyekabuddha and begged him to come and take as much butter as he wished in the future. Thereafter the saint came often to their house to obtain butter and, in order to repay their kindness, exhibited various supernormal powers for them such as soaring up into the sky, sitting there and making flames shoot from his body and water to flow. When the buttermaker and his wife saw these marvels, a mind of great serene faith was born in them and the husband said: 'By the merits we have gained by giving butter to this holy man, may we always be reborn man and wife.' The wife replied: 'Because you first gave only the dregs of butter to the sage, insulted him, and had no faith, you will be reborn ugly. How can I be your wife? I will run away and you will have to come after me and bring me back.' The husband and wife then dedicated their lives to the Pratyekabuddha and confessed their faults. The Pratyekabuddha told them: 'You two have cured my nervous disorder by giving me butter, and I shall fulfill whatever wish you may have.' In great joy, the man and his wife knelt and asked that wherever they would be reborn in the realms of gods or men, they would be together as man and wife.

"Your Majesty, Prince Stump was that buttermaker and his wife was the princess. Because he offended the Pratyekabuddha and gave him only the dregs of butter, throughout all his lives he was born ugly. Because he repented, confessed, and gave the saint good butter, he later became handsome, of enormous strength, invincible, and a Cakravartin, ruling over the four continents and possessing the five longed-for joys.

"Your Majesty, the effects of good and evil acts are never destroyed; like one's shadow, they never leave one. Therefore guard the workings of body, speech, and mind."

When the Buddha had thus spoken, King Bimbisāra, the princes and nobles, and the four parts of the great assembly together with men and gods, became streamwinners, once-returners, never-returners, and arhats. Some, desiring to become Pratyekabuddhas, established a root of virtue. Some established their minds in Supreme Enlightenment. All rejoiced greatly and believed.

15

The Kuṇḍa Beast Gives His Body

❧❧❧

Thus I have heard at one time: the Enlightened One was residing on the Vulture's Peak in Rājagṛha. Upon one occasion when the Buddha had a cold, the physicians compounded thirty-two kinds of medicine to cure him. Thereupon a thought of envy rose in the mind of Devadatta, who announced that he was the equal of the Buddha and that he would take the same medicine that had been given to the Lord. The physicians told him: "The Buddha's body is not the same as yours. If we give you the same medicine, your body will refuse to digest it and you will become ill." Devadatta said: "There is no difference between the Buddha's body and mine, and I shall take the same medicine. Give it to me." When the physicians had given Devadatta thirty-two measures of medicine, he was unable to digest it, it entered his veins, and he screamed in agony.

From a distance, the Buddha extended his hand and touched Devadatta's head in compassion and immediately his suffering ceased. Devadatta knew that this was because of the Buddha's compassion, but said: "Ah, Prince Siddhārta has studied and become an expert in medicine, but I have no need of him."

When Ānanda heard this, he was displeased and unhappy. Kneeling, he asked the Buddha: "In his compassion the Lord has healed Devadatta, but Devadatta is not grateful for the Lord's favor and constantly maligns you. Why is this?"

The Buddha said: "Ānanda, it is not only now that Devadatta maligns me. In times long past he did me great harm because of his evil mind."

Ānanda said: "Lord, relate, I beseech you, how in times long past Devadatta harmed you."

The Buddha said: "Ānanda, inconceivable, countless aeons ago there was, in this Jambudvīpa, in the land of Benares, a king by the name of Brahmadatta. This king was cruel, sinful, given to anger and attachment, and delighted in evil deeds. The king had a dream in which he saw the Kuṇḍa beast with golden hair, with brilliance emanating from its body and illuminating everything around it. When the king awoke, he thought: 'That animal I saw in my dream is real, and I shall send out hunters to capture it and take its skin.' Calling all the hunters in his country together, he told them: 'Listen! In a dream I saw an animal with a golden light emanating from its fur. That animal must be somewhere. Search for it, find it, skin it, and bring the skin to me. If you do this, I shall reward your families for seven generations. If you fail, I shall destroy you utterly.'

"The hunters were greatly troubled. Retiring to an isolated place, they took council among themselves, saying: 'This animal the king dreamed of has never been seen or even heard of. How are we going to find it? But if we don't the king will most certainly kill us.' Greatly worried, they continued: 'Not all of us should go to the distant lands, which are snake-infected and full of predatory animals—that would be our doom. But if there is anyone willing to risk his own life, it would be better if he went.' One of the hunters said: 'If there is anyone willing to go to such terrible places, find the animal, and return, I will reward him richly. If he were to die and not return, I will give his wife and children great wealth.'

"One of the hunters thought: 'It would be better for me to die than for all these men to perish,' and said: 'I will die in place of all of you.' Thereupon he took provisions and set out. While traveling through many lands his supplies exhausted, and he suffered greatly. At length he came to a desert which was scorching hot in the summer heat. He found himself knee-deep in the burning sands, without food or water, and at the point of death. In his agony he cried out: 'Oh, Great Merciful One, whoever you are I beseech you, save my wretched life!'

"At that time a Kuṇḍa beast with golden hair from which radiated golden light lived on a mountain. Hearing the man's cry from afar, it dipped its body in cold water and ran to the man and sprinkled him with it. Then he guided him to the edged of a stream and helped him enter it, then brought fruits of various kinds and fed him. When the man had regained consciousness, he saw the animal and thought: 'This must be the animal the king saw in his dream. When I was at death's door it saved my life. I can never repay its kindness, but how can I harm it? But if I do not, all the hunters and their families will be killed. What shall I do?' As he sat puzzling over this, his face became sad. The animal spoke to him: 'Man, why do you worry so?' Through his tears the man explained the reason for his coming. The Kuṇḍa beast said: 'There is no reason for you to be so worried, my skin is very easily removed. I know that, throughout all my former lives, I have occupied countless bodies and never done a single meritorious deed. Now I shall give you my skin in order to save your life. I give it to you with no thought of remorse.'

"The hunter carefully removed the beast's skin and the kuṇḍa beast prayed: 'By giving you this, my skin, I shall save the lives of many. I offer this merit for the sake of all living beings. May all beings attain Supreme Enlightenment and be delivered from the sufferings of the Round. And may I attain to the bliss of Nirvana!'

"At that moment the worlds of the Three-Thousand, Great Thousand trembled and shook in six ways, and all the palaces of the gods trembled. The gods became frightened, and seeing that the bodhisattva had offered the skin from his own body, descended from the firmament, came to the Kuṇḍa beast, strewed it with celestial flowers, and let fall a rain of their own tears. When the skin had been removed from the body and the blood flowed, insects and ants collected in great numbers and ate the flesh. Without moving, the beast offered it to them and then died. Those insects and ants which had eaten the bodhisattva's flesh were reborn as gods.

"The hunter took the skin to the king who rejoiced greatly and said: 'This is the only one of its kind.' Placing it on his throne, he slept on it.'

"Ānanda, I was that Kuṇḍa beast. Devadatta was King Brahmadatta. The eighty-thousand insects who ate the flesh were the deva-putras who attained the fruit when I first attained Enlightenment and turned the Wheel of the Law."

When the Buddha had thus spoken, the Noble Ānanda and all the great assembly had faith in the Supreme Law. Some attained the fruits of streamwinners and once-returners. Some brought forth the roots of virtue of a Pratyekabuddha. Some brought forth a mind of Supreme Enlightenment and entered the realm of no-return. All lauded what the Lord had taught and rejoiced.

16

In Praise of the Blessings of the Monk

❦

Exceedingly great and manifold are the blessings of him who has become a monk. Inconceivable are the blessings of him who has allowed his son, daughter, manservant or maidservant to enter the monastic life, or has himself become a monk.

The blessings of him who has become a monk, or allowed another to become a monk, far exceed the blessings of him who by means of the virtue of charity, has possessed wealth for ten lifetimes, or of him who has been born for many thousands of ages among the six realms of the gods.

One may ask why this is so. It is because the virtue which derives from charity will eventually become exhausted. But the blessings of becoming a monk go beyond the limits of time and are endless.

Again, through the virtue of observing the Precepts, one may become a sage who possesses the five supernormal powers, and even rejoice in the realm of the god Brahmā and be endowed with extreme wealth. But the blessings of him who has become a monk in the Teaching of the Enlightened One are beyond conception, and the blessing of the bliss of Nirvana is indestructible.

If one were to construct a stupa of the seven precious jewels so high that it reached the heaven of the gods of the Thirty-Three, the blessings from this would not equal those of becoming a monk. One may ask why this is so. It is because ignorant, benighted men could destroy the stupa of the seven precious jewels, but no one can ever destroy the blessings of him who has become a monk.

If one desires the dharma of blessings, he must realize that there is no other way than by becoming a monk in the Teaching of the Enlightened One. There is no dharma superior to this. It may be likened to a wise physician who heals the eyes of a hundred blind men and returns their sight to them. Or it is as when a man prevents a violent person from tearing out the eyes of a hundred men. Although the virtues of these two are beyond conception, the blessings of him who allows another to become a monk or himself becomes a monk are even greater. One may ask why this is so. It is because the first two, when they saved the sight of others, brought forth a worldly blessing. That happiness had to do with the fleshly eye and material existence. Yet those who allow others to become monks or themselves become monks, by aiding each other, will gradually, at the end of the kalpa in living beings, attain the eye of Supreme Wisdom. The self-nature of this eye of Wisdom will never be destroyed, even unto the end of the kalpa. Through the blessing of its virtue, men and gods will rejoice in inexhaustible possessions and, in the end, will attain the bliss of Enlightenment.

One may ask why this is so. It is because the dharma of the monk destroys the realm of Māra and causes the lineage of the Buddha to increase. It destroys virtueless, evil dharmas and gives birth to virtuous dharmas. It destroys the impurities and gives birth to supreme works of virtue.

The Buddhas have taught that the blessings of becoming a monk are higher than Mount Meru, deeper than the bottom of the sea, and more extensive than the firmament.

Grave indeed is the fault of him who obstructs or hinders another from becoming a monk. It may be likened to a man who enters a totally dark house in which he can see nothing, and falls into the pitch-black abyss of hell. The results of this sin may be likened to all the rivers emptying into the ocean. Thus sins accumulate within his being. It is like the great conflagration which occurs at the end of a world aeon, when majestic Mount Meru is reduced to flames. The man will be totally consumed by the flames of hell.

Thus the blessings of him who allows others to become monks, or who himself becomes a monk, are exceedingly great. He who becomes a monk becomes cleansed through the waters of the sutras, washes away all the defilements, totally alleviates the sufferings of the Round, and becomes a cause for the bliss of Nirvana. Through the Discipline, he courses within the realm of the pure Precepts. Through the clear eye of the Dharma, he sees the deeds of virtue and non-virtue throughout the entire universe, and through mindfulness he treads the Eightfold Path of the Nobles Ones and arrives at the city of Nirvana. He who allows older or younger people to become monks or himself becomes a monk—great are his blessings.

At one time the Enlightened One was residing in the Grove of the Kalandaka Bird in the city of Rājagṛha. There was, at that time, in the city of Rājagṛha, a householder by the name of Majestic Being who was a hundred years old. Having heard that the blessings of the monk were beyond measure, he asked himself why he, too, should not become a monk in the Teaching of the Buddha. When he told his wife, sons, men and women servants that he thought of becoming a monk, they, weary of the decrepit old man, rejoiced. "Yes," they told him, "the time has indeed come for you to join the Brotherhood. Do so quickly."

The old householder went to the Bamboo Grove where the Buddha was residing and spoke to the monks:

"Where is he who benefits gods and men, the Great Compassionate One, the Victor, he who has passed beyond phenomenal existence?"

The monks replied: "The Enlightened One has gone to other places for the benefit of many."

The householder asked: "Oh monks, who among the disciples of the Buddha is the chief in wisdom?"

The monks answered: "The monk Śāriputra."

The householder, leaning on his staff, went to Śāriputra, laid aside his staff, bowed, and spoke:

"Venerable one, I request you to ordain me in the Brotherhood."

The monk Śāriputra thought: "Certainly this old householder is incapable of study and meditation, or of doing the work of the Sangha." He said: "Householder, you cannot become a monk at your age. Return to your home."

The old man then went to the Venerable Mahākaśyapa, Upāli, and others and begged them to ordain him. These worthies asked him whether he had yet requested ordination from any of the other monks, and when he said that he had asked Śāriputra and that

Śāriputra had refused, they said to him: "Śāriputra is chief in wisdom. Since he has forbidden you from becoming a monk, how can we ordain you? It is as when an experienced physician treats a sick man. If he is unable to heal him, how can less-experienced doctors cure him? The man will certainly die. If Śāriputra, he of the wise mind, has rejected you, how can the other monks ordain you?"

In despair, the old householder left the Bamboo Grove, sat down at the gateway, wept loudly, and cried:

"Since the day I was born I have committed no great sin. Why is it that I am not allowed to become a monk? Upāli and other outcastes have become monks, scavengers and even Aṅgulimāla, who killed numberless human beings, and even brutal men like Āśīputra have taken the monastic vows. What sins have I committed that I am now prevented from becoming a monk?"

While he was saying this, the Buddha, his body radiant with the signs of the seven jewels of Indra, appeared to the householder Majestic Being, and asked:

"Householder, what is the cause of your sorrow?"

Hearing the voice of the Enlightened One, sweet as the melody of Brahmā, the householder suddenly became overjoyed and filled with adoration. His joy was that of a child who sees its parents. Folding his palms in reverence and kneeling, he worshipped the Enlightened One and said:

"Lord, outcastes, brutal men, liars and slanderers, and men of evil lineage have all been admitted to the Brotherhood. What sin could I have committed to be prevented from becoming a monk? Because I am old, my people at home have become tired of me and put me out. I can no longer go home. If I do not become a monk, I shall have no place to go and shall die here."

The Buddha asked: "Who was it that forbade you to become a monk?"

The householder replied: "He who turns the Wheel of the Law, he who is Master of the Law, he who is supreme in wisdom among your disciples, he who is the guide of those living in the world,—Śāriputra. It was he who refused to ordain me." Like a father speaking to his child, the great compassionate Teacher spoke comforting and loving words to the householder:

"Do not let your mind be troubled, householder. I myself shall ordain you. Śāriputra has not, during countless aeons, exerted himself in the austerities. Nor has he, for hundreds of aeons, brought forth virtues. Śāriputra has not, in previous births, allowed his head, eyes, bones, marrow, flesh, blood, skin, feet, hands, ears, and nose to be cut away and offered them freely. Śāriputra has never given his body to a tiger, has not been burnt in a pit of fire, has not had his body pierced by a thousand iron pins, has not had his body burnt by a thousand torches. Śāriputra has not given away his lands, his cities, his wives, sons, men and women slaves, elephants, chariots, or his seven precious jewels.

Śāriputra has not, during the first countless kalpas, honored a hundred-thousand kotis of Buddhas. Nor did he, during the intermediary countless kalpas, honor ninety-nine thousand Buddhas. Nor, during the final countless kalpas, has he honored a hundred-thousand Buddhas, become a monk in their presence and become perfect in the Precepts and the Pāramitās. Śāriputra is not one who zealously teaches the Dharma. How can he say that this one may become a monk and that one may not? I alone have authority to endow one with the Dharma and to extol the Six Perfections. I alone have put on the armor of patience. I alone sit on the Vajrāsana at the Tree of Enlightenment. I alone have overcome the hosts of Māra and attained the bliss of a perfect Buddha. There is no one like me. Therefore, follow me and I shall ordain you."

Thus the Lord comforted the householder in various ways, and rejoicing, he followed the Buddha to the monastery. The Enlightened One then spoke to Mahā Maudgalyāyana:

"You are to ordain this householder. It is your karma. It is you who are to ordain him a monk. Why is this? It is because if one being is related to another by karma, the latter should train him in the Discipline. If one is related to the Buddha by karma, another may not train him in the Discipline. If one is related to Śāriputra by karma, neither Maudgalyāyana nor Kāśyapa, nor Asaṅga, nor any other may train him in the Discipline. One is trained in the Dharma by him to whom he is related by karma."

When the Enlightened One had thus spoken Maudgalyāyana thought to himself: "This householder is too old to study, practice meditation, or do the work of the Sangha. But how dare I disobey the command of the Buddha, the King of the Dharma? To do so would be wrong." Therefore he ordained the householder and made him a monk.

*   *   *   *   *

This took place because in a former birth this man, through the power of accomplished virtue, had been caught by the hook of the Dharma just as a fish, caught on an iron hook, would be taken out of the water.

*   *   *   *   *

Now, accumulating the saving virtues, the old man day and night exerted himself in reading, studying, assiduously perusing the Sutras, the Vinaya, and the Abidharma, and attempted to understand them. Because he was old, he was unable to honor the teachers, bow, go forth with departing guests, welcome arriving visitors, speak clearly, and so on. The younger monks, who had been ordained before him and were his superiors, constantly offended him because they thought he was proud of what he read and learned, and he did not honor them.

The old monk thought: "When I lived in my own home my wife and children offended me. Now that I have become a monk, these young monks offend me. What former sins have I committed that such suffering should come about? It would be better to die than to live like this."

Going to the banks of the great river that flowed near the edge of the forest, he removed his monk's robe and hung it on the branch of a tree. Kneeling and weeping, he spoke the following vow:

"I do not renounce the Buddha, the Dharma, or the Sangha. I abandon this body. Through the merits of charity, keeping the Precepts, exertion, and studying the Scriptures, after I am separated from the body may I be born in the lineage of those who have perfect possessions and pride, and who cause their own people to be honored, those who hinder no one from following the Supreme Dharma. May I ever encounter the Three Treasures, become a monk, exert myself in the Dharma, and find a wise teacher who will teach me the way to Supreme Enlightenment." Making this firm resolve, he quickly threw himself into the swirling waters.

It so happened that at that very moment Maudgalyāyana was looking with his deva eye to see what his aged disciple was doing. Seeing the old man throw himself into the river, he appeared, through his spiritual powers, at the water's edge and said: "Son in the Dharma, why is it that you are perishing in the water?"

The old man was ashamed. He thought: "Now what shall I say? If I deceive my teacher I shall be born a dumb mute in all future lives. If I lie, the teacher, through his spiritual powers, will know it. He who is wise in the world, of an upright nature and without guide—him who all the gods honor. He who is unwise and cunning can never become the teacher of others, nor will he be honored. He who is of a good character but without knowledge can only benefit himself, he can never benefit others. If one is ignorant and stupid as well as cunning, all who see him will say that he is treacherous and a liar and even when he tells the truth will not be believed. It would be wrong to try to deceive the teacher. I shall tell him the truth."

He said: "Oh teacher, my wife and children became tired of me and no longer wanted me. I became a monk and went to the monastery, but the others abused me. Because I was unhappy, I decided to die and threw myself into the water."

Hearing these words, Maudgalyāyana thought: "Since neither birth nor death frighten this man, it was useless for him to have become a monk." He then said to him: "Disciple, hold tightly to the edge of my robe and do not let go."

Like chaff blown before the wind, like a magician holding a horsehair, like a falcon seizing a lark, like a man opening and closing his hand, they ascended into the sky and flew through the air until they came to the shores of the ocean. There on the beach they saw the corpse of a beautiful woman who had recently died. A snake was crawling into its mouth and out of its nose, into its eyes and out of its ears. When Maudgalyāyana showed this to his disciple, the latter asked who the beautiful woman had been. The teacher replied: "When the time comes, I shall tell you."

Going on, they came to a woman tending a large copper kettle. First she poured water into it, then kindled a fire beneath it. When the water began to boil she removed her clothing and jumped into the kettle. Her hair fell out, her flesh cooked, and as the water boiled harder, her bones were separated from her flesh and were scattered to the winds. The bones then turned into a man who tried to eat the flesh from the kettle. Standing behind the monk and watching, Majestic Being felt his hair rise in terror. When he asked who the person was who was eating the flesh, the teacher replied: "When the time comes, I shall tell you."

Going on, they came to an enormous tree with branches and foliage so dense that a needle could not have been inserted between them. Thousands of insects were gnawing at the tree and making a noise like the sounds of hell. Hearing this, Majestic Being asked what the hideous noise was. The teacher again answered: "When the time comes, I shall tell you."

Going on, they came to a man surrounded by many hungry ghosts with human bodies and animal heads who were shooting flaming arrows at the man whose body was in flames. Majestic Being asked who the man was and wondered how he could ever escape from the unbearable torture. The teacher told him: "When the time comes, I shall tell you."

Going on, they went to a far country where they saw a high mountain covered with sharp swords stabbing upward. A man was attempting to descend from the mountain-top but was constantly knocked to the ground and stabbed by the swords so he had not a moment's rest. When Majestic Being asked who the man was and what was the cause of his terrible suffering, the teacher again told him: "When the time comes, I shall tell you."

Going on, they came to a great mountain of bone, so high that it shut off the light of the sun and darkened the ocean...a mountain seven-hundred yojanas high. As Maudgalyāyana walked back and forth on one of the spurs of the mountain, Majestic Being followed him, thinking: "Soon I shall lose my way and become separated from the teacher. If only he would tell me about what we have seen!" Thinking this, he said: "Teacher, I implore you, explain to me what we have seen."

The teacher said: "The time has now come. I shall tell you. You wanted to know who the woman was. She had been the wife of a great merchant in the city of Rājagṛha. This woman was beautiful and charming and her husband loved her, and when he went to sea in search of precious jewels with five-hundred other merchants, he took her with him. When they had set sail and were at sea, the woman set up a mirror on a tripod and constantly looked at herself. Seeing herself lovely and attractive, she became greatly attached to her own form. The boat struck an enormous sea monster and capsized, and all were drowned. It is the nature of the sea that, when a person drowns, his body is soon washed up on the shore. What you saw was the body of that woman who had drowned. When people die, they are generally reborn as that to which they were attached."

Majestic Being asked: "If that is so, then why is it that, although no one desires to fall into hell, there are many who do?"

The teacher said: "Those who steal the property of the Three Treasures, those who steal the property of parents, those who take the life of living beings, that is, those who have committed grievous sins, fall into the terrible conflagration of hell when they die. Such persons first suffer from cold and crave fire, hence they enter the terrible fires of hell.

"Whoever steals a lamp lighted in honor of the Buddha, or the value of such a lamp, or a lamp belonging to the Sangha, or the property of the Sangha, or creates an obstacle to the Sangha assembling, or obstructs the teaching of the Dharma, or during the cold of winter steals another's cloak, or, because he is in a position of authority takes away a servant's or another's cloak in freezing cold weather, or throws water on anyone, will be born in the hell of ice because of these evil acts. Such people first suffer from heat and, constantly long for coolness, and for this reason are reborn in the cold hell. As the utpala blue water lily, the kumuda water lily, the kamala lotus, and the puṇḍarīka white lotus break open and split, so is it in this hell. The sufferings in the cold hell are like barley when it is parched and splits and bursts: one's head and bones split into a hundred-thousand pieces.

"Whoever, out of stinginess or greed, deprives others of food or does not give others food when they require it, will acquire a foul disease and be unable to eat. His wife and children will prepare various dishes and try to tempt him, saying: 'this is sweet, this is piquant, this is bitter, this is easy to digest,' but this will enrage the man because he will be unable to stand the very sight of food. When he dies, he will be reborn among the hungry ghosts.

"Whoever does not revere the Three Treasures or who humiliates the Sangha, such a one, in this very lifetime, will contract a vile sickness and will be unable to lie down. When the one who takes care of such a sick person, knowing that he is going to die, tells him: 'Now you should listen to the Dharma, observe the Precepts, have an image of the Buddha brought, invite the monks and pray with sincere devotion and create virtue, the man will be displeased, unhappy, and angry. He will think: 'I hope I go to a place where I never even hear of the Three Treasures or precious virtue.' When such a man dies, he will obtain birth among the animals.

"The man who strives for virtue, which is the foundation for gods and men, will not suffer when illness comes. At the hour of death his mind will not be disturbed. He will be at peace. When those who take care of him, or his relatives, see that he is going to die and ask: 'Do you wish to listen to the Supreme Dharma? Do you wish to contemplate the image of the Enlightened One? Do you wish to hear the monks recite the Sutras and verses? Do you wish to observe the Precepts and make a vow? Do you wish to make offerings to the Buddha and the Sangha?,' the man will say: 'How could I not wish to do this? Indeed, I do want to do all this.'

"And they will tell the sick man: 'By revering the image of the Buddha, you will receive the Buddha's blessing. By honoring the Dharma and making offerings of your possessions, in whatever realm you are reborn you will be endowed with knowledge and wisdom. By realizing the true nature of Reality in your mind, you will have understanding. By honoring the Sangha and making offerings of your possessions, wherever you are reborn you will be endowed with precious jewels and possessions.' Hearing this, the man will rejoice and have faith and will make the vow: 'In all future lives may I encounter the Three Treasures and hear the Dharma. Hearing it, may I understand it.' When such a man dies, he will obtain a human birth.

"Whoever wishes to be reborn among the gods should perform great acts of merit, should experience joy in giving, in observing the Precepts, and in listening to the Dharma. When such a person dies after having performed the ten works of virtue, he will lie down in peace and will see the Body of the Buddha, the palaces of the gods, the daughters of the gods, and will hear the profound voices of the gods. His appearance will be good when he dies, and, extending his hand upward, will be reborn in a higher birth, in the realm of the gods.

"Oh monk, the wife of the merchant attained an evil birth because she was attached to her own body. She has been reborn in the great hell where there is endless suffering."

Majestic Being asked: "Who was the woman eating her own flesh?"

The teacher said: "In the city of Śrāvastī there was once a woman lay-disciple who had a servant girl. This woman had invited a monk who kept the vows and maintained him in an outbuilding during the three summer months, and made daily offerings to him of various kinds of savory and fragrant food, which she prepared. These she sent to him by the servant girl at the noon-hour. The girl, when she came to a place where no one could see her, ate the best of the food and took the remaining scraps to the monk. When the woman noticed that the servant girl was putting on weight and that her appearance was improving, she asked her whether she had not been eating the offerings of food made to the monk. The girl answered: 'How would it be possible for me, who am very devout, to take the guru's food? The guru gives me what is left after he has eaten. If I am guilty of eating the guru's food, may I eat my own flesh in my next incarnation.' It is for this reason that the woman is now eating her own flesh. After experiencing indescribable sufferings, she will be reborn in hell where she will undergo sufferings unimaginable."

The aged monk then asked: "Teacher, what was that hideous noise that the insects made as they gnawed the tree?"

The teacher said: "Once there was a monk called Paladi, a custodian who administered the affairs of the Sangha. This monk appropriated the property of the Brotherhood—flowers, fruit, food and drink, and gave them away to people at a house in the city. For this, he was reborn with an evil reputation, has had to endure terrible sufferings, and because of his sins will later be reborn in hell. The insects gnawing at the tree are the people who ate the food that the monk took and gave to them. They were reborn as insects."

Majestic Being then asked: "Who was the man surrounded and being shot at by others?"

The teacher said: "That man was formerly a hunter. Because he killed many animals, he is now being shot at from all sides and undergoing unbearable suffering. When he dies, he will be reborn in hell and suffer even more. How will he ever find the Path of Liberation?"

The old monk asked: "Teacher, who was the man attempting to come down the mountain and falling on the sword blades, getting up and falling again?"

The teacher said: "That was once the powerful minister of a king. Because he killed many people, he now falls on the sword blades. When he dies, he will be reborn in the great hell and undergo unbearable sufferings."

Then the monk asked: "Teacher, what was that great mountain of bone?"

Maudgalyāyana replied: "Oh monk, if you really wish to know, that was your body in a former birth."

The monk's hair stood on end in horror. He said: "Teacher, my heart is ready to burst with anxiety. Explain this to me, I implore you."

The teacher said: "Oh monk, in the Round birth and death are without limits and end. When good or evil deeds disappear, they are not annihilated. Whatever deed is done produces a result. Listen carefully, monk. In times long past there was a king in this Jambudvīpa by the name of Excellent in the Law. This king was generous, observed the Precepts, was devout and compassionate, of good character, never deprived beings of their lives, was endowed with the signs of a monarch, and governed according to the Holy Dharma.

"When the king was twenty years old, it happened that on a certain occasion he was at leisure and playing chess. An official brought before him a man who had violated the law and asked how he should be punished. The king, interested in his chess game and paying no attention, said: 'Punish him according to the law.' Thereupon the official executed the man. When the king had finished the chess game he told the official: 'Bring the man before me, I want to hear what he has to say.' The official replied: 'But Your Majesty, we executed him because he had broken the law.'

"When the king heard this he fell to the ground in a faint. His ministers sprinkled him with cold water, and when he had regained consciousness he wept and said: 'I renounce my palace, my subjects, my elephants, horses, seven precious things, and all the rest. They are of no benefit to me now. You, official, have done a deed because of me which will lead to my rebirth in hell. Formerly, before I ascended the throne, the royal administration was righteous. When, within a short time, I die, it will be righteous again. Causing the death of a human being, I have become an unrighteous king and never, in any future lifetime, will I sit on a throne again.' Having renounced the throne, the king retired to a solitary place in the mountains.

"When he died, the king was reborn in the great ocean as a sea-monster seven-hundred yojanas long. (It should be known that a king and his officials, if guilty of killing, passion, anger, and harm done to living beings, are usually reborn as sea-monsters). On a certain occasion, many worms attached themselves to the body of that great sea-monster and irritated him. He rubbed his body against the crystal mountain and crushed them, and the ocean became red with their blood for five-hundred fathoms. For this sinful deed, he would be reborn in the great hell.

"On another occasion, when the sea-monster had been asleep for a hundred years, he awoke hungry and thirsty. He opened his mouth and the great ocean began to flow into it like the flowing of rivers and sea. At that time five-hundred merchants had gone to sea in search of precious jewels. When the monster opened its mouth their ship began to enter it. Screaming: 'Alas, we shall all perish,' each began to pray in his own way. Some called upon the Buddha and the Sangha, some called upon the gods of the earth, the mountains, and the sea some called for father and mother, wives and children, brothers and relatives, and all shouted: 'Alas, we shall perish! Never again shall we see our beloved Jambudvīpa.'

"Just as they were entering the monster's mouth, they called upon the Buddha in a great voice, with one accord, and with intense faith. Their cry was heard and the great gaping mouth closed. The waters were stilled and the merchants were delivered from death. The sea-monster starved to death and was reborn in the city of Rājagṛha as an insect. Its body washed upon the seashore, and baked by the sun and washed by the rain, the flesh disintegrated and its bones are now that mountain.

"Majestic Being, you should know that you were that king and that because you allowed a man to be killed, you were reborn as a sea-monster in the ocean. Now that you have obtained a human birth you must make good use of it, because if you do not, when you die you will fall into hell and rescue will be very difficult indeed."

When Majestic Being heard what the teacher had told him and looked at his former body, great fear of the Round overcame him. Striving earnestly, rigorously contemplating what had been explained to him with one-pointedness of mind, and observing his former skeleton, he understood the truth of the law of impermanence. He abandoned the sins of the Round, totally stopped the outflows of the defilements, and became an arhat.

The Mahā Maudgalyāyana rejoiced greatly and said: "Son in the Dharma, you have done in your own mind what was to be done. Until now you have depended upon my power. Now make use of your own powers and follow me." Then Maudgalyāyana flew into the upper firmament, the monk Majestic Being following him as a fledging follows its mother in flight, until they came to where the Buddha was.

The younger monks did not know that Majestic Being had become an arhat and, as formerly, looked upon him with disdain, but he sat respectfully and showed no irritation. The Buddha, however, did know, and to prevent the younger monks from offending him and to extol his attainment, called him to his side before the assembly and asked: "Have you been to the seashore, Majestic Being?"

Majestic Being answered: "Yes, Lord, I have been to the seashore."

The Enlightened One said: "Tell me what you saw there."

When Majestic Being had related all that he had seen, the Buddha said: "This is good, Majestic Being, this is good. All that you saw there is true. You have now abandoned all the suffering of the Round and have become an object of veneration among gods and men. Oh monk, you have done perfectly what was to be done."

When the younger monks heard this, they were filled with remorse and said with regret: "Not knowing that this Noble One was endowed with wisdom and knowledge, we, for no reason at all, offended him. Retribution will most certainly come upon us for this." They then went to the monk Majestic Being, prostrated themselves, and said: "Oh, Noble One, the Holy Ones are greatly compassionate. You, Noble One, are also greatly compassionate. We regret our sin of having offended you."

The monk said: "Your offenses did not harm me. You are forgiven." Seeing the sincere repentance of the younger monks, he taught them the Supreme Dharma. The monks, relying on the Dharma which leaves the Round behind, stopped their outflows by dint of great exertion and became arhats.

The fame of the householder Majestic Being spread throughout the city of Rājagṛha and all, in amazement, exclaimed: "Ah, what cannot be done if an old man, such as he, can become a monk in the Teaching of the Buddha, attain the fruits of arhatship, and teach the Supreme Dharma?" And thoughts of pure devotion and faith were born in the minds of the people of Rājagṛha. Some allowed their sons and daughters to join the Order, some allowed their men and maidservants. Some became monks themselves. All rejoiced and believed and said: "The blessings of becoming a monk are beyond time and are without limit. Since the hundred-year-old Majestic Being has attained the timeless blessing, why should the young and strong not become monks and attain the Supreme Bliss? Let them also become monks and exert themselves in the Dharma."

17

The Monk Keeps the Precepts

❧

Those who have taken the Precepts must never violate them, even at the cost of life or limb. Why is this? It is because the Precepts are the root which penetrates Enlightenment. They are the supreme of the non-defilements, the path which quickly leads to Nirvana. In truth, the merits of the Precepts are timeless and without parallel and the virtues of him who keeps them are timeless and beyond compare.

Just as the ocean is the great element of water in which dwell non-humans, turtles, sea-monsters, etc., the Precepts are the element in which dwell those many great beings who reside in the three Vehicles. And just as in the ocean there are to be found gold, silver, and many precious gems like lapis-lazuli, so in the ocean of the Precepts there are to be found precious jewels such as the cause of impermanence, the thirty-seven dharmas which lead to Enlightenment, dhyāna, and samādhi.

Why does the great ocean never overflow? Because the constant fires of hell cause it to evaporate. And just as the everflowing rivers never cause it to increase, so is the ocean of the Precepts never increased by knowledge nor is it decreased through the perfection of virtue.

It should therefore be known that the virtues of him who keeps the Precepts are great indeed.

After the Parinirvana of the Buddha, there lived in the country of Anta a monk of good conduct. He was a mendicant and did not reside within the Great Assembly praised by all the Buddhas. What was the reason for this? It was because the monk had few desires, was moderate, accumulated nothing, ate but once a day, and required no permanent dwelling, whereas the high ecclesiastics, the dignitaries, and the other monks who belonged to the Sangha and wore the monastic robes were immoderate and covetous, and for this reason never attained true glory. The mendicant monk, however, because of his virtue and good conduct, had attained the fruits of the monk: the six transcendental powers, the three knowledges, and the eight knowledges, and the eight liberations, and his fame had spread far and wide.

At that time there lived in the country of Anta a lay-disciple who greatly revered the Three Treasures and who kept the Five Precepts. He did not take life, did not take what had not been given, did not harbor sensual desires, did not speak what was not true, and did not drink intoxicating drinks. This lay-disciple honored and revered the mendicant. He prepared food and brought it to him each day, thinking that the merits would be greater than if he invited him to come to his home. This way, the monk would not have to experience heat and cold while coming and going.

In general, monks are like mangoes. There are those who pretend to have good conduct but are inwardly filled with attachment and desire. Such monks are not part of the Dharma, neglect the Precepts, and are similar to a mango which is ripe on the outside but green on the inside.

There are those who are outwardly crude and unbecoming in their behavior, but inwardly observe the monastic life, follow virtue and practice dhyāna, samādhi, and wisdom. These are like a mango that is ripe on the inside but green on the outside.

Still others exhibit crude behavior, faulty conduct, and break the Precepts. They are guilty of greed, anger, and delusion. These are like a mango green both inside and out.

Finally, there are those monks who behave themselves seemingly, keep the Precepts, and are endowed with samadhi and wisdom. Such monks are like a mango which is ripe both inside and out, and the mendicant was like this, ripe inside and out. Perfect in virtue and conduct, he was honored and respected.

At that time there was a householder who greatly venerated the Three Treasures, and who had a son whom he wished to become a monk. He asked himself the reason for this: "Why do I want my son to become a monk and the disciple of a wise teacher? It is because if one relies upon a holy teacher, virtues come into being, but if one relies upon sinners, sins come into being. It is like the nature of the wind, which is void. When it blows through a forest of sandalwood trees or through a campaka grove, it is perfumed. When it blows over a place of filth or a grove of elders, it has an unpleasant smell. It is also like a new garment which is placed in a chest containing incense and takes on the odor of the incense, but if placed in a filthy place, takes on the stench of filth. If one relies on a virtuous, holy teacher, virtues will gradually accumulate. If one relies on a sinful person, sins will accumulate and increase. Therefore I shall have my son become a monk and study with the mendicant. Going to the mendicant monk, he said:

"Venerable sir, I have brought my son to you and wish him to become a monk. Do you, in compassion, ordain him. Should you not approve, I shall take him back home with me."

The monk looked with his spiritual eye and saw that if the boy were ordained he would keep the Precepts and understand and disseminate the teachings of the Enlightened Ones, and immediately ordained him.

Upon a certain occasion a certain householder prepared a festival and invited the lay-disciple who sent food to the monk, his sons, daughters, men and women servants. The following day, while preparing to go to the feast, the lay-disciple thought: "Someone will have to stay home to watch the house," and said: "If anyone is willing to stay home, I will recompensate him for this when I return." One of his daughters said she would stay and her father told her: "It is very good of you to offer to stay home. Nothing bad will happen." As soon as the family had departed, the girl locked the door and remained alone in the house.

The lay-disciple, hurrying to get to the festival, had forgotten to send the food to the monk and when noon came the monk thought: "The sun has passed the door. The householder has forgotten to send my food because of the many things he has to do. It is wrong to eat at the improper time and I shall send my novice to bring it." Sending the novice, he told him: "Monk, guard your senses well. Go out on the alms-round remembering what the Buddha taught,—take alms from the city as a bee takes honey from a fragrant flower, with no thought of attachment. Guard your faculties against attachment to form, sound, smell, taste, and touch. If you keep the Precepts you will attain the fruit. Do not be like Devadatta, who read many sutras but committed many grievous sins and was reborn in the great hell, or like kokala, who abused the Holy Ones and, through breaking the Precepts, was also reborn in hell. Be like Colipanta who, although unable to remember one single verse of scripture, kept the Precepts and became an arhat. The Precepts are the gate through which one enters Nirvana. They are the source of great joy. Remember the rich brahmin who prepared a four-month feast for the mendicants who were wise and learned in the Vedas and observed the pure Precepts. Each was given a seal of honey on his wrist so it would be known that he had been invited. One brahmin licked off the seal because it was sweet and it disappeared. The next day when the feast convened and the gatekeeper examined the seals, the seal of that brahmin was missing and he was not permitted to enter. 'Where is your seal?' the gatekeeper asked. 'I licked it off because it was sweet,' the brahmin answered. Thus, for the sake of a single drop of honey that brahmin lost good food for four months, as well as many jewels. Oh monk, do not, like that brahmin, give in to the desire for unimportant things. Do not erase the seal of the Precepts. Do not abandon the thirty-seven dharmas which lead to Bodhi and are beyond the defilements, and the sweet savors of the five desires of gods and men. Do not relinquish the bliss of Nirvana and the inconceivably precious Dharma. Do not break the Precepts of the Buddhas of the three times. Do not disgrace the lineage of the Three Treasures, the Teacher, and the Brotherhood.'

When the monk had thus spoken, the novice bowed at his teacher's feet and went to the city. When he knocked on the householder's door, the girl asked who was there. When the novice said that he had come to get the teacher's food, the girl was pleased, opened the door, welcomed him, and the monk entered the house. The girl was sixteen years old, very beautiful, and, overcome with lust, she tempted the monk in many ways. The monk thought to himself: "The girl must be deranged. Either that, or she has given herself over completely to thoughts of lust and sensuality, and it is sensuality that destroys the Precepts." While he carefully guarded his behavior, the girl prostrated herself before him and said: "Oh monk, today I have found what I have always longed for. Have pity on me and satisfy my desire. In this house there are jewels, gold, silver, and many treasures—as many as in the house of Vaiśravaṇa—and they have no owner. I beg you to become the master here. I will be your slave and will honor and obey you. Do not despise my words, but fulfill my desire."

The monk thought: "What sins could I have committed to be subjected to such hopeless suffering? The Precepts of the Buddhas of the three times must not be broken. Formerly, when monks found themselves among lewd women, they entered fire rather than break the Precepts, When, in order to make them break the Precepts, they captured and bound them with ropes, exposed them to the sun and wind, and allowed them to be bitten by insects, they refused to break them. There was even a monk who, when shipwrecked and holding on to a plank, gave it to an elder monk in order to keep the Precepts and was drowned in the sea. But those monks had the Buddha, the Tathāgata, as their teacher, and we do not. It was as when the campaka flower was crushed together with sesame seeds and the seeds smelled like the campaka flowers. But I am not like that. If I truly adhered to a spiritual teacher, why would I even now be committing sins? Surely, it would be better to die. If I break the Precepts, this dishonors the Buddha, the Dharma, and the Sangha, the father, the mother, and the teacher. If I run away, this girl, because of her great passion which has not been satisfied, will shamelessly say that I abused her and escaped, and when the townspeople hear this, the Lineage will be put to shame. Certainly now, here in this very house, is the time to change births." Then he said to the girl: "Maiden, lock the gates and guard them, there is something I want to do, then I will join you."

When the girl went out to lock the gates, the monk locked the door and, looking around, found a razor. Rejoicing greatly, he removed his robe, hung it on a peg, folded his palms, and kneeling in the direction of Kuśināgara where the Buddha had attained Nirvana, prayed: "I do not renounce the Buddha, the Dharma, or the Sangha. I renounce this body for the sake of keeping the Precepts. In whatever place I may be reborn, may I become a monk in the Teaching of the Buddha and course in the pure course. May I stop the defilements and attain the fruit." Having made this vow, he cut his own throat. The blood flowed and his body became crimson.

The girl, wondering what he was doing, went to the door and called. When there was no answer, she broke down the door, looked in, and saw that he was dead. Knowing that her desires would not be fulfilled, her passion subsided, she became miserable, let down her hair, scratched her face with her nails, rolled on the floor and sobbed. While she was doing this her parents returned, knocked on the gate, and when there was no reply sent a man over the wall to see what the matter was. When they entered and saw the girl's condition, they asked what had happened. The girl thought: "If I say that the monk attacked me, I will have maligned the Holy Ones and will fall into hell and undergo terrible sufferings. I shall tell the truth." She then told what had happened and added: "This impure body of mine will never become a pure vessel and is now a source of misery." When her parents heard this, they were astonished to think that a totally defiled being could, in this manner, discern the Dharma Nature, and said to her: "Do not despair. All the components of being are impermanent."

Seeing the monk's body covered with blood like a red sandalwood tree, they bowed before it and lauded the monk for dying rather than breaking the Precepts of the Buddha.

It was a law of that country that when a monk died in the home of a layman a thousand gold coins were to be paid to the king. Taking a thousand pieces of gold, the lay-disciple went to the king and said: "Your Majesty, I have a great sin on my conscience. Take these gold coins, I beseech you." The king said: "In all my kingdom you alone have faith in the Three Treasures, are of good behavior, and speak the truth. Now tell me what sin you have committed." When the lay-disciple told what had happened, the king said: "You have committed no great crime. Take the money back. I shall come to your house to honor the remains of the monk." The golden drum was beaten, an entourage was formed, and all proceeded to the lay-disciple's house where they saw the monk's body like a red sandalwood tree. They paid their respects to it, praised the monk's virtues, adorned it with the seven kinds of jewels, laid it out on a chariot and took it to a level plane where all could view it. There they cremated it with sandalwood.

Because the girl was rare in the world for her beauty, the people all pointed her out and said: "How would it be possible not to be attracted by such loveliness? Marvelous indeed is it that the monk did not attain the fruit of this, but surrendered his body and died in order to keep the Precepts." They then invited the monk's teacher to come and teach them the Supreme Dharma. When he had taught it to them they had faith and some became monks and attempted to keep the Precepts. Some brought forth a mind of Supreme Enlightenment, and all had faith and rejoiced.

18

The Householder Without Organs

❧

Upon a certain occasion the Enlightened One was residing in the city of Śrāvastī at the Jetavana monastery in Anāthapiṇḍika's park, teaching the Dharma to great assembly of monks. At that time, there lived in that country a wealthy householder who possessed gold and silver, the seven kinds of precious jewels, elephants, horses, cattle, sheep, men and women slaves who worked for him, and storehouses filled with goods. This householder had five lovely, intelligent daughters, but no son.

At a time when the householder's wife was pregnant, the householder died. At that time, according to the laws of that country, if a man died leaving no male heir it was the right of the king to take the dead man's property. The king now sent an official to evaluate and confiscate all the householder's possessions. The daughters thought as follows: "It is impossible to know whether it is a boy or a girl in our mother's womb. If a girl is born, the king will, without question, take all our property, but if a son is born, the property will belong to him." Thereupon they went to the king and said: "Your Majesty, since our father died without a male heir, it is quite right for you to take our property. However, our mother is now pregnant. If a girl is born, we lose the property, of course, but if a son is born will not the property be his?" The king, Prasenajit, being a just man who ruled according to the Dharma, agreed that this would be so. Soon after, when the nine months had been fulfilled, a son was born whose body, although complete with the male organs, was without eyes, ears, nose, tongue, hands, or feet. He was named Mañjipila.

The girls reported this to the king who considered the case and thought: "If one is born with eyes, ears, nose, tongue, hands and feet, and so on, but without the male organs, he has no right to property. Yet if one is born with the male organs intact, even though he is without the other organs, his father's property belongs to him. Therefore, he told the girls: "Your father's property belongs to you and your baby brother." Thereupon they took possession of the property.

At that time the eldest daughter was married to a man of the same caste. When she was taken to his household she prepared his seat, made his bed, bowed to him, prepared fine food and offered it to him. She went out to meet him, and saw to it that all the men and women servants respected and honored him in the proper manner. The husband once said to her: "When a man and woman marry, there is usually not all this respect. Why is it that you honor me like this?" His wife explained to him all that had happened and concluded by saying: "If only one has the male organs, the king cannot take one's property. This is the reason that I honor you."

When the householder heard his wife's words, he was astonished. Taking her, he went to the Buddha and asked: "Lord, why was the householder's son born without organs and why did he inherit his father's wealth?"

The Enlightened One replied: "Householder, it is well that you have asked this. I shall explain the reason. Listen attentively and bear it well in mind."

The householder said: "Lord, I shall listen. Deign to tell me, I beseech you."

The Buddha said: "In times long past, there lived a householder who had two sons. One's name was Dāna, the other's was Śīla. From earliest age, these two brothers were of good character, modest, and spoke the truth. They rejoiced in giving, supported poverty-stricken beggars, and people respected and praised them. The king made the eldest brother a magistrate and his functions were those of a king's minister.

"At that time, according to the king's law, when people loaned property to each other they first were obliged to show it to a magistrate. Upon a certain occasion, a merchant who was going to sea requested the son named Dāna to lend him money and promised to repay him when he returned. Taking his son as a witness, he went to his elder brother, the magistrate, and said to him: 'Brother, this merchant is borrowing money from me and will repay me. If, while he is at sea, I should die, when the money is repaid it should be given to this young son of mine.' To this the elder brother agreed. Not long after, Dāna died.

When the merchant had gone to sea his ship was struck by a storm, capsized, and he alone of the crew as able to reach shore by holding to a piece of wood. When he arrived home alone, the son, knowing that the merchant had come alone and could not repay his father's money, made no claims.

"Again the merchant borrowed and went to sea and this time obtained many precious gems. Arriving home, he thought: 'Until now, the son of the householder has not demanded his money. Being young, he probably does not know that I borrowed from his father. I shall find out.' Donning an expensive silk robe and mounting a fine horse, he rode to the merchants' guild. When the son of the householder saw him attired in costly silks and riding a fine horse, he thought: 'The merchant has obtained great wealth. Now I shall get my money from him. He sent a go-between, requesting payment. The merchant thought: 'I did, indeed, borrow a certain sum from the householder, but right now I cannot repay it. I shall employ a ruse.' Taking a precious jewel, he went to the wife of the magistrate and said: 'Madame, deign to hear me. Formerly I borrowed a small sum from the householder Dāna. When his son comes to the magistrate to demand payment, tell him that he should say that he knows nothing about it. This will be a great kindness to me and to recompense you I offer you this jewel, which is valued at ten thousand ounces of silver.' The woman replied: 'My husband is very honest and quite incapable of telling a falsehood; nevertheless, I shall do as you say, and she accepted the jewel.

"That night, when the master of the house came home and his wife told him what the merchant had done, the magistrate was horrified and exclaimed: 'When I think of what righteousness is, I am ashamed. The king made me magistrate because I have never lied. If I were to lie now, I should betray the law.'

"The next day the merchant came again and the woman told him what her husband had said and returned the jewel to him. The merchant then offered her a jewel worth three-hundred thousand ounces of silver and said: 'Certainly there could be nothing wrong with taking such a jewel, just to say a few words about so trifling a matter. It is not the same as taking a bribe, and I offer it just to thank you.' The woman, coveting the jewel, agreed, and promised to do what the merchant asked.

"That night when the master came home, his wife again told him what had taken place. The magistrate said: 'It was because I never lied that I was appointed magistrate. If I lie now, no one will ever believe me in this lifetime and in the next I will undergo suffering for countless aeons.'

"The householder had a baby boy who was still at the toddling stage. The householder's wife said to him: 'Ever since we have been married you have never heard me ask for even a small favor. If you refuse this favor that I now ask, I shall kill both the child and myself.' When the magistrate heard this he thought: 'I am like a man in prison who will never be released and cannot escape. This is my only son. If he dies I will have no heir, but if I do what my wife demands, I will be mistrusted by everyone in the world and in future lives will experience endless sufferings.' Against his will, he agreed with his wife's request.

"The wife rejoiced greatly and told the merchant: 'I have done as you asked. When action is brought against you, do whatever you wish.' The merchant was delighted, returned to his home, caparisoned an elephant, put on a jeweled robe, and rode to the merchants' guild. When the son of the householder saw him he rejoiced, believing that now that the merchant had become wealthy he would repay what he had borrowed. Approaching him, he said: 'Ah, merchant, you remember the money that you borrowed from my father. Please repay me now.'

"The merchant feigned surprise: 'I know nothing about any money borrowed from you.'

"The boy said: 'The magistrate knows that in such and such a month of such and such a year you borrowed from my father. Why do you try to make difficulties?'

"The merchant said: 'I know nothing of borrowing anything from you. If you have proof, let us go to the magistrate.'

"Together they went to the magistrate. The boy said to his uncle: 'Formerly this man borrowed from my father. You, uncle, know this, but this man pretends to know nothing about it.'

"The uncle said: 'I have no knowledge of this.'

"The nephew, in astonishment, said: 'You yourself, with your own hands, evaluated the money, and now you say you know nothing about it?'

"The uncle replied: 'I have never heard of such a thing.'

"In anger, the boy reproached his uncle: 'And you are called a righteous man! A magistrate of the king! Praised by all the people as an honest man, you tell a hideous lie like this to your own nephew! If you deceive other people as you have deceived me, the truth will become known concerning you.'"

The Enlightened One then said: "Householder, who do you think was that magistrate? You should know that it was none other than the child who was born without organs. Because of his lie, the magistrate was reborn in the great hell and underwent various kinds of tortures. Delivered from the great hell, he was born in a body without organs five-hundred times. Because he had been charitable, he was born as a man of wealth although without organs. The fruits of sin and virtue never become exhausted. All of you, therefore, endeavor to guard the acts of body, speech and mind and cut off evil deeds."

The great assembly, having heard the word of the Buddha, believed. Some attained from the first to the fourth fruits, some brought forth a mind of Supreme Enlightenment. In faith, they rejoiced greatly.

19

The Beggar Woman Gives Her Clothing

☙❦❧

At one time the Lord was residing in Śrāvastī at the Jetavana monastery in Anāthapiṇḍika's park, teaching the Dharma to a great assembly of monks. At that time, in that country, there was born to the wife of a householder a girl child who was lovely and beautiful. Because at birth the child had been wrapped in a soft white cloth, her parents, in astonishment, took her to a soothsayer. The soothsayer examined the child and said: "This girl is endowed with great virtue," and named her Suci. As the child grew, the cloth also grew in proportion.

After the girl had grown, many sought her in marriage, and her parents searched for gold and silver for her wedding ornaments. Seeing this, the girl asked: "Father and mother, what are you going to do with all this gold and silver?" When told that it would be taken to a goldsmith to make ornaments for her wedding, she said: "I have no desire to be married, I wish to go forth into homelessness."

The parents consented to the girl's wish and brought out cloth with which to prepare the monastic robe. When the girl asked the purpose of the cloth and they told her it was for her robe, she said: "I have a robe. It is not necessary to sew one. Take me now to the Buddha, I beg you."

When her parents had taken her to the Enlightened One, she bowed at his feet and requested the going-forth. When the Lord said "Welcome," her hair fell away and the white robe which she wore became a mendicant's robe of five parts. The girl was made a novice and placed under the tutelage of Mahāprajāpatī. Due to her great diligence, in a short time she became an arhat.

Ānanda said to the Enlightened One: "Lord, by reason of what former virtue did this nun, born covered with a white cloth in the home of a householder, so quickly become an arhat?"

The Buddha said: "Ānanda, in times long past, when the Buddha called Virtuous Refuge and his disciples passed through this world for the benefit of beings, all the people made great offerings. At that time, for the benefit of many and that all might hear the Dharma, a certain monk went about enjoining the giving of alms.

"At that time there was a beggar woman by the name of Daniśka who, together with her husband, had only a single piece of cloth for their clothing. When the husband went out to beg, he put on the cloth and the wife lay down and covered herself with grass. When the wife went out begging it was she who put on the cloth while the husband lay down and covered himself with grass.

"Upon a certain occasion the exhorting monk came to the door of that couple's dwelling and, seeing the woman, said: 'Oh woman, go pay homage to the Enlightened One! Acquire merit!' He then lauded the virtues of giving, censured the evil of greediness, and continued: 'Oh woman, to meet a Buddha in this world is difficult. To obtain the human body is difficult. Why do you not go pay homage to the Enlightened One?'

"The woman said: 'Young monk, remain here a moment. I shall go into the house and return.' Entering the house, she said to her husband: 'A monk has come to the door. He says that one should pay homage to the Buddha, hear the Dharma, and give gifts. In a former life we were uncharitable and that is the reason we are now beggars. In some way, we should make provision for the next life.'

"The husband replied: 'We should, indeed, give gifts, but since we are beggars and have nothing, what can we give?'

"The woman answered: 'If it is true that because we formerly gave nothing we are now beggars, if we give nothing now, what will be our fate in the next life? I shall give something and you should be glad.'

"The man knew that there was only one thing to give, but said: 'If you have something to give, give it. But we have nothing else to wear when we go out begging, and begging is the only way we have of making a living.'

"The woman said: 'If we give the cloth and then die, what will be the loss? In this lifetime we have nothing, anyway, and there will be good fruits in the next lifetime. I think that if we give the gift and die, we shall be fortunate.'

"The husband was reluctant to do this, but said: 'Well, do whatever you wish.'

"The woman quickly went out to the monk and said to him: 'Monk, do not look at me. I shall give a gift.'

"The monk answered: 'When one gives a gift it must be given openly and given with one's hands. If you do this, I shall bless you with a verse.'

"The woman said: 'I have only this cloth with which to cover my body and that is to be my gift. How can you, a noble monk, look upon an evil, filthy body? I shall give it to you from within the house.' She entered the house, removed the cloth, and handed it to the monk who took the cloth, gave her his blessing, and went to the Buddha. The Buddha said: 'This cloth was given by a woman.'

"When the monk had offered the cloth to the Buddha and he had taken it into his hands, the assembly thought: 'A king would never take such a dirty old rag into his hands.'

"Knowing their thoughts, the Buddha said: 'Never has there been a gift to the Sangha more pure than this.' Thereupon the assembly was astonished. The king's wife, rejoicing greatly, removed her robes and jewels and sent them to the beggar woman. The king also sent jewels to the beggar and commanded him and his wife to appear in the assembly. When the Buddha, the Protector, the Helper, had taught the Supreme Dharma, many of those present were liberated."

Then the Buddha said to Ānanda: "Ānanda, this nun Suci was at that time that beggar woman. Because she gave, in great faith, that single piece of cloth, she was born for sixty-one kalpas wearing a cloth and endowed with possessions. Having requested from that Buddha and Supreme Dharma and the bliss of Liberation, she has now met me and attained arhatship. You should all, therefore, listen to the Dharma and make efforts to give gifts."

When the assembly had heard these words of the Buddha, they believed and rejoiced greatly.

20

The Slave Woman Sells Her Poverty to the Monk Mahākātyāyana

☙❧

At one time the Noble Mahākātyāyana was residing in the land of Apa. At that time, there was in that land a wealthy, but avaricious and cruel householder who owned an old female slave. Because this old woman did evil things, he gave her no clothing to cover her body, no food to eat, and constantly beat her. Unable to endure this suffering, the old slave decided to kill herself. Taking a water jug, she went to the water's edge and began to wail loudly.

At that time the monk Mahākātyāyana was passing by and heard her. He asked: "Old woman, why do you cry like this?"

The old woman answered: "Your Reverence, I have grown old. I am forced to do heavy labor and I am not given food or clothing. It would be better if I died. That is why I am wailing."

The monk said: "Would you like to sell your poverty?"

The old woman answered: "Your Reverence, how can one sell poverty? Who would buy it?"

Mahākātyāyana said: "Poverty can be sold." When he had said this three times, the old woman asked: "If that is true, how can it be sold?"

The monk said: "Old woman, if you truly want to sell your poverty, I will show you how. But you must do as I tell you."

When the old woman said that she would certainly do as the monk told her, he said: "First of all, you must wash your hands. Then you must make a gift."

The old woman said: "Your Reverence, I have nothing at all. How can I make a gift? Even this water-jug belongs to my mistress and is not mine. I have nothing."

When the monk said: "Old woman, fill your food-bowl with water and offer it to me, then I shall say a blessing," the woman filled her bowl with water and offered it. Then the monk took it into his hands, said a blessing, and invoked the name of the Buddha. He then exhorted the old woman to pray and to think, with firm faith, of all the Buddha's virtues. He then asked her if she had a place to live.

The old woman said: "I have no place of my own, but sometimes I stay in the place where I grind grain, eat, and work."

The monk said: "You must strive hard to cut off all thoughts of resentment and suffering, which are connected with evil deeds. At night, after you have slept outside, quietly open your mistress's door, go inside, spread clean grass in a corner, sit on it, think constantly of the Buddha, and pray."

The old woman did as the monk had told her and one night she died and was reborn among the gods of the Thirty-Three. The following morning when the mistress of the house awoke and saw that the old slave had died in the house, she was infuriated and screamed: "Drag this old woman outside! She was never allowed in the house. How could she have crept in and died here?" A grass rope was then tied to the old woman's legs and she was dragged to the burial ground.

When the old woman was reborn among the gods, five hundred goddesses had surrounded one of the gods and were playing games with him. Those of the gods with keen minds understood why the old woman had been reborn there, but the dull-witted ones did not. Even the old woman, although experiencing great happiness, did not understand the reason for this.

At that time Śāriputra was residing in the realm of the gods of the Thirty-Three. He asked the old woman: "By reason of what virtues have you been reborn here?" When she said that she herself didn't know he looked with his deva-eye, understood the reason and made this known. Then he and five-hundred goddesses proceeded to the burial-ground and made offerings of celestial flowers around the old woman's corpse. That great land was filled with the light of the gods, and the old woman's mistress and all the others were astonished. Going to the burial ground and seeing a host of goddesses honoring the old woman's corpse, they asked: "Oh goddesses, why do you honor this old woman's bones? While she was living, everyone hated her. Why do you do this now that she is dead?"

Thereupon the goddesses explained in detail the reason why the old woman had been reborn among the gods. They then proceeded to where the Noble Mahākātyāyana was. The noble monk taught them charity, the Precepts, birth in a higher state, and the Supreme Dharma. They then became freed from the defilements, attained the pure eye of the Dharma, and returned to their own realm. And the others, having heard the exposition of the Dharma, attained the fruits, from the first up to the fourth. All had faith and rejoiced.

21

Golden God

❦

Thus have I heard: at one time, the Enlightened One was residing in the city of Śrāvastī at the Jetavana monastery in Anāthapiṇḍika's park. At that time, there was in that country a wealthy householder who owned jewels, treasures, and great possessions. He had married a woman of his own caste, and a son had been born to him who was of a golden color. At the time of the birth, a soothsayer had been called who examined the child and named him Golden God. When the boy was born there appeared in the house a well which was eight cubits across, eight cubits deep, and when water was drawn from it, whatever one wished for appeared: food, clothing, drink, gold or silver, or wishing-gems.

When the child grew up, he became learned in the sciences, the householder, thinking that it was time for him to marry, searched for a girl who was of the same color and as lovely as the boy. At that time there lived in the land of Jampaka a wealthy householder who had a daughter called Golden Light, who was of exceptional beauty, form, and complexion, and in whose house a magic well had also appeared when she was born. The parents of this girl were seeking a husband for her who would be of the same golden color and as lovely as she, and when they heard of the householder with the golden son, they brought her to Śrāvastī and married her to the boy.

Golden God invited the Buddha and the Sangha to his home and honored them. When the Lord had taught the Supreme Dharma, the youth, his wife, and his parents were liberated from the grievous sins that had accumulated for two-hundred thousand kalpas, their minds became purified and they became streamwinners.

Golden God and Golden Light asked their parents' permission to join the Sangha. When this had been given, they went to the

Buddha, bowed their heads at his feet, joined their palms in reverence, and besought the Lord to compassionately admit them to the Order. When the Buddha said: "Welcome," their hair dropped away and they were clad in the red robes. Golden God became a monk in the Buddha's Sangha, and Golden Light resided as a nun with Mahāprajāpati. Within a short time, both became arhats endowed with the three knowledges, the six super-normal powers, the eight deliverances, and all blessings.

Thereupon the Noble Ānanda said to the Buddha: "Lord, this monk Golden God and the nun Golden Light—because of what previous merits did two wishing-wells appear when they were born, wishing-wells that gave everyone whatever they desired. What was the reason for this?"

The Buddha said: "Ānanda, in times long past, sixty-one kalpas ago, when the Buddha Vipaśyin had come to this world, taught the Dharma, and had attained final Nirvana, the monks who followed his teaching went through all the cities for the benefit of beings. At that time, there was a wealthy prince of the upper caste who gave his wealth to the monks for food and robes. There was also a man and his wife at that time who were beggars. This couple thought: 'When our parents were alive and we had jewels, great property and wealth, we never met the Noble Sangha. Now that we have been reduced to poverty and are beggars, the Sangha of holy men has come to aid all beings. All the princes and wealthy people are offering the necessities, and we have nothing to give. If, in this lifetime, we cannot make an offering, what we shall be in the next lifetime we do not know.' The wife said: 'Go and search in your parent's old treasure house. Perhaps you will find some small thing there. If you do, we can make an offering to the Sangha.' The beggar went there, dug in the earth, and found a gold coin. Buying a new pitcher, they filled it with water, dropped the gold coin into it, and covering the pitcher with a mirror which belonged to the wife, offered this to the Sangha. The offering was accepted and some of the monk used the pitcher to carry water, some used it to wash their hands, some to wash their begging bowls. When the beggar couple saw this, they rejoiced greatly and returned home. Not long thereafter, they died and were reborn among the gods of the Thirty-Three.

"Ānanda, these two, who are now called Golden God and Golden Light, were the beggar couple who filled the pitcher with water and offered it with the golden coin and the mirror. Through the power of that offering, they have been born beautiful and shining like gold for sixty-one kalpas. Because, at that time, they performed a very small act of virtue with a mind of firm faith, they have now reached the end of the Samsara and have become arhats.

"This, Ānanda, is the fruit of virtue and one should persevere in it. By giving a tiny gift, that beggar woman became endowed with an accumulation of virtue that is beyond conception."

When Ānanda and the great assembly heard the word of the Buddha, they believed. They then understood concerning the accumulation of the virtue of liberality, had complete faith, and rejoiced.

22

The Man With Two Families

❧

Thus have I heard: at one time, the Enlightened One was residing in the city of Śrāvastī at the Jetavana monastery in
Anāthapiṇḍika's park. At that time, there was a wealthy householder in that country who had married a woman of his own caste.
He was exceedingly sad because no son had been born to him. He
prayed to all the gods and finally his prayer was answered. His
wife became pregnant, and when her time was fulfilled a son was
born who was handsome and comely. The parents and relatives all
rejoiced and held the anointing ceremony on the banks of a great
river. During the celebration, while the child was being admired
and passed from hand to hand, it slipped into the water and was
carried away by the stream. Through the power of virtue, the child
did not die, but was swallowed by a fish and remained alive in the
fish's belly.

At the mouth of the river there was a city, and in that city there
lived a wealthy householder whose servants chanced to catch the
fish that had swallowed the child. When the fish was opened and
the child was found, a servant took it to the householder's wife,
who rejoiced greatly and exclaimed: "This is in answer to our
prayers to all the gods for a son." The child was then given to a
nurse who cared for it.

The first householder, hearing that a householder at the mouth
of the river had found a child in the belly of a fish, believed that it
was his child. Hurriedly going to that householder, said to him:
"The child that you found in the fish is my son. While we were
celebrating the anointing feast on the banks of the river, he fell
into the water. It is unquestionably ours."

The other householder said: "You only think it is your son. It
was found by us in the belly of a fish after we had prayed to all the
gods. By virtue of our prayers, the child came to us and it is ours."

the two householders argued and disputed, and finally took the case to the king for judgement.

The child's parents pleaded: "Your Majesty, the child is ours. While we were celebrating the anointing feast on the banks of the river, he fell into the water and was carried away. It is, without question, our child."

The other householder said: "Nothing of the kind. It is we who found the child in the belly of a fish." The dispute raged back and forth. The king, seeing the difficulty of rendering a decision, said: "There is no need of going on with the argument. Both of you will bring up the child. When it grows up, each of you will choose a wife for him and the children of each wife will belong to each family."

In accordance with the king's command, the two householders raised the child together. When it had come of age, the youth requested permission to become a monk. When the parents consented, he went to the Buddha, bowed at his feet, joined his palms in reverence, and said: "Lord, I beg to become a monk."

When the Buddha said: "Welcome," his hair and beard fell away, he became a monk, and was given the name "Two Families." When the Enlightened One had instructed him in the Dharma, he arrived at the end of suffering and attained the bliss of an arhat.

The Noble Ānanda said to the Buddha: "Lord, because of what former virtues did this monk not die when he fell into the river, was swallowed by a fish, and has now met the Buddha and become a monk? What is the reason for this?"

The Enlightened One said: "Ānanda, listen well and I shall explain it to you. Long ago, when the Buddha Vipaśyin had come to this earth, he instructed many people in the Dharma. At that time a certain householder, hearing the Buddha explain the virtue of giving and the merits of keeping the Precepts, had faith, and there arose in him a mind of great devotion. In the presence of the Enlightened One, he vowed to refrain from taking life and made an offering of a single gold coin. It was due to the merits of that virtuous deed that, wherever he was born, he was endowed with great wealth and was never poor.

"Ānanda, this monk called "Two Families" was at that time and under those circumstances the householder. Because he offered the Buddha that one golden coin with a mind of firm faith, he was born with great wealth for sixty-one kalpas. Now, in this birth, although he fell into the water, he did not die. He has been brought up by two mothers in homes of great wealth, and because he took refuge in the Three Treasures, he has now met me and attained to the state of an arhat."

Hearing these words of the Buddha, Ānanda and the great assembly believed and rejoiced greatly.

23

King Chandraprabha Gives His Head

☙❧

Thus have I heard at one time: upon a certain occasion when the
Enlightened One was residing in the Mango Grove at Vaiśālī,
he spoke to the Noble Ānanda: "Ānanda, when one attains to the
four bases of psychic power, one may remain in the world for an
entire kalpa. Having applied myself to the four bases of psychic
power, I now dwell in the world for as long as I desire." The Lord
repeated this three times, but Ānanda, having fallen into the snares
of Māra, sat without answering. Again the Buddha spoke to Ānanda;
"Ānanda, you should go into retreat and meditate upon what I have
told you." Thereupon Ānanda rose from his seat and went to a
remote place.

When Ānanda had gone, Māra came to the Buddha and said:
"Enlightened One, you have been in the world for a long time now.
You have tamed, protected, and liberated as many beings as the
sands of the Ganges. Now, you have grown old and it would be
well if you were to enter final Nirvana."

Thereupon the Buddha took a bit of sand, placed it upon his
finger nail, and said to Māra: "Māra, which is greater, the sands of
the earth or the sand on my finger nail?"

Māra answered: "Enlightened One, the sand of the earth is
ofcourse greater than the sand on your finger nail."

The Buddha said: "Māra, the beings which I have tamed and
liberated are like the sand on my finger nail. Those which have not
yet been tamed are like the sands of the great earth. But your wish
will be fulfilled. Within three months, I shall enter final Nirvana."
When Māra heard this, he rejoiced greatly.

At that time Ānanda was asleep in his retreat and dreaming. In
his dream, he saw a mighty tree which filled the entire sky. The
tree was filled with branches, leaves, flowers, and fruit and existed

for the welfare of all sentient beings. Suddenly the tree was shaken by a great wind, which tore away the leaves and branches and scattered them like dust. Then the tree disappeared and all beings mourned. When Ānanda awoke, his mind was upset and he thought to himself: "I dreamed of a great tree which was of benefit to men and gods, and suddenly a great wind caused it to split and destroyed it. The Buddha is like a great tree. He is the refuge and protector of all. Could this mean that the Lord intends to enter final Nirvana?" In great fear, he went to the Buddha, bowed his head at his feet, told his dream, and asked if the Lord intended to enter final Nirvana.

The Enlightened One said: "Thus it is, Ānanda; it is just as you say. Within three months I shall enter final Nirvana. He who attains the four bases of spiritual power abides for an entire kalpa. I told you this three times, but you did not respond. After you had gone, Māra came and requested me to enter final Nirvana, and I agreed."

When Ānanda heard this, he was overcome with grief. He told some of the brethren and they, in turn, told others, and stricken with grief, they all came before the Buddha.

The Buddha then spoke to the entire assembly: "Who among you is eternal? Everything is impermanent. All that I have done has been for your sake. I have completed the work of the Teaching. Do not grieve, but make every effort to exert yourselves."

When the Noble Śāriputra heard that the Enlightened One was going to enter final Nirvana, he grieved bitterly and thought: "Too soon does the Lord pass into final Nirvana. Who will now be a refuge and protector to those who are obstructed by ignorance, including the gods?" Then he thrice spoke to the Buddha: "Lord, I cannot bear to witness the Lord pass into final Nirvana. Grant that I may do this first."

The Buddha said: "If you are certain that the time has come for this, you may do as you wish. All the Noble Ones enter Nirvana when they have become quiescent."

When Śāriputra heard this, he arranged his robe, circumambulated the Lord a hundred times, lauded him with many verses, touched his hands and feet and thrice placed them on his head, and folding his palms said: "I salute the Buddha." Bowing, he then went with a monk named Kunti to the city of Rājagṛha, to the place where he had been born. There he said: "Kunti, go through the cities, the villages, to the king's court and to the ministers' residences and say: 'The Noble Śāriputra is going to enter Nirvana. Come and honor him.'" Thereupon the monk Kunti did as his teacher had bidden him, and went about proclaiming that the Noble Śāriputra had come to this place and was going to attain Nirvana, and that if they wished to witness this they should make haste.

The King Ajātaśatru and the noble princes, the dispensers of gifts, and the householders, hearing the proclamation, were unhappy. Their minds were troubled, and all exclaimed in one voice: "Alas, what shall we do? The Master of the Dharma, the leader of many beings, the holy Śāriputra, is now going to attain Nirvana." Going to Śāriputra, they bowed and said: "Noble One, if you now pass beyond sorrow, who will be a refuge and savior for us and all beings?"

Thereupon Śāriputra taught them as follows: "All beings are, without exception, impermanent. The end of every birth is death. The three worlds are subject to suffering. How will you escape death? By virtue of former good deeds, you have met the Enlightened One in the world. It is exceedingly difficult to hear the Dharma and the Sutras. It is very hard to obtain the human body. Now, bring forth virtue and exert yourselves in those acts which liberate from the Round."

When Śāriputra had taught this teaching, through skill in means such as when a physician gives remedies to the ill, all rejoiced, had faith, and some attained the first fruits. Some attained the second and third fruits, and some became monks and attained the fruits of the arhat. Some, wishing to attain the bliss of a Pratyekabuddha, made vows. All, hearing this teaching, bowed to the Noble One, and each went his own way.

Then, at midnight, Śāriputra attained to the equanimity of body and mind, and establishing his thoughts and reaching onepointedness, he entered dhyāna. Rising from the first dhyāna, he entered the second, third, and fourth. Rising from the fourth dhyāna, he entered the realm of the infinity of space. Rising from that realm, he entered the realm of no-thing-ness, and rising from that realm, he entered the realm of neither perception nor non-perception. Rising from that realm, he arrived at the cessation of perception and sensation.

Then Indra, ruler of the gods, knowing that Śāriputra had attained Nirvana, offered incense and flowers. Proceeding with many hundreds of thousands of the gods who together filled the sky, he came to where Śāriputra was and brought down showers of tears and flowers and said:

"Ah, the holy Śāriputra, who was profound like the sea who was endowed with the doors of wisdom, whose vigor of speech was like a flowing spring; who was perfect in the Precepts, samādhi, and wisdom; who was the great chief of the Dharma, and like unto whom, after the Buddha himself, there was no teacher of the Dharma; he has now attained Nirvana and gone beyond."

When all those who lived within and without the city heard that Śāriputra had attained Nirvana, they prepared oil-lamps, incense, flowers, and various offerings. They came with great sorrow and grief, each to make his offering. Then the lord of the gods, Indra, commanded Viśvakarman to construct a chariot adorned with many jewels, and when this had been done Śāriputra's body was placed in it. Accompanied by gods, nāgas, and yakṣas, the king and his princes and ministers and all the people of the country accompanied it to a beautiful level plain. Then Indra commanded the yakṣas to go to the ends of the earth for sandalwood. When they had brought it, it was formed into a pyre, the body was placed upon it, oil was poured over it, and it was cremated. Then each returned to his own country.

When the fire had gone out, the monk Kunti took his teacher's relics, begging-bowl, and three robes and went to the Buddha. Bowing at his feet and kneeling, he said: "Lord, I have brought my teacher's relics, begging-bowl, and robes."

When Ānanda heard the monk's words, he was greatly grieved and said to the Buddha: "Lord, now that Śāriputra, who was the foremost of the assembly, has attained Nirvana, upon whom shall we depend? To whom shall we look for help?"

The Buddha said: "Ānanda, Śāriputra who has now attained Nirvana, was not the Precepts, samādhi, wisdom, liberation, the Transcendental Wisdom of Enlightenment, the Dharmakāya, nor Nirvana. Ānanda, this is not the first time that Śāriputra has preceded me in Nirvana. In times long past he was also unable to bear my attaining Nirvana before he did and preceded me."

Then Ānanda folded his palms and said: "Lord, I beg you to relate in detail how in former times Śāriputra attained Nirvana before the Lord."

The Buddha said: "Ānanda, in times long past, aeons ago, aeons past reckoning, past conceiving, there was a king who ruled over this Jambudvīpa by the name of Chandraprabha who had eighty-four thousand minor kings subject to him, ruled over ninety-thousand countries, eighty-thousand cities, and had twenty-thousand wives. His first queen's name was Giver of Flowers. His second queen was called Large Eyes, and she had five-hundred sons. The eldest son's name was Good Precepts and the palace where he resided was called Pleasant Desire, was five-hundred yojanas long, and was constructed of gold, silver, lapis-lazuli, and crystal. Around the palace there were groves of trees bearing gold, silver, and lapis-lazuli. Some of the branches were of gold and the leaves of silver; some of the branches were of silver and leaves of gold. The sand at the bottom of the pools in the park was of the four kinds of jewels which had dropped into the water and sunk into the bottom. For a distance of thirty yojanas, the ground around the place was covered with gold, silver, lapis-lazuli and crystal. In that country everyone was happy. The crops thrived, there was an abundance of everything, and jewels without number.

"Upon a certain occasion the king sat in his palace and thought: 'To become a leader of all is the fruit of former virtues. For those who are mighty in the world and honored by all, the objects of the five desires appear as soon as they are wished for. It is like a farmer who labors in the spring and reaps a good crop in the autumn. Through the harvest of former virtues I have arrived at this abundance. But if I do not plant more seeds now, what will the future harvest be?' Calling his ministers together, he said to them: 'Ministers, collect and pile up all my jewels and treasures at the city gates and in the market place, and distribute them to all beings. Also convey my command to all the eighty-four thousand subject kings that they are to give their treasures to living beings.'

"When the king had given this command, the golden banner was furled, the golden drum was beaten, and the tidings spread in all directions. Then the monks, brahmins, beggars, all those without protection, and the destitute came together like a great cloud. Those who were naked were given clothing. The hungry were fed. Those who had nothing were given gold, silver, and jewels. The sick were given medicines and cared for, and the needs of all were met. Then the beings of Jambudvīpa lauded and praised the king for the happiness and welfare he had brought about. His name and fame spread to the ten directions, and there was no one who disobeyed his command.

"At that time, there was a minor king by the name of Siṃhasena who lived in a border country. He had grown so envious of King Candraprabha that he found no pleasure in life and could no longer sleep. This king thought: 'Unless Candraprabha is done away with, my fame will never be know. I shall bring together all the beggarfolk in my kingdom and find a way of putting an end to him.' He then invited all the beggars in his kingdom, fed them on various kinds of delicious foods for ten months, then said to them: 'Happiness eludes me day and night. Since you who follow the Dharma are the recipients of my hospitality, you should think of some way of removing my sufferings.' The mendicant brahmins said: 'Your Majesty, tell us the cause of your misery and we shall attempt to alleviate it.' The king said: 'Everyone praises the virtues of that king called Candraprabha. Everyone pays him special honors, and I alone am not praised for my virtues. It would be difficult to do away with that king, I know, but you must be able to think of some way of making him disappear.'

"When the brahmins heard this, they spoke among themselves: 'Ah, but King Candraprabha is greatly compassionate, and all beings are happy because of his benevolence. And he is like a father to all the mendicants. How could we possibly cause harm to such a king?' Immediately they dispersed and went to other places. When King Siṃhasena heard what the mendicants had said, he was not pleased nor did he rejoice. He sent a proclamation throughout his country saying: 'Whoever will cut off the head of King Candraprabha and bring it to me will share half my kingdom and have my daughter to wed.' A brahmin from the mountains heard this, went to see the king, and with beaming face said: 'Your Majesty, I can fulfill your desire.' The king said: 'When?' The brahmin told him: 'Please give me the necessary provisions, and within a week I shall set out.' For a week, the brahmin repeated magic formulas to protect himself, then started on his journey.

"At that time many evil omens appeared in the land of King Candraprabha. The earth split, lightning flashed, stars fell, people slept during both the day and the night. The nāgas thundered and roared, hail and lightning struck. Many birds made wailing sounds in the sky and fell to earth. Tigers, wolves, panthers, and other wild animals made ugly noises and seemed to be in misery. The eighty-four thousand minor kings dreamed that the golden drum had burst. The minister, Mahācandra, dreamed that a preta had come and stolen the king's golden crown. When the people saw these evil signs, they felt great fear.

"When the brahmin who sought the king's head came to the gateway of the royal city, the god who guarded it refused to let him enter. Slowly the brahmin walked around the city walls seven times, but could find no entry and sat down outside. Thereupon the gods of the pure realm, knowing that King Candraprabha might give his head in order to become perfect in giving, appeared to him in a dream and said: "Great King, you have vowed to give away everything you have. There is now a brahmin beggar at the city gates who cannot enter. You should be aware of this." When the king awoke, he was greatly astonished, and said to his minister Mahācandra: "Minister, go to the city gates and see if there is someone there who is not allowed to enter. If so, let him come in." When the minister arrived at the gates, the protecting god manifested himself to him said: "Minister, this evil-minded brahmin who is sitting here has come from a border region and seeks the king's head. I have been commanded to let him in. What should I do?"

"The minister said: "If this were true, there would have been some evil omen. The king's command cannot be disobeyed." The guardian-god then created no obstacles and allowed the brahmin to enter. Immediately the thought came to the minister that the brahmin did, indeed, want the king's head, and he thought: "I shall have five-hundred heads made of the seven precious jewels and offer those in place of the head of the king."

"The brahmin immediately went to the king's palace and cried out in a loud voice: "Oh King, I am a beggar who has come from a far country. I have heard that you have vowed to give whatever one desires. I have come from a great distance to for something from Your Majesty."

"When the king heard this he was delighted, bowed to the brahmin, asked if he was weary after his journey, and then asked him what he wanted: property, a whole city, wives and children, jewels, carriages, elephants, horses, the seven kinds of jewels, male and female slaves—and promised to give him whatever he wanted.

"The brahmin said: "Your Majesty, although a gift of goods and property is exceedingly valuable, it is not the greatest of gifts. But if one were to make a gift of the flesh from one's own body, that would be unsurpassed. King, I have come from a far country to ask for your head. Do not refuse my request, I beseech you."

"Hearing this, the king's joy knew no bounds and he promised to give his head to the brahmin. When asked when he would make the gift, the king said: "I shall give it to you within seven days."

"The minister Mahācandra then brought the heads made of the seven precious jewels, arranged them in a pile, and said to the brahmin: "Guru, the king's head is of flesh and blood and is unclean. What would you do with it? Let me give you these heads, which are made of the seven precious jewels. They will make you wealthy for the rest of your life. Take them and do not ask for the king's head."

"The brahmin replied: "I have no need for such things. What I require is the king's head. Do not create obstacles, but let my request be fulfilled." Knowing that the brahmin could not be dissuaded, the minister's heart broke in seven pieces and he died from horror and grief.

"The king then sent out a messenger on an elephant to announce that within seven days he would give his head to the brahmin and that all were to present themselves immediately. The minor kings came, bowed to the king, knelt, pressed their palms together, and spoke: "Your Majesty, you are the lord of all Jambudvīpa, and through your grace, all beings are happy. Why do you abandon all these beings for the sake of a single man?" Then the eighty-thousand ministers, the twenty-thousand queens, and the five-hundred princes all begged the king to refrain from giving his head.

"The king then spoke: "Listen, all of you. Since beginningless time, this body of mine has been circling in the cycle of births and deaths. It has participated in exceedingly sinful acts and has never once been the source of merit. For a long time, it was in hell where it was cooked in filthy water, burnt in pits of fire and underwent countless agonies. When born in the realm of the animals which kill each other, it deprived other living beings of life and ate their flesh, became putrid, and created not the slightest merit. When born among the hungry ghosts, it endured countless sufferings by having fire and flames shoot from it, its head hacked with a wheel of knives, being destroyed, and going through it all over again. Its eyes glittered with greed for wealth and property and women. As a preta, I fought with the other hungry ghosts, we killed each other, died countless times. Through the power of greed, hatred, and delusion, never attained to virtue. I now reject this body. It is engendered by filth. It is not eternal, and is quickly destroyed. And since the giving of my head will be of great merit, why should I not give it?" By virtue of giving my head to this brahmin, Supreme Enlightenment will be achieved. When the Enlightenment of a Buddha will have been realized, I will be perfect in all the virtues. Then, through skill in means, I shall deliver you from all your sufferings. Do not now create obstacles." When the minor kings, queens, and princes heard this, they could think of nothing to say.

"The great king then said to the brahmin: "Guru, the time has come. You may now have my head." The brahmin said: "Your Majesty, how could I dare to cut off your head here in the midst of this great assembly? If you truly deign to give me your head, let us go by ourselves into the forest." The king said to the ministers: "If you truly revere me, you will do no harm to the brahmin," and he and the brahmin went into the forest.

"The brahmin said: "Your Majesty, your body is very powerful and I fear that it will react when pain comes. Tie yourself to a tree." The king then tied himself to a tree which was covered with blossoms and flowers, knelt on the ground, and said to the brahmin: "Now, brahmin, cut off my head. I give it to you willingly. The virtue which I obtain from this is not to obtain birth as a Māra, a Brahmā, an Indra, or a Cakravartin. I do not seek the pleasures of the three worlds. I do this to attain Supreme Enlightenment and to lead all beings to Nirvana."

"Just as the brahmin raised his sword, the god of the tree said: "Why do you commit this sinful act?" and struck the brahmin across the face. The brahmin tripped and fell to the ground. The king, seeing the god of the tree, said: "In former times, I have given my head at this tree nine-hundred and ninety-nine times. By giving it once more, the perfection of giving will be complete. Do not create an obstacle to my attaining Supreme Enlightenment." Hearing this, the tree-god brought the brahmin back to consciousness. He got back on his feet, took his sword, and chopped off the king's head.

"Immediately the great earth trembled in six ways. The palaces of the gods shook, and the gods, seeking the reason for this and seeing that the bodhisattva had given his head for the sake of all living beings, came together and wept. Letting fall a shower of tears, they said: "King Candraprabha has given his head, and the pāramitā of giving has been perfected." When King Siṃhasena heard this, his heart burst and he died.

"When the brahmin had taken the king's head, all the minor kings, the ministers, queens, and princes threw themselves on the ground and wailed loudly. Some pulled out their hair. Some scratched their faces and screamed.

"The brahmin took the king's head, walked for a short distance, and threw it away. Other brahmins, seeing this, said to him: "You are evil. Why did you take the king's head?" and they refused to let him approach. All who met him on the road reviled him and refused to give him alms. As he went along starving, he heard that King Siṃhasena had died, and becoming terrified, his heart burst, he vomited blood and died.

"Ānanda, at that time Māra was King Siṃhasena. Devadatta was the evil brahmin. Maudgalyāyāna was the tree-god, and Śāriputra was the minister Mahācandra who, unable to bear his grief, died before the king. Now, having learned that I shall attain final Nirvana, he has attained it first."

When the Buddha had thus spoken, the Noble Ānanda and all the great assembly praised and lauded the amazing virtues of the Buddha, and by exertion in meditation, some attained the four fruits and some attained Supreme Enlightenment. All had faith in the Buddha's word and rejoiced.

24

The Seven Sons of Minister Mṛgara

ॐ

Thus have I heard at one time: the Enlightened One was residing in the city of Śrāvastī at the Jetavana monastery in Anāthapiṇḍika's park. At that time, King Prasenajit had a minister by the name of Mṛgara who was endowed with great wealth and property and who had seven sons, six of whom were married. The youngest son being still without a wife, his father thought: "Old age is upon me and death is approaching. I shall have a search made for a good wife for my youngest son." One day when he had met a brahmin who was a friend of his, he said: "Brahmin, I have never sought a wife for my youngest son and now I know not whom to ask. As you go about among the different people, look for a wife for my son. She should be virtuous and kind, wise, intelligent and beautiful. I shall recompense you for your trouble." The brahmin agreed, and as he went about among the different peoples he came to a land called Śridikta where he saw five-hundred girls playing, gathering flowers and making offerings to the Buddha. The brahmin followed them and watched. When the girls came to a small stream he noticed that all of them, except one, removed their shoes when they crossed. When they came to a river, all the girls removed their clothing before crossing, but the same girl did not. Going on, the girls came to a forest and climbed trees to pick blossoms, while the same girl remained on the ground and gathered more than the others. Thereupon the brahmin approached the girl and said: "Daughter, I wish to ask you a question and want you to answer properly." The girl said: "Ask whatever you wish." The brahmin said: "When you girls were crossing the stream, all took off their shoes except you. Why was this?" The girl said: "Brahmin, that is not hard to answer—when one walks on dry land one can see all the thorns, stones, and other obstacles and can avoid them. But if there are splinters, poisonous lizards or snakes in the water, one cannot see them. I left my shoes on so I would not step on such thing and hurt my feet." The brahmin then asked: "When the other girls crossed the river they rolled up their dresses or took them off, but you did not. Why?" The girl replied: "A person's body has both pleasing and ugly marks on it. If one rolls up one's dress and people see the attractive marks, they say nothing, but if they see the ugly marks, they make fun. That is the reason I didn't tuck up my dress." The brahmin said: "Very well, Now, when the other girls climbed the trees to gather blossoms, you stayed on the ground. Why was that?" The girl said: "Because if one climbs a tree and a branch breaks, one will fall and get hurt."

Now, this girl's father was King Prasenajit's younger brother, who had formerly committed an offense and been exiled. He came to this country, where he had married a girl called Anuradha who had born him this daughter.

The brahmin said: "Daughter, you are intelligent and honest. I wish to meet your parents." The girl agreed, and when they arrived at her home, she went in and told her father that a brahmin was outside waiting to meet him. The father went out, greeted the brahmin, introduced himself, and after the usual amenities had been exchanged, the brahmin asked whether the lovely girl was the man's daughter and whether she was engaged. When informed that she was not, the brahmin asked whether the man knew a minister in the city of Śrāvastī by the name of Mṛgara. The man replied: "Yes, we are relatives." The brahmin then said: "The minister has seven sons, the youngest of whom is unusually handsome. If you were asked to give your daughter in marriage to him, would have consent?" The man replied: "The minister is from a very noble family. If, as you say, he were to ask for my daughter, yes, I would consent."

When the brahmin returned and reported what had taken place, Mṛgara readied horses and carriages and he and his entourage proceeded to Sridikta to bring home the bride. As they drew near they sent a messenger ahead to announce their arrival. The girl's father prepared a great feast for the giving-away of the bride.

At the end of the feast, when all had been fed and entertained and the wedding party was about to leave, the girl's mother said to her in the presence of everyone: "Daughter, from today onward you must always wear only the finest clothing and eat only the best of food. Every day, without fail, you must look in the mirror." When the girl agreed to do this, the in-laws were displeased and thought to themselves: "Not every day is a holiday. Why should she always wear fine clothes and eat fine food? And why she should look in the mirror every day?" Grumbling, they finished the feast and left for home.

Along the road they came to a cool, pleasant pavilion, and as the bride's father-in-law had arrived there first, he entered and sat down to rest. As soon as the bride arrived, she told him: "You must not stay in this building. I beg all of you to leave immediately." All went out, except one of the in-laws, who remained sitting there. Suddenly, the horses and oxen rubbed against one of the beams, the building collapsed, and the man sitting inside was killed. The father-in-law thought: "This girl has saved me from a terrible death." Thereafter he favored her greatly.

As they rode on they came to a ready riverbed and sat down in it to rest. When the daughter-in-law rode up, she cried: "Do not sit there! Go away quickly, I beg you!" The people immediately moved away and at that moment, there was a cloud-burst and a flood which filled the riverbed. The father-in-law again thought: "This is the second time that this girl has saved me from disaster."

Going on, they finally came to their own country and invited all the relatives to a feast and ate and rejoiced. When the guests had departed, the father-in-law gathered together his family and said: "I have grown old, and I am no longer able to take care of my affairs. I shall have to turn them over to you. To whom shall I entrust the management of things, the property, and the keys?" The six daughters-in-law said that they were unable to take on the responsibility, but the new daughter-in-law said she was willing, and was given charge of the household.

She rose early each morning, cleaned the palace and sprinkled it with water, prepared food which she first served to her father and mother-in-law, then to the elders, then the children and servants, and only ate when the others had finished. The minister thought: "This girl is not like my other daughters-in-law. Nor is she doing what her mother instructed her to do." He asked her:

"Daughter, what did it mean when you mother told you to always wear the finest clothing, always eat the finest food, and always look in the mirror? The girl knelt and said: "When my mother said to wear the finest clothing, it meant to take care of my best clothes and wear them only when guests came. To eat only the best food means to eat after everyone else has finished, because it tastes better that way. To look in the mirror does not mean to look at oneself in a bronze or iron mirror, but to rise early in the morning, tidy up inside and outside, sprinkle water, and prepare the chairs and tables. This is what my mother meant."

Upon a certain occasion a bird flew from over the sea carrying rice in its bill which it dropped on the king's palace. Someone found the rice and took it to the king, who decided that such fine rice must be an excellent medicine. He gave orders that the rice should be planted and propagated, and gave some to the minister Mṛgara, who took it home and gave it to his daughter-in-law to plant. She, in turn, gave it to the servants and told them to work the soil properly, plant it, and cultivate it. This was done and the rice grew and multiplied. The others to whom the rice had been given did not cultivate the soil and had no harvest.

At one time the queen became ill. The physicians examined her and reported to the king: "Your Majesty, the only remedy that will save the queen is a certain type of rice from beyond the sea." The king recalled that he had given such rice to various persons to be planted, and asked them if the rice had grown. Some said that it would not grow. Others claimed that thieves had stolen it. But when Mṛgara went home and asked his daughter-in-law if she had planted the rice, explaining that it was needed as medicine for the queen, she told him that it had grown very well and that there was enough of it to feed the entire country. The minister then took the rice to the king, who was delighted and rewarded him richly.

At that time, King Prasenajit and the king of Śridikta disliked each other and constantly fought. Upon a certain occasion, the latter decided to learn whether King Prasenajit had a minister who was wise, intelligent, and honest. In order to do this, he sent the king two identical mares and asked which was the dam and which was the filly. The king called all his ministers together and consulted them, but none could tell. When Mṛgara came home from the palace and told what had happened, the daughter-in-law said: "There is nothing hard about that. Tie the two mares together and feed them good hay. The mother will push the best of the hay over to her filly." The minister reported this to the king, the mares were tied together, and it happened as the daughter-in-law had said.

Then the king of Śridikta sent two identical snakes and asked which was the male and which the female. Again King Prasenajit called his ministers, but they were unable to solve the problem. When Mṛgara went home and told of this, the daughter-in-law said: "That is quite simple. Spread out a soft cloth and place the snakes on it. The male snake will crawl back and forth, but the female will not move. That is because female snake likes to lie on light, soft surfaces, while the male likes rough, hard surfaces.' This was reported to the king, and again it happened just as the girl had said. Again, King Prasenajit rewarded his minister.

The king of Śridikta then sent two identical wooden poles which were two fathoms long, of equal size, neither rough nor smooth, neither thick nor thin, without visible top or bottom, and asked which ends of the poles were the top and which were the bottom. Again the ministers were unable to solve the problem, but when Mṛgara asked his daughter-in-law, she said: "That is not hard. Put the poles in water. The tops will float, the bottoms will sink." This was done and, again, it happened as the girl had said, and again the minister was richly rewarded. The messenger then returned to the king of Śridikta and reported. The king, seeing that the minister of King Prasenajit was indeed intelligent, sent a messenger with many treasures and the message: "Let us now live in peace," and King Prasenajit rejoiced.

Thereupon King Prasenajit inquired of his minister as to how he had known those things. The minister replied that he had not known, that it was his wise daughter-in-law who had known. The king was delighted and said that the girl would now be looked upon as his younger sister.

The girl became pregnant, and when the nine months had passed she gave birth to thirty-two eggs and out of the thirty-two eggs there came thirty-two handsome and comely boys. When they grew up, each was mightier than a thousand men. Although their father delighted in them and loved them, all the people of that country feared them greatly. At that time, brides were being sought for them.

Upon a certain occasion the boys' mother, with a mind of faith and devotion, invited the Buddha and the Sangha and made offerings to them. When the Lord had taught the Dharma, the people of the household attained the fruit of stream winners except the youngest son who, mounting an elephant, rode out of the city. While crossing a bridge which spanned a river he met the son of a great minister crossing from the other side. Since both were of the same caste, neither gave way to the other. The first boy became enraged, urged on his elephant, and forced the minister's son off the bridge. Falling into the river, he broke both his arms and legs. When he returned home wailing and told his parents what had happened, the minister regretfully thought: "Those boys are exceedingly strong, but they are friends of the king it is impossible to harm them. I shall employ a ruse. He then fashioned thirty-two canes out of the seven jewels, concealed a sword in each, and presented these to the boys saying: "Boys, you are young and enjoy playing. Here are some canes to play with. Have fun with them." The boys were delighted and accepted the canes.

According the royal command, those who came into the presence of the king were prohibited from bearing arms. When the boys, carrying their canes, came before the king, the minister made an accusation: "Your Majesty, these thirty-two boys are too powerful for their age, and they certainly have evil intention toward Your Majesty." When the king said that he trusted them, the minister said: "What I have told you is true. May Your Majesty himself ascertain whether or not I am telling the truth. In their canes, those boys have swords hidden and their intentions are unquestionably evil. Examine the canes." When the king opened the canes and found the swords, he had the boys executed. Putting their heads in a box, he sent it to the daughter-in-law of the minister Mṛgara.

At that time, the boys' mother had again invited the Buddha and the Sangha and was honoring them in her home. When the box which the king had sent arrived, she thought it was a gift for the Buddha and began to open it, but the Buddha said: Open it after we have eaten."

When food had been prepared and eaten, the Buddha taught the following:

"This body is truly impermanent.
It is subject to suffering,
Void, and without a self.
Being without essence,
It is of short duration.
By its very nature
It is bound to the defilements.
It is tortured by misery.
It is separated from what it wants.
Because of suffering
This body is useless and without profit.
Wise is he who understands this."

The woman did understand, because she had attained the fruit of a never-returner. She rejoiced, had faith, and folding her palms in reverence, said to the Buddha: "Lord, I desire to do four things. May the Lord, in his compassion, permit this. The first is to provide healing medicine, food and drink for sick monks. The second is to care for sick monks and provide them with nourishment. The third is to prepare and offer the necessities to the monks. The fourth is to give provisions to those monks who have come from afar. Why is this? It is because a monk who is ill, if he does not obtain healing medicine, food, and drink, will have great difficulty in recovering and his life will be in danger. If there is no one to look after him and he obtains no food, he will be obliged to go out for alms. If he does not obtain them at the proper time he will become angry and his illness will be difficult to cure. Therefore, I shall offer food. When a monk comes from afar, if he has no friends or relatives or does not make friends among the people, he will have to beg, and if the housewives or evil people mistreat him, his patience will be exhausted. And if a monk travels to a far country and has no company or friends and is without supplies, he may be attacked by savage beasts or thieves, and his life will be in danger. Therefore I shall offer supplies."

The Buddha approved and said: "Great indeed is the virtue of these four things. It is the same as making offerings to the Enlightened

One himself." Thereupon he and his disciples returned to the Jetavana monastery.

When the Buddha had departed, the mother opened the box and found the heads of her sons. Because she had become separated from attachment, she experienced no anguish and said: "When a son is born, death is inescapable. A son is not eternal and death may come quickly. Now, in whatever realm these boys are born, they will undergo suffering."

When the relatives of the boys heard what had happened, they became enraged and exclaimed: "How could the great king murder these innocent boys? We shall gather together a great army and ruin him." Taking counsel, they formed an army and surrounded the king's palace. In terror, the king escaped and went to the Buddha, and the army followed him and surrounded the Jetavana monastery. Ānanda learned that King Prasenajit had killed the thirty-two boys, and that their relatives had armed themselves and come. Then he knelt before the Buddha, pressed his palms together, and said: "Lord, what is the reason that those thirty-two boys all died together at the same time?"

The Buddha said: "Ānanda, this is not the first time that the king has killed the thirty-two sons of that woman. Listen well and I shall tell you how they were killed once before.

"Ānanda, in times long past, these thirty-two boys were born as thirty-two men who were devoted to each other and lived in accord. Upon a certain occasion, they banded together and stole a man's cow. Then took it to the house of an old, childless, beggar-woman who lived in that country who, when they killed the cow, rejoiced and cooked the meat for them. Before it was killed, the cow made a vow, saying: "If you kill me now, in future times, regardless of what you become, may I kill you!' The men killed it, some ate it boiled, some ate it roasted. The old woman ate her full of beef and delightedly told the men: 'Even when princes stayed overnight here, none of them ever treated me this well!"

"Ānanda, King Prasenajit was that cow. the woman's thirty-two sons were those thirty-two men who stole and killed the cow. The boys' mother was that old woman. The result of their deed is that for five-hundred lifetimes they have been killed. Because that old woman rejoiced at what was done, she has always been reborn as the boys' mother and undergone suffering. But now, having met me, she has attained the fruit."

Then Ānanda pressed his palms together and said: "Lord, what was the reason and because of what virtue, were these boys born into a noble family and endowed with great wealth and strength?"

The Buddha said: "Ānanda, in former times when the Buddha Kāśyapa had come to the world, there was in an old woman who greatly venerated the Three Treasures. She purchased a great deal of fragrant powder, and dissolving it in oil, constantly anointed a stupa. Upon a certain occasion while this old woman sat at the crossroads anointing the stupa, thirty-two men came up and helped her. This so delighted the old woman that she made the vow: "By virtue of having helped me anoint this stupa with fragrant powders, may you, wherever you are born, be handsome and comely and be endowed with unusual strength.' This pleased the men and they in turn made a vow: 'By virtue of having helped this old woman anoint the stupa, wherever we take birth may be born in a high caste, endowed with wealth, and may this old woman always be our mother. May we always encounter the Buddha, hear the Dharma, and quickly obtain the fruits. May the same be true for this old woman.' It was because of this vow that they were born in a high caste for five-hundred births.

"Ānanda, she who was the mother of those boys was that old woman. These thirty-two boys were those thirty-two men."

When the army heard the Buddha's word, their anger abated and they said: "The king is without guilt. This is the fruit of an act performed long ago—the killing of a cow. King Prasenajit is our king, why should we think to do him evil?" Laying down their arms, they went before the king, confessed their guilt, and the king forgave them.

The Enlightened One then explained what he had told them, instructed the four groups of hearers in the Supreme Dharma. When he had shown them that one should make efforts toward virtue and remove all non-virtue and sin and had taught them the Four Noble Truths, they had faith, lauded the Buddha's words, and rejoiced.

25

Mahā Kapina

❦

Thus have I heard at one time: the Enlightened One was residing in the city of Śrāvastī at the Jetavana monastery in Anāthapiṇḍika's park. At that time, the king of the country was Prasenajit. To the south of him lay the country of Golden Land, whose king had been Kapina, but was now ruled by his son, Mahā Kapina. King Mahā Kapina was a straight-forward man, of enormous strength, and kept an army of thirty-six thousand troops. His army, wherever it went, was like the force of the great wind and none were able to resist it. King Mahā Kapina was unacquainted with King Prasenajit of Magadha, but it so happened that a merchant from Magadha went to the city of Kapali and took with him four rolls of fine cloth, which he presented to Mahā Kapina. The king examined the cloth and asked where such excellent merchandise had come from. When the merchant told that cloth of that sort could be found in Magadha, the king asked him where that was. When told that it contained the cities of Rājagṛha and Śrāvastī and that there were many such cities there, the king asked why the rulers of those cities did not come to pay him homage. The merchant replied: "Your Majesty, each of those kings is a sovereign ruler. Why would they pay homage to you?" The king thought: "My power is great enough to conquer them all. Why could it be that they refuse to pay me homage? I shall subdue them with my might." He then asked the merchant: "Which of the kings of Magadha is the greatest?" When the merchant told him that it was the king of Śrāvastī, the king commanded him to take the following communication to him:

"In view of the fact that my power is sufficient to conquer all of India, how is it that you refuse to send ambassadors to me? I am herewith sending this messenger to you. If you receive it while you are reclining, stand up! If while sitting, get to your feet! If while eating and swallowing your food, vomit! If while combining your hair, muss it up! If between sitting and standing, run! You are to come to pay homage to me within a period of seven days. Should you not do this, I shall come with my army and utterly lay waste to your country."

The messenger went to King Prasenajit and reported. The king was terrified, went to the Buddha, bowed down before him, and told what King Mahā Kapina had said. The Buddha said: "Have no fear, Your Majesty. Tell the messenger to give Mahā Kapina this message. "I, Prasenajit, am not the greatest king in this country. There is one even greater than I. Not far from me there is magic king." When the messenger was passing through Anāthapiṇḍika's park, the Buddha transformed himself into a Cakravartin king, Mahā Maudgalyāyana into his great minister. The Jetavana monastery became a jewel-park which was surrounded by seven jewel-moats, between which there were the seven kinds of jewel-trees and countless exquisite lotuses blaxing with radiance. The mighty emperor sat within a palace built of the various kinds of jewels. When the messenger approached the palace and saw the great king, he was afraid and thought:

"This king is mightier than ours. We can never overcome him." He then sent in a written message of greeting, but the magic king put it under his feet and said to the messenger: "I am the ruler over the four continents. Why does your stupid, evil king disobey me? Go to him quickly and give him this message: "King, when you hear my command, if you are reclining, arise! If sitting, move! If walking, run! If you disobey my command and fail to come and pay homage within seven days, I shall punish you."

The messenger returned and gave the message to the king. When he heard it, he was troubled and wondered whether he should present himself together with the minor kings who were subject to him. He sent the messenger back to inquire, saying; "Great King, when I come to pay homage, should all my three hundred and sixty-thousand subject kings also come, or only some of them?" The message came back: "Assemble some of them and bring them."

Thereupon the king of Golden Land took many hundreds of thousands of his subjects and proceeded to the magic king in Śrāvastī.

Bowing to him, he thought: "This king is, indeed, more magnificent than I, but as far as might is concerned, he cannot compete with me." As he was thinking this, the magic king said to his minister: "Minister, give your bow to the king of Golden Land." The minister handed his bow to Mahā Kapina, but he was unable to pull it back. The magic king then took the bow, pulled back the bowstring with his little finger, and caused the string to produce a sound that was audible throughout the worlds of the Three-Thousand, Great Thousand. He then shot five arrows, and from their tips there came forth countless rays of light, each of which contained the seven jewels which contained a Cakravartin king. This light filled all the worlds of the Three Thousand, Great Thousand and brought benefit to all beings in the five realms of existence. When the light struck the realm of the gods, the teaching of the Dharma was clearly heard and the minds and bodies of the gods became totally pure. Some became streamwinners, some became arhats. Some brought forth a mind of Supreme Enlightenment, some entered the realm of no-return. When those who were in the realm of humans saw the light and heard the Dharma, they rejoiced and believed. Some became streamwinners, some became once-returners, some became monks and attained the bliss of arhats. Some brought forth a mind of Supreme Enlightenment and attained the realm of no-return. When this light of the Buddha reached the pretas, their minds and bodies ceased to be tormented because they could hear the Dharma, and they became at ease. Compassion arose in all of them, and honoring the Buddha, they were liberated from the state of hungry ghosts and were reborn as gods and men. When those beings who were imprisoned in the realm of animals saw the Buddha's light, their minds of craving and anger were pacified. Those who were subject to the sleep of ignorance awakened from their sleep, rejoiced and believed in the Buddha, and were delivered from the animal state and reborn as gods and men. When the light of the Buddha reached the beings in hell, those who were freezing became warm, their sufferings disappeared and when, with a mind of rejoicing, they had faith in the Buddha, they were liberated from hell and reborn as gods and men.

When King Mahā Kapina and all the minor kings saw this spiritual feat of the Lord, they were astonished. Because they attained a mind of firm faith, the dust was removed from their eyes, they attained the pure eye of the Dharma, and their minds were pacified.

Then the Enlightened One withdrew the phantom form and appeared as usual, sitting surrounded by the assembly of monks. The king of Golden Land joined his palms together in reverence and said: "Lord, I beg to become a monk." When the Buddha said: "Welcome," the king's hair and beard fell away by themselves, he was dressed in the red robe, and became a monk. By meditating on the Dharma, his outflows were stopped and he became an arhat.

Thereupon Ānanda folded his palms in reverence and said to the Buddha: "Lord, this king of Golden Land—by performing what former virtues was he born in this high position and now, having met the Enlightened One, has stopped the outflows? What was the reason for this?"

The Buddha said: "Ānanda, every act performed by a living being is followed by results. In times long past when the Buddha Kāśyapa had come to this world, had brought benefits to living beings, and had attained final Nirvana, a householder built a stupa and a resident monastery for the Sangha. In time, the stupa disintegrated and supplies were no longer given to the monks. This householder had a son who became a monk and taught the Dharma to many people. Eventually, the stupa was restored and food, clothing, beds, seats, and so on were again distributed to the Sangha. The many people who were in accord with the thoughts of the monk prepared countless necessities and made the following vow: 'In future times may we be born in a high caste, be wealthy, live long, and meet the Buddha when he comes to this world. By hearing the Dharma, may we attain to the fruit.' Ānanda, Mahā Kapina, the king of Golden land, was that monk, the son of the householder. Those many thousands of minor kings present were those to whom the monk taught the Dharma, who repaired the stupa and offered their property."

When the Buddha had taught thus, many brought forth a mind of Supreme Enlightenment, believed and rejoiced.

26

Utpalā the Nun

❦

Thus have I heard at one time: the Enlightened One was resid-ing in the city of Śrāvastī at the Jetavana monastery in Anāthapiṇḍika's park. After the death of King Prasenajit, his son Vaidurya ascended the throne. Because the minor kings did not reign in accordance with the Dharma, countless beings were killed by being trampled by elephants. Many women of the higher castes, seeing this, abandoned worldly life and became nuns. Some of these women were from the Śākyas and the royal family, and they were lovely and beautiful beyond compare. When five-hundred such women abandoned desire and pleasure and joined the Sangha, all the people of the country rejoiced and provided them with the necessities.

These nuns once said to each other: "Although we have taken vows, we have not tasted the flavor of the Dharma, have not given up attachment, hatred, or ignorance, and this is an error. Let us go to the nun Prajāpatī and hear the Dharma." They then proceeded to the nun Prajāpatī, bowed, and said: "Sister, when we were ordained we did not taste the nectar of the Dharma. We beseech you to give it to us." The nun Prajāpatī told them: "You are all from the highest castes and have the seven treasures, elephants, horses, ministers, men and women servants, fields and property. Why did you give these up but cannot, like me, separate yourselves from the pleasures of the de-filements and enter the Teaching? You may as well return to your homes, enjoy yourselves with your husbands and children, and be happy during this lifetime." Hearing this, the women wept and re-turned. They then went to a nun called Utpalā, bowed to her, asked after her health, and said: "Sister, although we have renounced the world and become nuns, we are still gripped by desire and pleasure and are unable to free ourselves from the defilements. We beseech you, sister, instruct us in the Supreme Dharma."

The nun Utpalā said: "Ask whatever you desire concerning the past, present, or future, and I shall tell you."

The nuns said: "Sister, leaving the past and the future for a moment, we beg you to teach the Dharma of the present and remove our doubts."

Utpalā said: "Attachment is like fire. Even rivers and mountains are consumed by it and eventually it burns everything like grass. Through the power of attachment, one harms other, and thereby falls into the three evil births and then there is no means of deliverance. When a woman is married, she is truly subjected to suffering. If she is separated from her husband, that is sorrow. Birth, sickness, old-age, death, punishment from the king—all these are unmitigated miseries. If, when one dies he is reborn in hell, that also is endless suffering. For a married person there is little happiness and much sorrow."

The nun continued: "My parents were mendicants, although they belonged to a high caste. They married me to a wise, intelligent mendicant, one who had heard much, and a son was born to us. Later, when my husband's parents had passed on, I again became pregnant. When the time came for the child to be born, I told my husband that I wished to return to my parents' house and have the child there. My husband agreed, and the three of us set out. When we arrived at the Central Province, my pains came, I became ill, laid down beneath a tree and gave birth at midnight. My husband was sleeping some distance away. During the night, he was bitten by a poisonous snake and was unable to call out. In the morning, just at dawn, I found him dead, his body already beginning to disintegrate. I fainted, but my son, seeing his father lying there dead, began to scream. His screams brought me back to consciousness. I got up, put the older child on my back, carried the baby next to my breast and, weeping now that I had no dear husband, started out. We passed through a desolate wasteland and came to a deep, broad river. Unable to carry both children over at the same time, I left the older child on the bank and carried the baby over. Then, when I returned to get the first child, he jumped into the water as soon as he saw me and was carried away by the current. When I got back to the other shore I found that a wolf had eaten my baby and his blood was still on the ground. I started out alone and met a mendicant along the road who was a relative of ours. He asked me where I was going and whether I was traveling alone. When I asked concerning my parents, he said: "Your parents' house has burned down and all the people in it were burned to death. Your parents are no longer among the living." I fainted upon hearing this, but my relative put me on my feet again and took me to his home, where he cared for me as tenderly, as though I were his own child. I lived there happily for awhile, then another mendicant asked me to marry him. I married him and we were happy. I became pregnant again, and when the time came for me to have the baby, my husband was at a festival. I locked the door and was sitting in my labor pains when my husband returned drunk, pounded on the door, and as there was no one to open it, kicked it down, came in and began to beat me. When I screamed: 'Don't strike me! Don't you see that I am going to have a baby?' he became furious. He killed the baby which had now been born, fried it in oil, and forced me to eat it although I protested that I could not eat the flesh of my own child. Later I left him and went to Benares. As I was sitting under a tree on the outskirts of Benares, they carried out the body of the wife of a young householder. While the householder sat weeping because he was greatly attached to his wife, he saw me and drew near with the words: 'Woman, what is the reason that you are sitting here alone?' I told him all that had happened and he said: 'You and I will be man and wife.' I agreed to this, we were married, and not long after he died. It was the custom of that place that, when a man died, his wife was abandoned with his corpse and I was buried with him. During the night, a thief came to steal the belongings of the corpse, and while digging in the grave, found me and took me for himself. He was apprehended while stealing and was executed by the king's order. His brothers then buried me in the ground together with his corpse. Three days later a wolf dug me up and I escaped. Then I thought: 'Because of what former evil deeds have I met disaster so many times but somehow recovered? I have heard that a son of the Śākyas has achieved Enlightenment. He is called the Buddha and is famous for knowing the past and the future. I shall go to him and he will deliver me.' I then went to Anāthapiṇḍika's park and from a distance saw the Buddha sitting like a tree in full bloom, like the full moon among many stars. And the Buddha, by his unimpeded knowledge, knew that I had come to be converted, arose, and said to me: 'Come' I was embarrassed and ashamed, and clasping my breast, sat down on the ground. Then the Lord said to Ānanda: 'Ānanda, clad this woman in your own robe.' Ānanda gave me his robe, I put it on and bowed at the Buddha's feet, joined my palms, and said: 'Lord, in great compassion ordain me.' The Buddha said to Ānanda: 'Ānanda, this woman is to be ordained a nun. Take her to the nun Prajāpati.' When the nun Prajāpati ordained me and had taught me the Law of the Four Truths, I quickly applied myself and attained the fruit of an arhat and now know all things past, present, and to come."

Then the nuns asked: "Sister, because of having done what deeds have you attained such fruit?"

Utpalā said: "Listen well, all of you, and bear it well in mind, and I shall explain. In former times, there was a very wealthy man who, because he had no son born to his first wife, married again and his second wife soon bore him a son. The father and mother loved the child and cared for it with great tenderness. The first wife thought: 'Although my family is of high caste, there is no son to continue it. When this boy grows up, he will inherit all the property, will give me nothing, and I shall be miserable.' Then thoughts of malice and ill-will arose in her and she decided to kill the child. Taking a needle, she pierced the soft-spot on its head and the baby soon died. As there was no scar, no one knew what had happened, but the second wife accused her of murdering her baby. The first wife solemnly swore: 'If I have killed your child, may my husbands, in all future lifetimes, be bitten by a poisonous serpent. If I have a son, may he be devoured by a wolf! May I be buried alive and eat my own son's flesh! May my father and mother be burned alive in their own house! It is I who was that first wife who swore that oath at that time, and now all the sins from that oath have come to pass."

The nuns then said: "Sister, because of performing what acts of virtue did the Buddha welcome you and ordain you, and now you have reached the end of the Samsara?"

Utpalā said: "Long ago, in the land of Benares, there was a mountain called the Meeting Place of the Rishis on which there lived many Prateyekabuddhas, Śrāvakas, and those endowed with spiritual powers. Upon a certain occasion, when a saintly Pratyekabuddha had gone to the city for alms, the wife of a householder saw him, rejoiced, and offered him food. Thereupon the Pratyekabuddha soared into the sky, from his body light blazed and water flowed, and he walked, sat, lay down in the sky and exhibited many powers. The householder's wife made the vow: 'Ah, holy one, in future times may I become like you!' It was I who made that vow at that time, and it is through the power of that vow that I have now met the Buddha and my mind has been liberated. But before I attained the fruit of an arhat, I underwent suffering as though I had been pierced from the top of my head to the soles of my feet with a red-hot iron chisel."

When the five-hundred nuns heard this, they understood that desire and pleasure are like pits of fire and their thoughts of attachment ceased. They understood that the sufferings of married life are like those of a prison, and cut them away. Their impurities ceased, and when they had entered the samādhi of the three times, they became arhats. Then the nuns, in one accord, said to the nun Utpalā: "Because you have taught the Dharma to us, to us who were totally bound by attachment, we have reached the end of the cycle of birth and death. We praise and thank you. When one teaches the Dharma to others and the fruit is realized, one truly becomes the son or daughter of the Buddha."

27

Śudolagarne

Thus have I heard at one time: the Enlightened One was residing in Rājagṛha in the Bamboo Grove of the Kalandaka Bird. Upon a certain occasion the Noble Ānanda rose from his seat, arranged his robe, kneeled, folded his palms in reverence, and said to the Buddha: "Lord, when you turned the Wheel of the Law, you allowed the five disciples led by Kaundinya to be the first taste the nectar of the Dharma. I beseech you to make know the reason for this."

The Buddha said: "Ānanda, in times long past I fed those five monks with my own flesh. Now I have liberated them by giving them the nectar of the Dharma to taste."

Ānanda said: "I beg the Lord to relate what things those monks formerly did."

The Buddha said: "Ānanda, long ago, in an aeons past reckoning, past conceiving, there was an emperor in this Jambudvīpa by the name of Śudolagarne who ruled over eighty-four thousand minor kings. At one time a soothsayer foretold that there would be no rain for fifteen years. This saddened the emperor. As he thought of the great drought and famine and starvation that would come, and he summoned his minor kings and ministers and took counsel. They decided to calculate the amount of grain in the storehouses and the number of people, then dole out the grain to each person, but found that there was not enough grain to last for twelve years.

"When the great famine came and many people were starving, the emperor tried to think of how he could save lives. One day when he and the queen and their entourage had gone to a park and were reclining in a pleasant place, the emperor stood up and with a firm mind bowed in the four directions and made the solemn vow: 'Because of the drought there is no food and the people are perishing. May I leave this body, take birth as an enormous fish, and nourish the people with my flesh.' Climbing up into a tree, he jumped down, was killed, and was immediately reborn in a great river as an enormous fish five-hundred yojanas long.

At that time, there were five woodcutters in that country who had come to the banks of the river to gather wood. When the fish saw them, it cried out in a human voice: 'Oh men, if you are starving, cut away my flesh and assuage your hunger. When you have eaten, take as much with you as you can carry. You are the first to eat of my flesh, and in future times when I have attained Supreme Enlightenment, I shall let you be the first to taste the nectar of the Dharma. Make known to all the people of this land that they may come and eat my flesh.'

"Thereupon the five men cut flesh from the fish, ate it, and took away as much as they could carry. They then proclaimed to all what had happened, the people told each other of this, came and ate. When the flesh from one side was exhausted, the fish turned around and they ate from the other side. They then ate its back and breast and the fish nourished all the people for twelve years. As the people ate the fish, a mind of compassion arose in them and when they died they were reborn among the gods.

"Ānanda, I was that emperor who took birth as a fish. The five woodsmen who first ate of the fish are now the five monks led by Kaundinya. The eighty-thousand disciples and those to be liberated are those who at that time ate the fish. At that time I saved the lives of the people with my own body. Now, through the Body of the Dharma, I extinguish the fires of the three poisons."

When the Lord had thus spoken, Ānanda and the great assembly had faith and rejoiced.

28

King Aśoka

❦

Thus have I heard at one time: the Enlightened One was residing in the city of Śrāvastī at the Jetavana monastery in Anāthapiṇḍika's park. Upon a certain occasion when the Buddha and Ānanda were going on the alms-round, there were some children playing along the roadside, building toy treasure houses. One of the children, seeing the Buddha approach, rejoiced, and thinking that he would acquire merit, took a handful of earth and tried to offer it to the Buddha, but because he was so tiny could not reach the alms-bowl and asked another boy to let him climb upon on his shoulders. The boy did this, and when the Buddha lowered his bowl, he dropped his handful of earth into the begging bowl. The Buddha accepted it, handed the bowl to Ānanda, and said: "Take this earth to the monastery and scatter it. Ānanda, a hundred years after I have attained final Nirvana, this little boy, by virtue of having made an offering in great joy and by virtue of its having been scattered at the monastery, will be reborn as the Emperor Aśoka. The child who let him climb up on his shoulders will be reborn as his minister. The emperor will rule all India and will make known to all the blessings of the Three Treasures. He will venerate my relics by erecting eighty-four thousand stupas."

Ānanda rejoiced, believed and said to the Buddha: "Lord, by reason of having performed what virtues will so many stupas be erected for the Tathagata's relics?"

The Buddha said: "Listen well, Ānanda, and bear it well in mind. In ages long past, there was a king in this Jambudvīpa by the name of Clear-Seer who had eighty-four thousand minor kings subject to him. At that time, the Buddha Burśa had come to this world, and the king and his ministers prepared the four necessities and offered them to the Buddha and the Sangha. Although the king and all his people constantly honored the Buddha and made offerings, the minor kings did not bring forth virtue in this way. In order that the minor kings and the other people might learn the Dharma, the king thought to have an image of the Buddha painted to send to them. He called together his artists and commanded them to paint a perfect image of the Buddha. When the artists came before the Buddha and saw his signs, they were unable to reproduce them. Thereupon the Buddha himself prepared colors, painted his own image and gave it to them. From that image, the artists prepared eighty-four thousand images and the king sent one to each of the minor kings with the proclamation: 'Ye kings and all the people! Honor these images of the Lord with flowers and incense and make offerings of the necessities.' When the people saw those images of the Tathagata, they rejoiced, had faith, and honored them. Ānanda, I was at that time that king Because I had eighty-four thousand images made of the Tathāgata and gave them to those minor kings, wherever I was reborn, it was as an Indra, ruler of the highest gods. Now I have attained Buddhahood and am endowed with the thirty-two marks of a great being and the eighty secondary marks of perfection, and when I attain final Nirvana eighty-four thousand stupas will be constructed for my relics."

When the Buddha had thus spoken, Ānanda and the great assembly rejoiced and believed.

29

The Pot of Gold

Thus have I heard at one time: the Enlightened One was residing in the city of Śrāvastī at the Jetavana monastery in Anāthapiṇḍika's park. At that time the monks, having been in hermitage during the rainy season, came out and went to where the Buddha was. The Lord had not seen them in a long time and lovingly raised his hand, which was adorned with the wheel of a thousand spokes, and asked the monks concerning their welfare. When Ānanda saw the Buddha, who was endowed with supreme virtue, honor the monks, he was astonished and said: "Lord, you are the supreme in the world, endowed with virtue beyond compare and wisdom beyond conceiving. Why is it that you condescend to honor the monks?"

The Buddha said: "Ānanda, in times long past, aeons beyond counting or recall, there lived in Benares a householder who was a genius at creating wealth. Whatever he did not require for his personal use he changed into gold, placed the gold in a golden urn, and put the urn under his pillow. As time went on he filled seven urns with gold and buried them in the ground. Finally, the man became ill and died and, because of his attachment to the gold, was reborn as a poisonous serpent which guarded the gold. Later, the city was destroyed and became a wasteland with none living in it, but the serpent continued to die and he reborn in the same place guarding the gold. This went on for tens of thousands of years. Finally the serpent became weary of constant rebirth in that form and thought: 'Because of my attachment to that gold I have had to undergo endless births as a serpent. Now it would be well to put the gold to some virtuous use.' He hid himself in the deep grass along a well-travelled highway, and when he saw a man approaching called out to him. The man looked all about but could see no one and continued his way. The serpent called: 'Man, come near,' and when the man said: 'what do you want? You are a poisonous serpent and will probably kill me,' the serpent replied: 'I will indeed bite you if you do not approach.' The man became terrified and came near to the serpent. The serpent told him: 'I have a pot of gold. If, in order to create virtue, I give it to you, will you put it to virtuous use? Because if you do not, I will certainly harm you.' When the man said he would create virtue, the serpent gave him the gold and said: 'You are to take this gold and make an offering with it to the Noble Sangha. When the virtue has been established, come back and rescue me.' The man took the pot of gold, took it to the Sangha, offered it, and said: 'This gold comes from a poisonous serpent who asked me to offer it to the Sangha. Use it to obtain food and the necessities. On the day that virtue is created the serpent will come here.'

The Sangha approved, obtained food and the necessities with the gold. On the day that virtue was established, the man put a large basket on his shoulders and went to the serpent who, seeing the man, rejoiced. The man put the serpent into the basket and as they were going along the road, met a man who asked: 'Where are you coming from and what do you have in that basket?' The man carrying the serpent made no reply and the other man asked the question three times. This enraged the serpent and it thought: 'What ails this man? He was asked a question three times and refuses to answer. I shall bite him.' Then he thought: 'No, it would be an error to harm this man who has created virtue for my sake and has benefitted me. I shall be patient.' When they came to a deserted place, the snake said: 'Let me out a minute,' but the man, knowing that it was angry, humbly said: 'I repent having committed a fault out of ignorance and having offended you,' and carry it to where the Sangha was residing.

"It was then the hour of the daily meal and the Sangha had gathered. The man offered food and gold and a mind of faith arose in the serpent. As the man spread flowers, the serpent watched with delight. When the Sangha had finished eating, they washed their hands and rinsed their mouths. They taught the Dharma to the serpent, who rejoiced and brought six more pots of gold and offered them. After this virtue had been created, the serpent died and, because of the fruition of that virtue, was reborn among the gods of the Thirty-Three.

"Ānanda, I was the man who at that time carried the serpent. Śāriputra was the poisonous serpent. Just as, at that time, I humbly begged the serpent's forgiveness when it became angry, so now do I humbly honor the monks."

Thereupon Ānanda and the assembly believed the Buddha's word and rejoiced.

30

Joy, the Brahmin's Wife

༄༅

Thus have I heard at one time: the Enlightened One was residing in the Bamboo Grove of the Kalandaka Bird together with countless monks. At that time, there lived in that country a poverty-stricken brahmin who went about asking everyone what one should do to obtain well-being in this life. A certain person told him: "Do you not know that the Buddha has come to this world and resides here in order to benefit all beings? The Buddha's disciples have healed Mahā Kāśyapa, Mahā Maudgalyāyana, Śāriputra, and Aniruddha, and they constantly aid beggars and those who are in need. If you, with a mind of faith, will make an offering of food to those holy ones, they will fulfill your every desire." When the brahmin heard this he was overjoyed, and by constant begging and working for wages, he obtained a little money. He returned to his home, prepared food, and invited the Noble Sangha with the wish that, in this lifetime, he might attain well-being. The brahmin's wife, whose name was Joy, was that day observing a single-day vow, and she served the Noble Ones.

That day King Prasenajit had gone to the country, and upon returning, saw a criminal who had been left tied to a tree as punishment. Seeing the king, he cried out for food. The king, promising that he would send something to eat, went on to the palace and immediately forgot all about it. At midnight he suddenly remembered that he should send food to the man, but knew that because there were demons, rakśas, and other fearful things along the road, no one would go. In pity for the starving man, he issued a proclamation saying that if there was anyone in his kingdom willing to take him food he would reward him with a thousand measures of silver, but no one dared go.

When Joy, the wife of the brahmin, heard the king's proclamation, she thought: "Demons and other fearful things can do no harm to anyone in this world who is observing a one-day vow. I will carry out the king's command.' She went to the king and told him she would take the food. The king gave her the food, told her where she would find the man, and promised to reward her. The woman took the food, and guarding her vow, set out. As she passed outside the city gates she met a female rakśa who had just given birth to five-hundred rakśa whelps and was watching the road. Seeing Joy approach, she was delighted and was on the point of eating her, but because of the power of the vow, was afraid, moved back from the road, and said: "Oh woman, give me a bit of the food you are carrying, I beg you." When Joy gave her a little of the food, the rakśa increased it with her magic powers and both she and her starving whelps ate their fill. The rakśa then asked the brahmin' wife her name and when she told her that it was Joy, said to her: "There is a pot of gold where I live and you, who have fed and nourished a mother and her babies, may have it when you return. Up ahead you will meet my younger sister whose name is Alamba, and you are to say to her: 'Younger sister, are you not happy? Five-hundred babies have been born.'"

The woman walked on and met the rakśa-sister, Alamba, and told her what her elder sister had said. Alamba rejoiced and told Joy that there was a pot of gold where she lived and that, when she came back, she would give it to her. She also told her that she would meet her brother along the road, and that she should tell him the good news about the birth of the five hundred rakśas. Joy went on, met the rakśa-brother, told him about the arrival of the rakśa-babies, and he was delighted. He also promised to give her a pot of gold when she returned.

The brahmin's wife went on, found the starving man tied to a tree, gave him the food, and returned bringing the three pots of gold with her. The king rewarded her with a thousand measures of gold, and the brahmin and his wife lived joyfully in that land and became wealthy. The king, learning of the virtue of the brahmin and his wife, elevated them to the rank of government officials. They rejoiced and a mind of firm faith was born in them. They invited the Buddha and his disciples and made great offerings to them. When the Lord had taught them the Dharma, their minds became enlightened and they obtained the fruit of streamwinners.

31

Great Charity Goes to the Sea

❧❦❧

Thus have I heard at one time: the Enlightened One was residing in Rajagṛha on the Vulture's Peak together with a great assembly of one-thousand, two-hundred and fifty monks. Upon a certain occasion, the Lord spoke to the Noble, all-knowing Kaundinya and the others: "Select someone to accompany and serve me." Thereupon Kaundinya arose from his seat, folded his robe over one shoulder, pressed his palms together in the direction of the Buddha, and bowing, said: "Lord I will accompany you and carry your robes and begging-bowl!." The Enlightened One said: "Kaundinya, you yourself have grown old and require someone to accompany you. You cannot accompany and serve me. Kaundinya, you remain where you are." Then Kāśyapa, Śariputra, Mahā Maudgalyāyana, and all five hundred of the disciples each volunteered to serve the Buddha, but the Lord did not accept them. While the Noble Aniruddha was wondering who it was that would accompany the Buddha, the thought came to all like a sunbeam that comes through a chink in the eastern wall of a palace and illuminates the western wall, that it was Ānanda, whom the Buddha wished to accompany him. Thereupon Śariputra, Mahā Maudgalyāyana, and the others went to Ānanda, sat down beside him, and told him the happy news: "Noble Ānanda, it is for you to accompany the Enlightened one and serve him. The Lord wishes this. Great indeed will be your merits if you serve the Buddha."

Ānanda replied: "Monk Śariputra, it is not my wish to stay near the Enlightened One and serve him. Why is this? It is because it is difficult to care for the Buddha. It is difficult to be patient. Just as it is a difficult thing to care for and be patient with a flaming fire, so is it difficult to care for and be patient with the Buddha. These are the reasons I do not wish to accompany the Buddha or take care of him."

Then the Noble Maudgalyāyana said to Ānanda: "Ānanda, the Buddha's desire for you to accompany him is like the rays of the sun entering a crack on the eastern wall of the palace and shining on the western wall. It is you alone of all the other disciples whom the Buddha wishes to accompany him. If you do this, the benefits which you will obtain will be great indeed."

Ānanda said: "Monk Mahā Maudgalyāyana, if I were to serve the Lord and accompany him there are three conditions. First, I would never consent to wear a robe that the Lord has worn. Second, I would never eat a morsel of the Buddha's food. Third, I would request that the Buddha never teach the Dharma when I am absent. If the Lord grants me these three wishes, I will accompany him and serve him."

Thereupon the monk Śāriputra and Mahā Maudgalyāyana approved what Ānanda had said, went to the Buddha and told him.

The Enlightened One approved, and said: "This, Mahā Maudgalyāyana, is the amazing dharma of Ānanda. Ānanda is wise and knows the time. To know the time means to understand when it is appropriate for the four classes of disciples to come to see the Buddha, when it is appropriate for the non-Buddhist mendicants to approach the Buddha and when it is not, to know when the non-Buddhist mendicants should dispute the Buddha's teaching, and to know whether the Buddha would be content with this or that kind of food. Knowing this, Mahā Maudgalyāyana, is the amazing dharma of Ānanda."

Then both Śāriputra and Mahā Maudgalyāyana lauded the fact that it would be Ānanda who was to accompany the Lord, and that the Buddha had pronounced Ānanda wise and knowing the times. Certain of the other monks, however, had doubts and said to the Buddha: "Lord, for what reason, for what cause, does the monk Ānanda know the times and the occasion?"

The Buddha said: "Śāriputra, countless aeons ago there was an emperor in this Jambudvīpa who ruled over eighty-four thousand minor kings. At that time, in the city of Varuna, there was a brahmin by the name of Nyagrodha who had learned the sciences of medicine, mathematics, and astronomy, whom the emperor made his preceptor and honored greatly. The wealth of this brahmin could be compared with the wealth of Vaiśravaṇa, the god of riches, but because he had no son he was miserable and constantly sought to obtain one. He prayed and made offerings to Brahmā and Indra, to the sun and moon, to the stars, to the gods of the mountains and waters and forests, and finally, after twelve years, his first wife became pregnant. Being a wise woman, she knew that the child in her womb was a boy and told the brahmin, who rejoiced and honored his wife greatly. When the months had passed, a son was born who had black hair and a golden skin, was handsome and comely, and perfect in all his organs. At the anointing ceremony a soothsayer was called who examined the child and named it 'Great Charity.' As the years passed, the boy was made happy in the spring—, summer—, fall—, and winter-residences that his parents had built for him. He grew in wisdom and became perfect in the eighteen sciences.

Upon a certain occasion, the boy said to his parents: 'I wish to go out and see the world.' His parents approved the request and had the road swept clean, set up banners and streamers, and strewed flowers and fragrant incense along it. Then they mounted him on an elephant caparisoned with the seven jewels, and he rode out of the city with an entourage of many hundreds of thousands of people to the accompaniment of cymbals, drums, and music. As the people watched from both sides of the road and from the house-tops, they proclaimed: 'Ah, this splendor and magnificence is like that of the god Indra!'

"As the procession moved along, some poverty-stricken people dressed in rags and holding broken bowls approached and cried out for alms. When Great Charity asked them the cause of their misery, some told him that they had no parents or relatives. Others said that they had been ill for a long time, and still others told him that they had been attacked by brigands who had stolen everything they had. When the boy saw their wretched condition, he wept and went on.

Soon they came to some butchers who were slaughtering animals and skinning them. When asked why they were committing this evil deed, they said that they had inherited this profession from their parents and that it was the only way they had of surviving.

Unhappily, Great Charity rode on and came to some farmers plowing. He saw the worms coming out the plowed soil and birds and snakes catching and eating them. When he asked the farmers why they were doing this, they told him that by turning the soil and planting seed they hoped to obtain a good harvest by which they could support themselves and pay the king's taxes.

"Sadly, Great Charity rode on and came to a fowler who had caught many birds in a net. The birds lay pinned to the ground, beating their wings, and crying pitifully. When the fowler was asked why he was doing this evil thing to living beings, he replied that this was the profession of his caste which lived by killing birds and eating them.

"Deeply moved, Great Charity went on and came to a fisherman catching fish and throwing them onto the banks of the river, where they lay flopping miserably. When he asked the fisherman what he was going to do with the fish, the fisherman told him that they would be eaten and that this was the only way he had of making a living. Great Charity thought: 'Alas, it is because these people are poverty-stricken that they have no way to live except by killing. When they die, they will fall into the three evil states and go from darkness to darkness. How will they ever be liberated?'

"Returning to the palace, he thought day and night of the misery of those beings. He then went to his father and said: 'Father, I have a request to make and beg you not to refuse.' The father replied: 'Son, I will give you whatever you desire.' The boy said: 'Lately, when I went out, I saw many people who, because they were without food or clothing, were poor and miserable and committed various kinds of sins by killing and lying. I constantly think of making gifts to those beings and beseech you to give me your great treasures. With them I shall relieve the sufferings of those people.' The father replied: 'Son, it is only for you that I have gathered together all my jewels and treasures. How, then, can I deny you this? Make whatever gifts you desire.'

"Great Charity then made a proclamation to all the people: 'Come! Gifts will be given.' Then the people, monks, brahmins, beggars, the starving, the sick assembled and filled the space outside the city to overflowing. People came from a distance of a hundred yojanas, five-hundred, a thousand, five-thousand, even ten-thousand yojanas, and when all were assembled it was like a great cloud. Those who wanted clothing were given clothing. Those who wanted food were given food. Those who wanted jewels, gold, silver, lapis-lazuli, horses, carriages, parks, dwellings, or animals, were given to them.

"This giving continued for a long time and when a third of the treasury had been depleted, the keeper of the treasury said to the brahmin: 'Your son has given away a third of your treasures. Only two-thirds remain. If all is given away, what will you do?' The brahmin said: 'But I love my son. How can I refuse to let him give gifts? What if the treasury is depleted?' Later, when two-thirds of the treasury was gone, the keeper again spoke to the brahmin: 'My lord, your son's giving alms has left only a third of your treasures. What am I to do?' The brahmin replied: 'I myself am unable to prevent my son from giving gifts. If you know what to do, do it.' Then the keeper of the treasury locked the doors of the treasure house and went about his business. When the beggars came and found the doors locked they looked for the keeper, but when they found him he refused to give them anything. Great Charity then thought: 'This must be according to my father's orders. It would not be right to totally deplete his treasury and I shall find some other means of aiding beings.' Then he began to ask people what one did to obtain endless wealth. Some told him that one might become wealthy by raising cattle. Others recommended agriculture. Still others advised trade with distant countries. Some said that it would be well to go to sea in search of jewels and the cintamani.

"When Great Charity heard what these people said, he thought: 'It is not for me to till the soil or raise cattle or trade with distant lands. It is for me to go to sea and find the cintamani.' Then he spoke to his parents: 'Father and mother, I beg your permission to go to sea in search of the cintamani, that I may give gifts to the poor and destitute.' When his parents heard this they trembled with fear and told him: 'Son, in this world poverty is a matter of fate. Why waste your life? Think of what you are going to do. If you wish to give gifts, give all we have here in the palace, but do not go to sea. What will save you from the terrible dangers of the sea:—drowning, the mighty waves, sea monsters, the poisonous nāgas, the female yakśas, the water colored mountains? Why throw away your life? Think of yourself!' Great Charity was not convinced and made the vow: 'Until my intention has been realized I shall lie here on my belly and never get up!' The unhappy parents then called together all their relatives and friends and took counsel. They repeated to the boy all the dangers of the sea, and told him that for twelve years his father had made offerings to the gods to obtain an only son and that now it would be wrong to endanger himself. They reasoned with him for one day, two days, six days, and when they saw that it was useless, knew that it would be wrong not to allow him to carry out his intentions. His parents then said to him: 'Son, get up and eat. We give you our permission to go in search of the cintamani.'

"Then Great Charity arose, ate and drank, and going out, proclaimed to the many: 'I go in search of jewels and will provide with the necessities all those willing to go with me.' Five-hundred merchants agreed to go, and Great Charity prepared the necessities for each and set the time of departure. When the time came, his parents, the king, princes, ministers, and all the people came to bid him farewell and offer gifts, and when they had departed his father and mother returned to their homes weeping.

"After many days had passed, they came to a desolate place where all their supplies were stolen by brigands. They continued their journey until they arrived at a city called Supara in which there lived a brahmin by the name of Kapali whose house they visited, and from whom Great Charity wished to borrow three thousand measures of gold. This brahmin had a black-haired daughter whose complexion was like gold and for whom eighty four thousand minor kings had sued, but in vain. When Great Charity arrived at the brahmin's door and asked for the brahmin Kapali, the daughter, hearing his voice from within the house, said to her parents: 'This is the voice of him who will be my husband.' When the brahmin opened the door and saw the boy, he thought: 'This boy is indeed superior to all others.' When he was asked for the gold, he agreed to give it and held the gold in one hand, his daughter in the

other, and said: 'Son, I give you my daughter to wed, also.' Great
Charity answered: 'I am going to sea in search of jewels, and because there are great dangers, it is not certain that I shall return. It
would therefore be wrong for me to marry your daughter.' The
brahmin said: 'If you do return safely, marry this girl,' to which
Great Charity agreed. The brahmin then gave him the three-thousand measures of gold and they left the city. They came to the
shores of the sea and there constructed a ship and outfitted it with
seven hawsers. Then Great Charity said to the merchants: 'Great
are the dangers of the sea! The black winds, the yakśas, the waves
and billows, the deadly nāgas, the water-colored mountains, the
sea monsters! If you have qualms, now is the time to go back, so
that you may have no regrets later. But if you have no care for life
or limbs, and are not attached to parents, wife, children, brothers,
or relatives, we shall go on together. If we return safely and if we
find the seven kinds of jewels, we shall have wealth for seven
generations and own possessions beyond count.' He spoke thus
for seven days, each day cutting loose one of the hawsers. When
he cut the seventh hawser, the wind filled the sails and the ship
shot out into the sea like an arrow that has been loosened from the
bow.

"They sailed until they came to the isle of jewels. There Great
Charity, being wise in the value of jewels, showed the merchants
which jewels were of great value and which were not, and soon
they had loaded the ship and it was time to return. Thereupon Great
Charity told them: 'Merchants, may your return be a safe one. I
shall not go back until I have obtained the cintamani from the palace of the king of the nāgas.'

"The merchants wailed loudly: 'Oh, noble one, we have come
as your servants. If you abandon us now in a place like this, we
shall never get home safely, but will surely loose our way and
perish!' Great Charity said: 'I shall pray that you arrive safely and
without mishap.' Taking a vessel of incense, he offered it in the
four directions and spoke a vow: 'May I find the cintamani and
make gifts to destitute people! Through the virtue of giving, may I
attain Enlightenment! If my words are true, may these merchants
arrive safely in Jambudvīpa without obstacle or mishap, and with

all their jewels!' When he had made this vow the sails were furled, the hawsers loosened, the wind filled the sails, and the ship quickly set course for Jambudvīpa.

"When the ship had gone, Great Charity entered the sea alone. He waded for seven days until the water reached his thighs, for seven days more until the water reached his waist, for seven days more until it reached his shoulders, and for seven days more until it reached his hair. Then he began to swim and swam until he came to a mountain. Grasping the branch of a tree, he climbed up onto the mountain and in seven days reached its peak. He stayed on the mountain for seven days, then walked down to the shore where he saw poisonous serpent wrapped around the root of a golden lotus. Then the bodhisattva sat down cross-legged, and with one-pointedness of mind, entered the samadhi of love and saw that the serpent had attained this evil birth because of anger and lust. With a great mind of compassion, he pacified the serpent's evil thoughts and the evil thoughts of all serpents. He then stepped over the lotus and walked on for seven days. Soon a cloud of deadly insects, smelling a human, came in search of him. The bodhisattva pacified their minds with his one-pointed mind of love and compassion, and they said to him: 'Noble One, whence have you come and where do you go?' When Great Charity told them that he was seeking the cintamani, the insects were delighted and thought: 'Ah, this entails great virtue. The palace of the nāga king is far distant and he can arrive there only with great difficulty. With our great powers we shall take him there.' Taking him up into the sky, they carried him for four-hundred yojanas, then let him down to earth. Great Charity went on from there, and seeing a city of silver and thinking that this must be the nāga king's palace, approached it. The city was surrounded with seven moats which were filled with poisonous snakes. Seeing them, and knowing that the snakes had attained this fearful birth because of former great anger, and knowing that they suffered greatly, Great Charity loved them as one loves an only son, and had pity on them with a mind of great compassion. The snakes' poisonous minds were pacified, and he walked over them in the direction of the palace of the nāga king. Before the city stood a gate and two serpents lay with their heads on the gateposts. Seeing Great Charity, they raised their heads to strike, but he meditated on thoughts of love and the serpents lowered their heads and lay as before.

"Great Charity walked over the snakes, entered the city, and saw the nāga king sitting in his incomparably beautiful palace which was made of the seven jewels. When the nāga king saw the bodhisattva, he was terrified and thought: 'My palace is surrounded by seven moats which are full of poisonous snakes and no one can enter except nāgas and yakśas. Who, then, is this who has come?' Rising from his seat, he bowed to Great Charity, honored him, sat him on a jeweled throne and offered him various kinds of food. When he had eaten, the nāga king said: 'How did you overcome the obstacles of this place and what is your purpose in coming here?' The bodhisattva said: 'The people of Jambudvīpa are destitute and suffering. For the sake of food and clothing, they harm and kill each other, and when they die they attain the three evil births. I pity them, and in order to save them I have surmounted the long, difficult way with no thought for life or limb. I have come to you, great king, to request the cintamani. With that wishing jewel, I shall aid all beings and through the fruit of that virtue I shall obtain perfect Buddhahood. Your Majesty, do not, I beseech you, refuse my request. Grant me the cintamani.'

"The nāga king said: 'To obtain the cintamani is exceedingly difficult, but since you have come for it, stay here in my palace for a month, accept my small offerings, and grant us the gift of the Dharma. Then I will give you the cintamani.' The bodhisattva agreed to this, and the nāga king prepared a hundred savory dishes each day and offered them. When Great Charity had taught the dharma of mindfulness, the nāga king rejoiced, took the cintamani from his head, and gave it to the bodhisattva with the words: 'Great being, your mind has become firmly established for the sake of sentient beings and you are certain to attain Buddhahood. When you do attain the perfection of Enlightenment, may I become the chief of your disciples!' The bodhisattva then asked what the power of this cintamani was and was told that it would cause all things desired to appear for a distance of two-thousand yojanas. Knowing that it could not create the great good that he desired, he departed. The nāga king and his entourage accompanied him for a great distance.

"Going on, he came to a city of lapis-lazuli which, like the former city, was surrounded by seven moats filled with poisonous snakes, the gates guarded by two serpents. The bodhisattva did as before, came into the presence of the nāga king, and asked for his cintamani. He remained there for two months, accepting the nāga king's offerings, and taught the four supramundane powers. This nāga king also gave him his cintamani with the prayer that when the bodhisattva attained Enlightenment he would become his disciple, and told him that the cintamani had power to grant wishes over a distance of four-thousand yojanas.

"Going on, Great Charity came to a golden city, again pacified the snakes in the moats and the guardian serpents. He remained there for four months teaching the Supreme Dharma, was given the nāga king's cintamani with the wish that the king might become his disciple when he attained Enlightenment. He was told that the cintamani had the power of bringing down showers of jewels for a distance of eight-thousand yojanas and would fulfill all desires. Putting all the cintamanis in the hem of his robe, the bodhisattva departed.

"When Great Charity came to the land of Naliyan he took the wishing jewels into his hand and said: 'If these be true cintamanis, may I fly through the sky.' Immediately he found himself soaring through the firmament. When he came to the seashore, he rested and slept. The lesser nāgas of the sea saw him and took counsel saying: 'Because this man has the great cintamanis, the other cintamanis will disappear from the sea. He must not be allowed to take them away.' While the bodhisattva was asleep, they stole them. When he awoke and found them gone he knew that the sea nāgas had taken them and thought: 'I shall pour out all the water of the sea and cause it to evaporate.' Making a mighty vow, he walked to the water's edge, took a hollow tortoise shell and began to dip out the sea water. The nāgas, seeing this, said to him: 'Man, are you trying to empty the sea? This sea is very deep and is thirty-thousand yojanas across. All the men in Jambudvīpa could not empty it. How can you do it alone?' The bodhisattva replied: 'There is nothing one cannot do if one truly wishes to. By means of the cintamani which I have obtained, I shall reach Buddhahood, aid all beings and cause them to rejoice. For this reason my mind knows no fatigue. Since my mind never wearies, why cannot I cause the sea to dry up by pouring it out?' Thereupon Viṣnu and other gods, seeing from afar the resolve of the bodhisattva and the mighty deed he was performing for the sake of all beings, thought: 'Come, let us go watch the bodhisattva.' They came one by one, and watched him pour out the water of the sea. Then, removing their divine robes, they themselves plunged into the sea and helped and the water evaporated for a distance of forty yojanas. A second time they plunged in, drew out water, and the sea evaporated for eighty yojanas. When they plunged in a third time and the water evaporated for a hundred and twenty yojanas, the nāgas became frightened, came to the bodhisattva, and pleaded: 'Bodhisattva, do not cause the sea to dry up. What were you going to do with the cintamanis?' The bodhisattva said: 'I require them in order to aid all beings.' The nāgas said: 'If that is true, since there are many living beings in the sea, why do you not aid them, too?' Great Charity replied: 'It is true that there are many living beings in the sea, but they are not subject to poverty and suffering.' All the beings of Jambudvīpa harm each other for the sake of material things and thereby commit the ten sins. When they die, they are reborn in hell. It is to deliver those beings that I have searched for the cintamani.' Then the nāgas returned the cintamanis to the bodhisattva.

"The gods, knowing the firm endeavor of the bodhisattva, thought: 'This man is certain to obtain Buddhahood.' They made the following vow: 'Ah, bodhisattva, when you attain Enlightenment, may we be among your disciples.'

"The bodhisattva then took the cintamani, flew up into the sky, and came to his own land. Seeing the merchants whom he had befriended, he asked if they had a good journey. The merchants were amazed and delighted to see him. He then went to the house of the Brahmin Kapila and when the brahmin learned that Great Charity had returned, he rejoiced and went out to meet him. When the bodhisattva entered the brahmin's house, such was the power

of the cintamani that all the brahmin's wealth was restored. Then
the brahmin adorned his daughter with many jewels, filling a precious vessel with water washed the bodhisattva's hands and feet,
and taking his daughter by the hand, offered her to him and when
she was accepted rejoiced greatly. He then adorned five-hundred
girls and caparisoned five-hundred elephants, mounted the
bodhisattva and his bride, and to the accompaniment of music and
singing, sent them on their way.

"When Great Charity had left home, his father and mother,
went blind from constantly weeping because of the sorrow of being separated from their son. When he arrived home, he bowed to
his parents and took them by the hand. When they knew that this
was their son, they said to him: 'Ah, Great Charity, when you left
us we became blind. What did you find at sea to bring back?' Great
Charity put the cintamanis in his parents' hands and said: 'This is
what I have found.' Feeling of the jewels, his father said: 'I have
many stones like this in my treasury. Was it only for this that you
have gone to so much trouble?' The bodhisattva took the jewels
and rubbed them across his parents' eyes and it was as when a
great wind drives away the clouds. Their eyes were opened and
they could see. Rejoicing, they said: 'Ah son, this is truly the
cintamani, and if you have suffered greatly to obtain it, the value is
indeed great.'

"Then Great Charity took the jewels into his hands and said to
them: 'If you are truly the cintamanis, may there appear beneath
my parents a throne of the seven jewels and above them a garland
of jewels.' And it happened as he said. Then his father's treasuries
were replenished. A messenger was then sent out for a distance of
eighty yojanas to proclaim to the people of Jambudvīpa that Great
Charity had brought the precious cintamani from the sea. For seven
days, there would be showers of jewels, food, clothing, and everything one desired, and that the people might come and obtain what
they wished.

"Then Great Charity bathed, donned a new robe, and furled
the victory-banner. Holding a vessel of incense in his hands, he
made the following prayer: 'The people of Jambudvīpa have ever
been destitute and poverty-stricken. I shall aid them. You, cintamani

jewel, if you are truly real, bring down a rain of whatever it is that each person wishes!' Immediately a wild wind sprang up, blew from the four directions, and removed all the impurities from the earth. Then there descended a fine shower which settled all the dust. There appeared a shower of various kinds of delicious food and drink, a shower of the fruits of the fields, a shower of silks and robes, then jewels descended like rain and totally filled all of Jambudvīpa. When all the people were satisfied, the bodhisattva commanded them: 'Ye beings of Jambudvīpa! For the sake of food and clothing and things, you do evil to one another and constantly commit sins. At death, you will fall into the three evil states and go from darkness to darkness. I pity all of you and in order to liberate you, have undergone great sufferings and passed through great dangers to obtain the cintamani from the sea. Now I have met your needs, and you must cease to commit evil, sinful acts and enter the path of the ten virtues. Guard body, spirit, and mind and be zealous in virtue.' He then set them on the path of supreme virtue and, because they made efforts on that path, at death they were reborn among the noble gods.

"At that time King Śuddhodana, who is now my father, was that brahmin called Nyagrodha. My mother, Queen Mahāmāyā, was his wife. I myself was Great Charity and Śāriputra was the nāga king of the silver city. Mahā Maudgalyayana was the nāga king of the city of lapis-lazuli, and Ānanda was the nāga king of the city of gold. Aniruddha was the god of the sea. Ānanda, who had taken birth at that time as a king of the nāgas and honored me, was wise then and he has remained wise from that time until now. I grant him his three wishes."

When the Buddha had thus spoken, Ānanda rejoiced, had faith, and kneeling on his right knee and folding his palms in reverence, said: "Lord, may I serve you as long as I live." Happily, the Buddha approved. Some of the assembly attained the fruit of streamwinners, some of arhats, some brought forth the thoughts of a Pratyekabuddha, some reached the realm of no-return, and all rejoiced.

32

King Mirror-Face

᙮

Thus have I heard at one time: the Enlightened One was residing in Rājagṛha in the Nyagrodha Grove. Upon a certain occasion the Lord sat surrounded by Indra, Brahmā, and other gods. When the disciples saw his body adorned with the signs and shining with a golden color, they were astonished and praised and extolled him. But as the Lord sat thus in splendor as the supreme of all, doubts arose in the minds of many of the monks and folding their palms, they said: "What is that which sits here, the supreme in splendor among the great assembly?"

The Buddha said: "Oh monks, this is not the first time that I have been supreme among all. In aeons long past, aeons past counting, past reckoning, aeons beyond compare, there lived in this Jambudvīpa a great king who ruled over eighty four thousand minor kings and had five-hundred sons. Late in life, his first queen gave birth to a son whose body was the color of gold, whose hair was jet-black, whose palms bore the sign of the wheel of a thousand spokes, whose left sole bore the mark of a horse's hoof, whose right sole had the mark of an elephant's foot, and who was endowed with perfect wisdom and virtue. This son was named 'Mirror-Face.'

"When the king became ill and death was approaching, his ministers said to him: 'Your Majesty, when you pass beyond sorrow, which of your sons is to succeed to the throne?' The king replied: 'Whichever of my sons is endowed with the ten signs. What are the ten? His body will be the color of gold and his hair will be black. The palms of his hands will bear the sign of the wheel, the sole of his right foot will have the mark of a horse's hoof, and when he dons the royal robe, it will be neither too long nor too short, but will fit him perfectly. When he sits on the royal throne, he will be splendid. He will be greatly honored by the lesser kings, and when wives and friends see him, they will rejoice and bow. If he goes to the realms of the gods all the gods will return his homage. He will bring down showers of the seven kinds of jewels through the power of wisdom and virtue, and he will satisfy the longings of all beings. Whichever of my sons is born of the great queen and is endowed with these signs should ascend the throne.' Then, in accordance with the law of impermanence, the king passed on.

"Thereupon all the princes and ministers came together to ascertain who among the great princes was endowed with the signs, but none had them except the youngest son. On the day of the full moon, early in the morning as the sun was rising, the lesser kings and the princes and ministers raised him to the throne. A golden wheel with a thousand spokes, a yojana in breadth, appeared in the east, passed across the sky, and rested in the southern sky. Thereupon the prince knelt and spoke: 'If I am truly the king endowed with virtues, may the wheel draw near me.' And immediately the wheel descended from the sky and came to him. Then the precious elephant came from the fragrant mountain of incense, its tail adorned with the cintamani. The king mounted the elephant and flew through the sky, and by mid-day had circled the four continents. Wherever he put down his foot there appeared sand of gold. Then the precious horse appeared with black mane and red tail, adorned with the seven jewels. The king mounted the horse and, in the time that it takes to eat a meal, he had visited the four continents without growing weary. The precious jewel came and shone by day and night over a hundred and thirty lands, and there fell a shower of the seven jewels which fulfilled all wishes. The precious minister appeared, brought forth the seven precious substances and made them inexhaustible. The precious general came, assembled and reviewed the four armies, and with great might overcame the enemy.

"Thereupon the king thought: 'It is because of former virtues that I have become endowed with the seven precious things. Now the root of virtue must not be cut off.' Bathing himself in fragrant water and putting on a new robe, he held a vessel of incense, knelt toward the east, and prayed: 'Oh ye Noble Ones who reside in the eastern quarter, come, I beseech you, in accordance with my request.' Then twenty-thousand Noble Ones came to the king's palace. He then prayed in the same manner toward the south, the west, and the north, and twenty-thousand noble Pratyekabuddhas came to the king's palace from each direction. The king himself, the princes, and the ministers made offerings of the four necessities to those Noble Ones. The eighty-four thousand lesser kings paid homage to the king as they departed to their own countries, and made offerings to the Noble Ones. For four-thousand years, the king and his princes and ministers made offerings and honored the Noble Ones. When they died, they were reborn among the gods.

"Oh monks, I was that king called Mirror-Face. My father, Śuddhodana, was his father and my mother Mahāmāyā, was his mother. The five-hundred Śākyas were the five-hundred princes. At that time I was the supreme of all, and now that I have attained Buddhahood and am endowed with the signs, I am the supreme."

When the great assembly heard the Buddha's word, they believed and rejoiced.

33

Good Searcher and Evil Searcher

❦

Thus have I heard at one time: the Enlightened One was residing in the city of Śrāvastī at the Jetavana monastery in Anāthapiṇḍika's park. At that time the monk Devadatta, fearing the future results of the evil deeds he had committed for the sake of personal gain—oppressing the Buddha, stabbing his feet with wooden splinters, letting loose an elephant to kill him, vilifying the Noble Sangha, and harming the monks who had stopped the outflows, went to the six heretic-teachers and requested their teachings. When they taught him the false doctrine that evil deeds are not sinful and that virtuous deeds are without virtue, he took these as his refuge and cut off the root of virtue. Thereupon Ānanda, having pity for his relative, became exceedingly sad and wept. He said to the Buddha: "Lord, Devadatta has become infected with ignorance, and he commits stupid, sinful deeds. He has cut off the root of virtue, and vilifies and dishonors the tribe of the Śākyas."

The Buddha said: "Ānanda, it is not only in this lifetime that Devadatta has cut off the root of virtue for the sake of gain and fame. In former lifetimes, he frequently destroyed life and limb for the sake of gain and fame." When the Lord had thus spoken, the monks wondered about this and Ānanda said: "Lord, how did Devadatta destroy life and limb in former times?"

The Buddha said: "Ānanda, in aeons long past, aeons beyond count, beyond recall, beyond imagining, there lived in Benares a brahmin by the name of Mahā Māyi, who had married a woman of his own caste and to whom a son had been born. After the son was born, they held a great anointing feast and named the boy 'Good-Searcher.' The boy was then given over to a nurse who cared for him. The nurse herself then became pregnant, and whereas she had formerly been of a good disposition, she now became ill-natured, angry, and violent. When the months had passed, she gave birth to a son who was given the name 'Evil-Searcher.' The boys were raised as brothers and when they grew up they decided to go to sea in search of the cintamani. They set out, each with five-hundred followers.

"When seven days had passed, their supplies were gone and they were in danger of starving to death. Good-Searcher made offerings to all the gods, and presently they came to a desolate, uninhabited place. Spying a tree from afar, they went to the tree and they found a spring from which they all drank. 'This,' they said, 'is because we made offerings to the gods.' Thereupon a god appeared to them and told them that if they would break off the branches of the tree, their every wish would be fulfilled. The travellers broke off branches and delicious beverages appeared. Then they broke off more branches and a hundred kinds of delicious food appeared. They ate and drank until they were satisfied. They then broke off still more branches and various sorts of clothing and jewels appeared, as much as they could carry.

"Evil-Searcher and his followers then came to a tree and, seeing that Good-Searcher and his followers had obtained many jewels by breaking off the branches of the tree, decided that if they were to dig up the roots of the tree they would obtain still more jewels. Good-Searcher said: 'Younger brother, why do you dig up the tree? We were starving and the tree saved our lives. Do not dig it up.' After he had departed, Evil-Searcher dug up the roots of the tree. Five hundred rakśas came out from under it and ate Evil-Searcher and his followers.

"Ānanda, I was that person called Good-Searcher, my father Śuddhodana was that father and my mother Mahāmāyā was that mother. Devadatta was Evil-Searcher. It is not only now, Ānanda, that Devadatta has harmed me. He has done me harm in every lifetime, but I help him by teaching him the Good Law. Still, he makes himself my enemy."

When the Buddha had thus spoken, the many disciples had faith and rejoiced.

34

Prince Virtuous

Thus have I heard at one time: the Enlightened One was residing together with the Sangha on the Vulture's Peak in Rājagṛha.
At that time Ānanda saw Devadatta's evil designs toward the Buddha, the Lord's refusal to make any distinction between Rāhula
and Devadatta, and his compassion toward Devadatta. He said:
"Lord, when Devadatta does evil to the Buddha, what is the reason
that the Lord has compassion on him?" The Buddha said: "Ānanda,
this is not the first time that Devadatta has harmed me. He did me
great harm in other lifetimes as well." When the monks wondered
about this, Ānanda said to the Buddha: "Lord, in what manner did
Devadatta do evil to you in other lifetimes?"

The Buddha said: "Ānanda, in aeons long past, aeons beyond
count, beyond reckoning, beyond conception, there lived in this
Jambudvīpa a king by the name of Precious Armor. This king had
five-hundred queens, five-hundred palaces, but no son, and although
he prayed for many years to the sun, the moon, and all the gods, no
son was born to him. In great sorrow the king thought: 'If I continue without an heir, the five-hundred minor kings will be in disa-
greement and the people will suffer.' Pressing his hands against
his cheeks in misery, he sat there in grief. One of the gods, seeing
his thought, appeared to him in a dream and said: 'Your Majesty,
two rishis live outside your palace in the forest. One of them has a
body the color of gold. If you will go to him and pray, a son will be
born to you.'

"When the king awoke he went in search of the two rishis and
when he found them said: 'Holy sages, I have no son to succeed
me and I beg you to fulfil my desire and be born as my son.' The
one rishi said: 'May it be as you desire.' The second rishi also
said: 'I also wish to be born in your family.' The king rejoiced and

said: 'Yes, may you both be born into my family.' He then returned to his palace and, sometime later, the rishi with the golden body died and entered the womb of the king's first queen. When the nine months had passed, a son was born who was of a golden color and had black hair. The king rejoiced and prepared a great feast to which a soothsayer was invited. When he examined the boy, he named him 'Virtuous.' When the other rishi died, he also entered the womb of one of the queens. When he was born a soothsayer was invited who examined his signs and called the boy 'Sinful.'

"The king loved his first son greatly and constructed spring-summer-autumn-and winter-residences for him and when Prince Virtuous grew up he became learned in the eight sciences. Upon a certain occasion, he said to his father: 'Father, I wish to go out into the world and see things.' The king approved and had the road that led from the palace and the great highway swept and made clean, set up flags and banners, strewed flowers and sweet-smelling fragrances, mounted the prince on an elephant caparisoned with jewels, and to the accompaniment of cymbals and drums the prince rode out of the city with an entourage of a hundred-thousand followers. All the people exclaimed: 'Ah, the magnificence and splendor of this prince are like unto the ruler of the gods!' As the procession proceeded, it came to a group of people who were dressed in rags. Holding broken vessels, they cried out in a loud voice: 'Give us anything! Anything!' When the prince asked them the cause of their misery, some said they were homeless orphans without families, others said they had been long ill, still others said they had been reduced to begging because robbers had stolen everything they had. Going on, he came to people of the candala caste who had killed an animal, skinned it, and were eating its flesh. When asked why they were doing this, they told the prince that it was their way of life and that there was no other way for them to survive. Soon he came to men working in the fields and turning up worms which were eaten by the birds. The men told him that this was the way they earned their living. Going on, he saw hunters who had caught birds in a net and were crying piteously. The hunters told him that this was their inherited profession

and that they knew no other. Further along the road, he met fisher-
men who told him the same thing. Realizing that these people's
sins were the result of their poverty, he returned sadly to the palace and asked his father's permission to give away his treasures to
the poor and needy. His father, out of love for him, allowed him to
do this. When two-thirds of the treasures had been given away the
treasure-keeper locked the doors and no more could be given. Thereupon, Prince Virtuous decided to go to sea in search of the
cintamani.

"At that time, there were five-hundred merchants in that country who were preparing to go to sea in search of jewels. There was
also an old man, a guide, who had gone to sea many times. Prince
Virtuous went to him and said: 'Sir, I am going to sea in search of
the cintamani, come and be my guide.' The old man replied: 'Ah,
Prince, I am a feeble, old man, and almost blind. I cannot go.' The
prince then went to his father and said: 'Father, there is a man of
our country who knows the sea and has often been to search for
jewels. I beg you to command him to go with me as a guide.' The
king went to the man and said: 'Guide, you must not disagree with
my son, the prince. You are to go to sea with him and be his guide.'
The guide told the king: 'Your Majesty, I am old, feeble and cannot see well, but I cannot disobey your command. I shall go.' The
king then returned to the palace and announced: 'My son is going
to sea in search of the cintamani. Who will accompany him?' Prince
Sinful said: 'I will go with my elder brother and be a servant to
him.' Believing that this would be of benefit to the prince, the king
gave his permission.

"Then Prince Virtuous took from the treasury three-thousand
measure of silver, and with a third of this outfitted a ship, keeping
the remaining two-thirds for supplies for the journey. When it was
time to depart, the king, queen and all the people accompanied the
prince to the seashore. When all were on board the prince told the
merchants: 'There are many dangers in the sea. Some of you may
not return. If you have doubts and wish to go back, now is the time
to do it. But if you have no fear for life or limb and are not attached
to father, mother, brothers and sisters, wives, children, friends or
relatives, if we do arrive at the Isle of Jewels and return safely, you

will be wealthy for seven generations.' For seven days he spoke to them thus, each day cutting one of the hawsers, and when he cut the seventh, the ship shot out into the sea like an arrow.

"Eventually they arrived at the Jewel Island and the prince, being wise in jewels, showed the merchants how to distinguish the valuable ones from the others. While they were searching for them, the prince and the guide sailed on. When they had gone away, the guide asked: 'Has a white mountain become visible?' When the prince said that he could see one, the guide told him that it was a mountain of silver. When they came to a blue mountain, the guide said that it was a mountain of lapis-lazuli. They then came to a yellow mountain, and the guide told him that this was gold. They sailed to the golden mountain, sat down on the golden sand, and the guide said: 'I am old, feeble and can go no further; it is here that I shall die. You must continue your journey. Soon you will come to the city of the seven jewels. The city gates will be locked, but near them you will find a diamond pestle. Take it, strike the gates, and five-hundred goddesses will come out of the city, each with a jewel in her hand which she will offer to you. Then a goddess with a blue jewel will appear. This is the cintamani. Grasp it with all your might, because the other goddesses will try to take it from you. Also take the jewels from the other goddesses, but guard your senses well and do not speak to them. Now I am weak and will die here. Think of the service I have rendered you and kindly bury my bones.' Thereupon the guide passed on and the prince buried him, covering his body with golden sand. Following the guide's advice, he went on and came to the city made of the seven precious jewels, the gates of which were locked. When he struck the gate with the diamond pestle they opened by themselves and five-hundred goddesses appeared, each with a jewel in her hand, and offered them to him. One of the goddesses held a blue jewel which he took, hid in his robe, and departed.

"After Prince Virtuous had left the merchants, Prince Sinful commanded them to load the ship with as many jewels as possible. This they did, but when they had set sail the ship began to sink. At that moment, Prince Virtuous returned and Prince Sinful, seeing him, cried out: 'We are perishing, elder brother, save us!' As Prince

Virtuous was pulling them to shore, the ship sank and the merchants were drowned. Then Prince Sinful said: 'Ah, elder brother, we have left father and mother and now will return empty-handed. How shameful this is.' Prince Virtuous, being of a pure heart, did not attempt to conceal the jewels he had obtained and said: 'There is no cause for shame, we have many jewels,' and showed them to him. Prince Sinful thought: 'Although we are brothers, Prince Virtuous is loved and I am not. We have gone to seek jewels. He has found them and I have not. When we return, he will be in greater favor than I and they will dislike me more than ever. When he is asleep I shall kill him, take the jewels return and say that he drowned at sea.'

"He then said: 'Elder brother, we should not both sleep at the same time. While one of us is asleep the other should stay awake and guard the jewels.' To this the elder brother agreed and thereafter they slept in turns. One night when the elder brother had kept watch, he went to awaken the other but could not find him, so he continued his watch until he fell asleep. Then Prince Sinful came out of the forest, and with two sharp thorns he pierced the eyes of the elder brother, took the jewels, and fled. When Prince Virtuous awoke he thought that brigands had done this and called the younger brother, but there was no answer. Thereupon a tree-god appeared to him and said: 'This is not the work of brigands, but of your enemy, your younger brother.'

"Slowly and painfully, because of his blindness, Prince Virtuous walked away. Eventually he came to a place called Liśivar, where he found an elephant-herder who cared for five-hundred elephants. Among the elephants was a bull-elephant who, seeing that the prince's eyes had been wounded, licked them while all the others elephants stood around in a circle. The herder, wondering what all this might be, came and saw a man rolling about on the ground and, coming closer, saw that he had thorns in his eyes. He gently drew them out and took him to his home where he bathed his eyes with milk and butter and fed him. When the prince's eyes began to heal, he wished to go on, but the elephant-herder dissuaded him. Later, when his wounds were completely healed, the elephant-herder accompanied him to the city.

"When they arrived at the city, the prince asked for a lute. When this was given to him, he sat down to play and sing beautiful songs. The people of the city brought him food and drink in abundance, so much that he was able to feed five-hundred beggars. An orchard-keeper, delighted with his melodious voice, asked him to come to his orchards to sing and guard the trees. The prince told him that he was unable to watch the trees because he was blind, but the man told him: 'It does not matter, we shall hang a rope with bells on the trees, you will hold the rope, shake it, and the birds will be frightened away.' The prince agreed, and the man took to his orchard, where he played the lute and sang.

"Meanwhile, Prince Sinful had returned and the king asked concerning his son and the merchants. He told them that Prince Virtuous had found many jewels, but while returning the ship had capsized and all had drowned and that he, Prince Sinful, had been the only one to escape. Hearing this, the king and queen fainted and all who heard this wept and mourned. When the king recovered, he said: 'Evil son, it would have been better if you, too, had died.'

"At the palace there was a tame yellow duck that had belonged to Prince Virtuous. The king went to the duck and said: 'Our Prince Virtuous went to sea in search of jewels and it has been reported that he has drowned. Go and see whether he has really perished or not.' He then wrote a note and tied it to the duck's leg. The duck flew to distant lands and finally came to the orchard where Prince Virtuous sat beneath a tree singing. Recognizing his voice, he flew down beside him. The prince recognized the duck's voice, took the note from its leg and had it read to him. When he learned what his parents had written, he had a letter written which described how his younger brother had put his eyes out, tied it to the duck's neck, and sent it back.

"The king of that country had a daughter rare in the world for beauty who, seeing the wretched state of the prince, his hair matted, his face dirty, and his robe soiled, came and stayed with him and took care of him. When the king called his daughter at meal times, she refused to go to the palace and ordered food to be brought. She offered this to the prince, but he refused it, saying: 'I am only a blind beggar and it would be improper for me to eat with a princess.' The princess insisted and said that if he refused to eat with her, she also would not eat. Thereupon the two ate together, had pleasant talk, and the princess stayed with the blind prince and found pleasure in the company of no one else. At sunset the king called his daughter, who sent word to him that she was going to marry the gardener's boy and begged him not to reproach her. Hearing this, the king thought: 'What strange words are these? The girl has promised to marry the son of King Precious Armor who has gone to sea. Now, before he returns, she says that she will marry this foul beggar! My line will be disgraced and I will be put to shame by every man.' Again he summoned her, but the girl refused to alter her decision or come. Finally, out of love for his daughter, the king brought the boy and girl to the palace and allowed them to marry.

"When some time had passed, the wife began to absent herself each day and returned only at night. The prince became suspicious and told her: 'You became my wife and we are married, but each day you go away and return only at night. You are certainly seeing others and you humiliate me.' The girl replied: 'I have no thought at all of anyone else. If my words are true, by the power of truth of the spoken word, may you recover sight in one eye!' And immediately the prince could see in one eye. Then, as they talked, the girl asked him where his country was and who his parents were. The prince asked her if she had ever heard of King Precious Armor and his son, Prince Virtuous, and when she told him that she had, he revealed to her that he was that prince. Alarmed, the girl asked him why he had suffered so. The prince explained to her in detail all that had taken place, and the girl said: 'Wherever Prince Sinful may be in the world, his evil karma will be there with him for having put out your eyes. If I should ever meet him, how should I act?' The prince said: 'It is not his fault. When we were small I disliked him and refused to play with him.' The girl said: 'That is hard to believe. How can I be sure that, having done the great evil which he has, you are not offended with him?' The prince said: 'I do not hate Prince Sinful. If what I say is true, by the power of the truth of the spoken word, may I receive sight of my other eye!' And immediately he could see clearly in his other eye.

"The girl then went to her father and said: 'Father do you know of a Prince Virtuous, son of King Precious Armor?' The king asked: 'Where is the prince now?' The girl replied: 'That prince is now my husband.' The king laughed and said: 'The girl is either mad or her mind is disturbed. The prince went to seek for jewels, and while he is away this beggar pretends to be he.' The girl replied: 'Father, if you do not believe me, come and see: When the king went and saw the splendor of Prince Virtuous, he knew that this was indeed the prince. The king said: 'Ah Prince, I am indeed at fault for not having recognized you and for having humiliated you,' and took him to another place. He called all his princes and ministers together and told them: 'Princes and Ministers, hear! Prince Virtuous has now returned from the sea and you must all know who he is." And they all paid homage and applauded the king for having given his daughter to him.

"When the duck had brought back the message from Prince Virtuous, it was opened and read and the king and queen and all the people were greatly grieved. They learned of the prince's suffering, threw Prince Sinful into a dungeon, and sent a message to the king of the Liśivar country saying: 'It has come to our knowledge that our son is undergoing grief and suffering in your realm. What is the reason that you have not informed us of this? You are to come immediately with my son, accompanied by many hundreds of horsemen. Should you not do this, I shall come out to do battle with you.'

"Meanwhile, in order to return the kindness shown him by the elephant-herder, the Prince begged the king to give him a gift. The king sent gifts of white elephants, horses, robes, dwellings, farms, gold and silver, jewels, servants, men and women-slaves, and much more—enough to make him happy for the rest of his life.

"When the messenger arrived from King Precious Armor, the king of Liśivar caparisoned five-hundred elephants with jewels, took servants and five-hundred young maidens and five-hundred chariots as a dowry, and with a retinue of a hundred-thousand ministers and servants beating drums and cymbals, went forth with the bride, having sent a messenger in advance. King Precious Armor and his entourage went out to meet them, and Prince Virtuous descended from his chariot, bowed to his father and mother, asked after their health. Rejoicing, they all proceeded to the palace. Prince Virtuous then asked where his younger brother, Prince Sinful was, and when told that he had been cast into a dungeon, he said: 'Prince Sinful must be released.' The king protested: 'But how can I release him when he has committed so terrible a crime?' The prince said: 'I cannot remain in the palace unless my younger brother is freed,' whereupon the king brought him out from the dungeon. When Prince Sinful saw his elder brother, he bowed to him and the two embraced. All were astonished that the prince showed great love for Prince Sinful.

"Prince Sinful persuaded Prince Virtuous to tell him where were the jewels which he had brought, and he told him where they were hidden along the road. He asked him to go bring them, and Prince Sinful went but was unable to find them. They both then went together, found them, and returned to the palace, where Prince Virtuous gave one jewel each to all the minor princes. Then he took the cintamani and said: 'Oh, cintamani, if you are real, may the throne upon which my parents sit be of the seven jewels and may the canopy above them also be made of the seven jewels.' And immediately this came to pass. Then the prince said: 'Formerly, through giving gifts, I depleted my father's treasury. May the treasury again be filled. And when he pointed the cintamani at the treasury, it again filled with precious jewels.

"Then the prince proclaimed: 'All ye people, hear! For seven days I will cause a shower of jewels to fall. Assemble, all of you!' Then, bathing in perfumed water and donning new robes, he placed the cintamani on the banner of victory, and holding a vessel of incense, bowed in the four directions and cried: 'Cintamani, if you are in truth the cintamani, fulfill the wishes of all these people like showers of rain!' At that moment clouds appeared from the four directions, a wind sprang up and swept away all impurities, and a fine shower descended and laid the dust. Then there came down showers of a hundred kinds of delicious foods, of silken robes, of the seven jewels, enough to fill the entire country. Thereupon the prince proclaimed: 'There is now nothing you lack to satisfy your wants. All of you must guard your bodies, speech, and minds, and exert yourselves in the path of the ten virtues.' Then the people abandoned their evil, sinful deeds and making rapid progress on the path of the ten virtues, attained birth in a higher realm when they died.

"Ānanda, my father, King Śuddhodana, was King Precious Armor. My mother, Mahāmāyā, was his queen. I was Prince Virtuous and Kāśyapa was the king of Liśivar. The nun Prajāpatī was his daughter. Devadatta was Prince Sinful. The eighty thousand devaputras who have come to me and those of my followers who have been given prophecies were those beings of Jambudvīpa whom I benefitted and made happy. Ānanda, when Devadatta did me great evil, I was compassionate to him in return. Now that I have stopped the defilements and attained Supreme Enlightenment and have total compassion, why, when he does some small evil act to me, should I withhold my compassion?"

When the Buddha had thus spoken, all believed and rejoiced.

35

The Householder Named 'Pacifier'

☙❧

Thus have I heard at one time: the Enlightened One was residing in the city of Śrāvastī at the Jetavana monastery in Anāthapiṇḍika's park. At that time there were five-hundred beggars in that country who relied upon the Buddha and the Sangha for sustenance. Upon a certain occasion, they decided to join the Order, went to the Buddha and said: "Lord, through the compassion of the Lord and the Brotherhood we have been fed. Now we beg to become monks."

The Buddha said: "The Dharma which I teach is totally pure and makes no distinction between race or caste, between rich or poor, between good and bad. It is like washing in pure water. The water washes all races and castes, rich and poor, good and bad, without distinction. It is like fire which burns all substances without exception: mountain, rocks, sky, and earth. My Teaching is like the sky under which all find a place: men, women, boys, girls, rich and poor, all without exception."

The beggars rejoiced and believed when they heard what the Lord said, and again requested permission to join the Order. When the Enlightened One said: "Welcome," their hair and beards fell away by themselves, they were dressed in the ochre robes of the Order, and became monks. When the Lord had instructed them in the Dharma, their minds became liberated, their outflows were stopped, and they became arhats.

When certain high-caste householders and merchant princes who lived in that country heard that the wretched beggars had been accepted into the Order, they were offended and said to each other: "If we were to invite the Buddha and the Noble Sangha in order to create virtue, and these beggars were to sit above us, we would be defiled."

Upon a certain occasion, Prince Victorious invited the Buddha and the Sangha, but said to the Buddha: "Lord, I invite the Buddha and the Sangha, but those beggars who have lately become monks are not invited." The next day, when it was time for the Lord and his disciples to go to the prince's house, the Buddha told those monks who had not been invited: "The master of gifts has not invited you. Go to the Northern Continent and obtain wild rice that has been neither sown nor reaped, bring it to the master of gift's house, and eat it." Immediately, in accordance with the Buddha's command, they flew with the spiritual powers of the arhats to the Northern Continent and filled their begging bowls with rice. Then in beautiful formation, like wild geese in the sky, they flew back to the palace of Prince Victorious, sat down in a row, and ate the rice.

When Prince Victorious saw the monks come flying through the sky in lovely formation, he was astonished, rejoiced, and believed. He then asked the Buddha: "Lord, where have these magnificent, splendid, virtuous, holy men come from?" The Buddha said: "You should recognize them. Listen well, Prince, and I shall tell you about them. These monks are those whom you did not invite. Because you did not invite them, they went to the Northern Continent and obtained wild rice to eat."

When Prince Victorious heard this he was overcome with shame, repented what he had done, and said: "It was because I was obstructed by ignorance that I did not understand about these holy men and refused to invite them. Lord, your virtue is beyond conception. Although these holy men were low-caste beggars in this country, through the Lord's mercy they have found joy in the world and have obtained benefits for long to come. Lord, your coming into the world is for such as these. I beg you to explain what root of virtue these beggars planted in order to meet you and attain liberation, and because of what former sins were they first born as beggars?"

The Buddha said: "In times long past, aeons beyond recall, there was a mountain called 'Many Rishis' in the land of Benares where many Pratyekabuddhas lived and would continue to live until a Buddha appeared in the world. If Pratyekabuddhas did not reside there, rishis with magic powers lived there. At one time when there were two-thousand rishis living on the mountain, a soothsayer foretold that for twelve years there would be no rain. The rishis thereupon went to a wealthy householder by the name of Pacifier, who lived in that land, and asked if he would offer them food and drink for twelve years. They said that if he would not, they would go elsewhere. The householder told them: 'Holy rishis, do not go anywhere else, remain here, I beg you, and I shall make offerings for twelve years.' The householder then asked his treasurer if there were enough supplies to feed the holy men for twelve years, and when told that there was enough, the householder appointed five hundred men to serve the rishis. When the five-hundred men had served for some time, they became tired of serving and began to murmur among themselves that it was too much trouble to care for the beggars.

"At that time, there was a certain man who called the rishis at mealtime and who had a dog that followed him. One day the man forgot to call the rishis but the dog ran to them, began to bark, and the rishis knew that their food was ready and went to receive it. Sometime later, the rishis told the householder that the rains were soon coming and that he must prepare his fields for the sowing. The householder directed his field workers to begin work in the fields and they planted barley, wheat, and many other kinds of crops. When the seeds had sprouted and were as high as water pots, the householder went to the rishis and asked if there would be a good yield. The rishis said that the crops would be good and advised him to irrigate from time to time. When the crops were harvested, it was found that the yield was manifold and the householder rejoiced when his granaries were filled.

"When the five-hundred men who had served the rishis saw this, they were ashamed, felt remorse, and confessed to the holy men, saying: 'Holy ones, we humiliated you with our evil words and we confess our sin. In future times, may we again meet you and attain Liberation.' It was because of those evil words against the rishis that those five-hundred men were reborn as miserable beggars throughout five-hundred lifetimes. Later, by having confessed their sins and having made a vow, they have met me and reached the end of the round of birth and death. Prince, you should understand this: I was the householder called Pacifier. Udiyana was the treasurer. You, Prince Victorious, were the man who daily called the rishis at mealtimes. You whose name is Good Voice were the dog, and because you called the holy ones by barking, have had a good voice throughout all your lifetimes. These five-hundred beggars are the five-hundred serving men."

When the Buddha had thus spoken, some in the great assembly attained from the first to the fourth fruits. Some brought forth a mind of Supreme Enlightenment. All had faith in the word of the Lord and rejoiced.

36

The Prince Whose Eyes Were Opened

ॐ

Thus have I heard at one time: the Enlightened One was residing in the city of Śrāvastī at the Jetavana monastery in
Anāthapiṇḍika's park, teaching the Dharma to many people. At
that time there was in that city a blind brahmin who used to sit
along the highway. When many people passed by him to go hear
the Dharma, he asked where they were going, and they told him:
"Brahmin, have you not heard? The Enlightened One has come to
this world and is now residing in this country and teaching the
Dharma. Because it is exceedingly difficult to meet a Buddha in
the world, we are going to hear the Dharma from him."

This brahmin was wise concerning the eight different kinds of
voices and, as soon as he heard a person's voice, he could tell that
person's lot in life and how long that person would live. Should
one ask what the eight different kinds of voices are, they are the
voice of the nighthawk, the raven, the hoarse voice, the voice of
the elephant, of the horse, of the dragon, of the bell, and the voice
of Brahmā. Those who speak with the voice of the nighthawk are
shameless and return favors. Those who speak with the voice of
the raven are of an angry disposition, take pleasure in killing, and
have no mercy. When one speaks with a hoarse voice, this means
that a man speaks with the voice of a woman or a woman speaks
with the voice of a man. Such people are of low nature and do not
have good fortune. Those who speak with the elephant's voice
stand firm in their own true nature and are intent on aiding friends
and relatives. Those who speak with the voice of the horse are
wise in speech, are learned in the sciences, and are the instructors
of kings. Those who speak with the dragon's voice are quick to
anger but are wise in the Dharma. Those who speak with the voice
of the bell are rich in possessions and guard hundreds of thousands

of measures of gold. Those who speak with the voice of Brahmā are endowed with virtue and fortune. If they are married they become universal monarchs, but if monks, attain to Buddhahood.

The brahmin said to the people: "I am wise in the knowledge of voices. If this is truly the Buddha you are going to see, he will speak with the voice of Brahmā. Take me there." The people led the blind brahmin and, as they drew near the Lord and heard him speaking with the voice of Brahmā, the brahmin rejoiced greatly. Because of his faith, his eyes were opened and he saw the body of the Buddha, like unto gold and endowed with the thirty-two signs, as clearly as the sun. He bowed his head at the Buddha's feet and boundless joy arose in him, and when the Lord had taught him the Dharma and he had attained absolute faith in the Buddha. Two-hundred-thousand sins were erased and he attained the fruit of a streamwinner. He became endowed with wisdom and begged the Buddha to ordain him as a monk. When the Lord approved, saying: "Welcome, brahmin," he became a monk, and when the Lord had instructed him in the Dharma, he attained the bliss of an arhat.

As the people all wondered about this, the Noble Ānanda rose from his seat, pressed his palms together in reverence, and spoke to the Buddha: "Lord, of all beings whom you have aided, you have shown the greatest compassion to this blind brahmin. He has recovered his fleshly eyes and has attained the eye of wisdom."

The Buddha said to Ānanda: "Ānanda, this is not the first time that I have restored that brahmin's eyes to him. In former times, I also returned his sight to him and allowed him to see."

Ānanda said: "Lord, I beseech you to relate how in former times you restored his sight."

The Buddha said: "In times long past, aeons ago, aeons past counting, beyond conceiving, there lived in this Jambudvīpa in a land called Pukalada a king by the name of 'Opened Eyes.' He was called this because he could see into cliffs and mountains for a distance of forty yojanas. This king ruled over eighty-four thousand lesser kings, had twenty-thousand palaces and wives, and five-hundred sons, the eldest of which was named Good Morality. Interested only in the welfare of his people, he thought of them all as his own sons. During his reign, the rains came in season, the crops

were abundant, and the people enjoyed peace. Upon a certain occasion the king was sitting in a secluded place and thought to himself: 'By the power of virtue of a former life I have become a king
of men, obtained great wealth, and all obey me. Yet life is like the
tender grass that is blown hither and yon by the wind. If, during
this lifetime, I do not prepare for future lives, suffering is certain
to come. It is as when a farmer does not sow in the spring. In the
autumn, he will have nothing to harvest. If in the spring of this
lifetime I do not sow and plant, in the fall of the next life there will
be no harvest. I must not be idle now. I shall plant the seeds of
virtue during this very lifetime.'

"The king then called his ministers together and said to them:
'You are to move my treasuries to the gates of the city and assemble all the people and make gifts to them. The treasuries of all the
eighty-four thousand minor kings are also to be distributed in the
same manner.' He then unfurled the golden banner and proclaimed:
'Come all! Monks and brahmins, beggars and old people, and all
the sick of Jambudvīpa. Whatever your needs, they will be fulfilled from the treasuries.'

"When the people had all assembled and their wants had been
satisfied, they lauded and praised the king in one accord. There
was one king, however, from one of the border regions who disobeyed the king's command. This was King Doer of Evil Deeds.
This king had a minister by the name of Lodari, who told him:
'Your Majesty, you are quick to anger and think neither of the past
or the future. Later you will regret this. King Opened Eyes is of a
truly compassionate nature and all the beings of Jambudvīpa are
happy because of his grace. All the minor kings have obeyed his
command and will therefore be happy for eight generations.' These
words enraged the king and he disregarded what the minister had
advised.

"The minister then became worried and thought: 'My king is
committing evil acts, and when I give him valuable advice, he
reproaches me and becomes furious. I shall consult with the people and advise them not to obey the king's order.' When he did
this and news of it reached the king, he called out the army to
arrest the minister. Learning of this, the minister mounted a good

horse and escaped. The army gave chase and when it had almost captured him, the minister, being a good marksman, shot and killed fifteen men. The army then returned, and the minister made his way to the kingdom of King Opened Eyes. Coming before the king, he pressed his palms together in reverence and explained in detail what had taken place. The king was pleased and placed him among his own ministers.

"The ministers then advised the king: 'Your Majesty, that minor king in the border region has disobeyed your command and is committing unusually evil deeds.' When the king asked the ministers whether that king was his subject and the ministers assured him that he was, they all took counsel and proposed called out the army to ride against the subject king. The king approved and appointed the minister who had come from the border region to lead the army. When King Doer of Evil Deeds learned that an army had been sent against him, he became exceedingly worried. Unable to think of any means of escape, he put on an old, dirty robe and hid himself in a dark building.

"At that time there lived in that country an evil brahmin. This brahmin came to the king and said: 'Your Majesty, what seems to be the trouble?' The king replied: 'Haven't you heard? Lodari, my minister, has turned traitor and gone over to King Opened Eyes, and I've heard that he's leading the king's army against me. If the army does come, it will be my undoing. That's what I'm worried about!'

"The brahmin said: 'Your Majesty, assemble all your ministers and call a council.' When all had assembled, the brahmin told them: 'Listen, all of you. I have heard that King Opened Eyes' only real attachment is to his father and his son, and that he is a great giver of gifts. Now, in our country there is a blind brahmin whom we shall send to beg for one of the king's eyes. If the king gives it to him, the army will probably not come.' The king agreed to this plan and had the blind brahmin called. When he came, the king instructed him: 'Brahmin, there is something I want you to do for me.' The brahmin replied: 'Your Majesty, in view of the fact that I am totally blind, what could I possibly do for you?' The king said: 'I have heard a rumor to the effect that King Opened Eyes is mobilizing an army and that it is coming here. If that is really true, we can save ourselves only if we have eyes to see with. You, a sightless brahmin, could never escape. It has been reported to me that King Opened eyes promises to give strangers anything they ask for. You are to go to the king and ask him for one of his eyes. If he gives it to you, the army will not be likely to come. Now go and do as you have been told.' The brahmin demurred: 'But since I can see nothing, how can I go?' The king said: 'Brahmin, you are most certainly going. I shall prepare everything you need and, if you are given the king's eye, I will reward you richly,' and sent him on his way.

"At that time there appeared many ill omens in the land of King Opened Eyes: voices heard in the sky, thunderbolts falling, shooting stars, people losing their minds, the earth splitting open, birds making unpleasant sounds and falling to earth, lions, tigers, and wolves howling and coming near to people, then rolling on the ground, and many others.

"The blind brahmin made his way to the land of King Opened Eyes and, arriving at the palace gate, cried out in a loud voice: 'Oh, King, I have come from another land to beg. Oh, King, your name and fame have spread far and wide. I have heard that you have promised that whatever a beggar asks for he will receive. With great difficulty I have come from a far country, not sparing life or limb, to beg from you. Oh, King, satisfy my desire.'

"When the king heard this he went out to meet the brahmin and joyfully said: 'Ah, brahmin, are you tired and weary from your journey? Have you arrived in good health? Brahmin, do you wish a king's realm? Do you wish jewels? Do you wish horses, food, clothing? Do you wish medicine to cure your ills? Whatever you require, tell me and I shall satisfy your desire.'

"The brahmin said: 'Oh deva of devas, when one gives a gift of material things there is no great virtue. But when one makes a gift of his own body the virtue is great indeed. Oh King, my eyes are blind and I have suffered for long. I ask for the king's eyes.' When the king heard this, he rejoiced greatly and said: 'Oh brahmin, I give you my eyes.' The brahmin asked: 'When will you do this?' The king replied that he would make this gift within seven days and thereupon issued a proclamation to all the eighty-four thousand minor kings saying: 'Now, within seven days, King Opened Eyes will give his eyes to a brahmin. All of you are to come and be present for this occasion.'

"When the people of Jambudvīpa heard this they all feared greatly and, with the eighty-four thousand minor kings, they came to the palace, knelt, and with tears streaming down their faces and their palms pressed together in supplication, they said: 'Lord, all the beings in Jambudvīpa rely on you alone. They have been living in peace and tranquillity. What, Your Majesty, is the reason that you abandon all your people for the sake of a single person?' Then the ministers, queens and the people of the palace prostrated themselves and in a great voice cried: 'Oh King, now can you abandon your great realm for the sake of a single person?' The five-hundred princes wailed: 'Alas, King and Father, why are you planning your own downfall? Who will be our protector? In your great compassion, give up this evil deed of giving away your eyes.' Then the eldest prince, Good Morality, said: 'Father, let me give my eyes in your stead. If someone like me dies it is no great loss, but if the king is without eyes there will be no protector or refuge in all Jambudvīpa.

"Then the king spoke to all the minor kings, princes, ministers, and queens: 'Hear me, all of you! While circling long in the cycle of births and deaths I have experienced countless births. If one were to pile up my bones from former births, they would be higher than Mount Meru. The blood that I have shed would be greater than the four great oceans. The mothers' milk that I have drunk would be more than the four great rivers. The tears which I have shed over parting from loved ones would fill the great ocean. Beyond count are the pains I have undergone by having been born in hell. I have been burnt, boiled, chopped, cut with sharp knives, stuck with spears, and my eyes have been torn out. When born as a preta, I experienced countless sufferings, like flames covering my entire body. When born as an animal, I brought about inconceivable evil by eating others and being eaten. When born as a human, I died untimely deaths, countless numbers of times, and few indeed were the times that I lived to reach maturity. Many were the times when I killed and was killed because of passion. Wherever I took birth in any of the six forms of being in the triple world, I created evil with my body through the power of ignorance, anger, and attachment and never did I make any effort toward Enlightenment. Now, if I make a gift of this stinking body which was born from filth, it will be well. By giving these, my fleshly eyes, may I attain the eyes of an omniscient Buddha. When I attain to Enlightenment I shall give you the immaculate eye of the Dharma. Do not create obstacles to my attaining Supreme Enlightenment!' When the king had thus spoken, all remained silent and despaired.

"Then the king commanded that one of the ministers should remove his eyes, but the minister replied: 'Your Majesty, may we perish, but none of us will so much as harm one of the hairs of your head, much less touch your eyes.' Then the king said: 'Find and bring here a coal-black man whose lower eyelids have been cut off.' The ministers searched here and there and found such a person whom they brought before the king. The king commanded: 'Remove my eyes and place them in my hand.' The man then took out the king's eyes and put them in his hand. Thereupon the king, holding his eyes, made the vow: 'By virtue of giving my eyes to this brahmin, may I attain to perfect Buddhahood. If I am truly to attain Enlightenment, may my eyes grow in the sockets of that brahmin and may he have sight!' When the king placed his eyes in the eye-sockets of the brahmin, he could see and cried out: 'I see!' At that moment the heavens and earth trembled and the palaces of the gods shook and the gods, astonished, looked and saw the bodhisattva-king on earth who had given his eyes. They lauded him and sent down offerings of divine flowers from the highest firmament. Indra, king of the gods, descended and asked: 'Your Majesty, what is it that you expect in return for this difficult feat?' The king answered: 'I have not done this in order to become an Indra, a Brahmā, a Māra king, one of the Four Mahārājas, or a Cakravartin in this triple world. I have done it in order to attain Supreme Enlightenment and to lead all beings to the bliss of Nirvana.' Indra said: 'Your Majesty, when your eyes were taken out, did you feel no regret or anger?' The king replied: 'I felt no regret whatsoever.' Indra said: 'Yes, but I saw tears streaming down your face and your entire countenance was troubled. It is difficult to believe that you felt no regret.' The king said: 'If I truly felt no regret and if I truly am to attain Supreme Enlightenment, may I, by the power of the truth of these words, regain my sight.' Immediately the king's sight was restored. He could see even better than before, and gods and men rejoiced greatly and believed.

"Then the king said to the brahmin: 'By giving you my eyes you have attained sight. When I shall have attained Supreme Enlightenment I shall give you the eye of the Dharma.' Giving him many jewels, he said: 'Brahmin, accept these jewels and return to your own country.' Taking the jewels, the brahmin went back to his own land and when the king asked him if his mission had been accomplished, the brahmin reported that it had and that he was now able to see. When the king asked whether King Opened Eyes was dead and the brahmin said that he not only was not dead, but could see better than before. When he told him that the gods had come to the king and praised and lauded him, king Doer of Evil Deeds was terrified, his heart burst, and he died.

"Ānanda, I was King Opened Eyes and Devadatta was King Doer of Evil Deeds. This blind brahmin, who has obtained his sight and become an arhat, was that brahmin who asked for the king's eyes. Through the virtue of having given my eyes, I attained the eye of wisdom. Throughout all births, I have overcome all the obstacles and have now attained Supreme Enlightenment. You, also, should make efforts in good works."

When the Buddha had thus spoken, some of the great assembly became streamwinners. Some became never-returners, some became arhats, and some brought forth a mind of Supreme Enlightenment. Ānanda and the great assembly believed the Lord's word and rejoiced.

37

Aṅgulimāla, or Finger-Necklace

Thus have I heard at one time: the Enlightened One was residing in the city of Śrāvastī at the Jetavana monastery in Anāthapiṇḍika's park. At that time, King Prasenajit had a minister who belonged to the highest caste and who was wise, intelligent and exceedingly wealthy. When his wife became pregnant and the months had passed, a son was born who was incomparably handsome, comely and physically perfect. A soothsayer was called and, when he examined the child, said with beaming countenance: "This child is perfectly endowed with the signs of virtue. He will be wise and intelligent and exceed all others." When the father asked the soothsayer to give the child a name, he asked if there had been any unusual signs at the child's birth. He was told that, although the mother had always been of a gentle nature, as soon as the child had entered her womb she had become even more gentle. She rejoiced when she heard of others' virtues and goodness and became unhappy when she heard of evils or faults, and that she had great compassion on destitute beggars. The soothsayer said: "The child's name must be that of one who performs virtue. His name will be Aṅgulimāla."

When the boy grew up he was exceedingly strong—stronger than the great elephant, and could overcome a thousand people. He could jump into the sky as high as the birds fly, and could run as swiftly as a horse. He was greatly loved by his parents. At that time, there was a brahmin in that country who was learned in the sciences and who had five-hundred pupils who studied under him. The minister placed his son with this brahmin, and Aṅgulimāla was able to learn in one day what the other students learned in a year. The brahmin praised the boy, constantly kept him at his side, and honored him more than the other students. The brahmin's wife, seeing that he was more handsome and intelligent than the others, fell in love with him, but because he was always with the brahmin, had no opportunity of talking with him.

Upon a certain occasion, a master of gifts invited the brahmin and his students and prepared the necessities for a period of three months. The brahmin accepted and told his wife that he and the students would go, but that he would leave one at home to help her with the work. He asked her who it should be. The woman was delighted and said that since Aṅgulimāla was strong and intelligent, it should be he. The brahmin then told Aṅgulimāla to remain behind and help his wife.

As soon as the brahmin and his students had departed, the wife adorned herself and spoke to Aṅgulimāla with a mind of passion. She said that he was always in her thoughts, and that, now that the teacher had gone, they could enjoy themselves together. Aṅgulimāla said: "But I am a member of the Brahmin caste and it is improper for me to be together with the wife of my religious teacher. If I were to do such a thing I would no longer be a brahmin, and if I were to die I would lose the grace of my teacher." When the brahmin's wife saw that she could not fulfil her desire, she was enraged and thought of how she might take revenge. When the brahmin returned she tore off her dress, scratched her face, threw dust over herself, and lay down on the floor. When the brahmin entered the house and saw her in that condition, he asked her what the matter was. The women burst into tears and said that what had happened was too shameful to tell. When the brahmin pressed her, she sobbed and said: "While you were gone, your student Aṅ gulimāla, the one you always praised, tried to force me and I rejected him. Because I refused, he ripped my dress and put me in this condition. I don't think you need evil students of this sort." The brahmin was infuriated and said to his wife: "Aṅgulimāla is so powerful that a thousand men cannot overpower him. Besides, he is the son of a nobleman and of a high caste. I will have to employ a ruse to punish him."

Thereupon he went to Aṅgulimāla and spoke to him in a friendly manner: "Aṅgulimāla, while I was gone you did a great deal of work and took care of things well. It was a lot of trouble, wasn't it?" Aṅgulimāla said: "Teacher, because of your grace, it was no trouble at all and I was happy." The brahmin said: "Añ gulimāla, your looking after things was a great help to me. I have a secret teaching which I have never taught to anyone, and I am going to impart it to you. It will cause you a little suffering, but you will be reborn as the god Brahmā." Añgulimāla knelt and said: "Ah teacher, I beseech you to impart this teaching to me." The brahmin said: "You must fast for seven days and seven nights. Then you will cut off the heads of a thousand people, take one finger from each, make a necklace with the fingers, then hang the necklace around your neck. As soon as you die you will be reborn as the god Brahmā." Añgulimāla doubted what the brahmin said and asked: "But teacher, is destroying life the way to become a Brahmā?" The brahmin said: "If you are truly my disciple, how can you not believe what I tell you? If you doubt my word you can no longer stay here with me and will have to go somewhere else." Taking a sword, he enchanted it with a magic spell and plunged it into the earth. By the power of that incantation, a terrible rage arose in Añgulimāla. When the brahmin saw that he had become mad, he place the sword in his hand. Añgulimāla took the sword, ran out, and within a short time had killed ninety persons, made a necklace with their fingers, and hung it around his neck.

At the end of the seven days he had killed nine-hundred and ninety-nine people and lacked only one. But all the people of that country knew what was happening and had hidden themselves. Search as he might, Añgulimāla was unable to find the thousandth person. Añgulimāla's mother, learning that he had eaten nothing for seven days, tried to send food to him but everyone was terrified and refused to take it to him. The mother then prepared food and went to find him.

When he saw his mother coming Añgulimāla drew his sword and went to kill her. The mother said: "Son, why do you commit these terrible sins of killing?" The son said: "My teacher told me that if I killed a thousand people within seven days and hung their fingers around my neck, I would be reborn as the god Brahmā. I have followed his instruction and killed nine-hundred and ninety-nine and lack but one. Now I shall kill you." The mother said: "You are not going to kill me or take my fingers."

While they were talking, the Buddha, seeing from afar that the time had come to tame Aṅgulimāla, changed his appearance into that of a monk and drew near. When he saw the monk approach, Aṅgulimāla decided to kill him instead of his mother and ran toward him. As the Buddha watched him approach he continued to walk slowly on and suddenly Aṅgulimāla's great strength was drained from him and he found himself unable to run. He shouted: "Monk, sit down for a bit!" The Buddha said: "I am always sitting, but you are not because you have been led astray through terrible sins." Aṅgulimāla asked: "How is it that you are always sitting and I never am? What is the reason for this?" The Buddha said: "I am always sitting because all my senses have become calmed and I have attained the power of the samādhis. But you, because you have learned the wrong teaching from an evil teacher, rely on evil acts. Because your mind has been hypnotized, you commit countless evils day and night."

Then Aṅgulimāla came to himself, bowed, and cried out: "Holy One, have pity on me!" The Buddha then showed his true body, shining with light and endowed with the thirty-two signs and when Aṅgulimāla saw this he felt remorse, threw himself on the ground and confessed his sins to the Lord. When the Buddha had instructed him in the Dharma, Aṅgulimāla attained the eye of the Dharma, was endowed with firm faith, and said: "Lord, I wish to become a monk." When the Buddha said "Welcome", his hair and beard fell away and he was a monk. When the Buddha had taught him the Dharma, his mind was cleansed of the defilements and he became an arhat. The Lord then took him to Anāthapiṇḍika's park.

At that time, all the people of that country were paralysed with terror when they heard the name Aṅgulimāla. Pregnant women and even animals, if they so much as heard the name, were unable to give birth because of their fear. When a cow elephant could not give birth to her calf, the Buddha said to Aṅgulimāla: "Aṅgulimāla, go to the mother elephant and speak these words of truth: 'Unborn from the very beginning, I have killed no man.'" Aṅgulimāla replied: "But Lord, how can I say such a thing since I have, indeed, killed many people?" The Buddha said: "Aṅgulimāla, you have been born anew in the Dharma of the Holy Ones and you may say this." Thereupon the monk Aṅgulimāla put on the religious robe, went to the cow elephant and said to her what the Lord had told him to say.

Meanwhile King Prasenajit and his army were searching for Aṅgulimāla and had come to Anāthapiṇḍika's park. Hearing a short, ugly monk reciting the scriptures in the monastery in a sweet, melodious voice, the army stopped to listen and even the horses and elephants halted and pricked up their ears. The king was astonished and asked: "Why have the horses and elephants stopped?" His entourage said: "Because the army and the horses and the elephants are giving themselves over to the joy of listening to the Good Word." The king said: "If even animals take pleasure in hearing the Dharma, why should we humans not find joy in it too?" Then the king entered the park, dismounted from his elephant, laid aside his weapons and went before the Buddha. He bowed his head, pressed his palms together and said: "Lord, who is that monk with the sweet voice? I shall make an offering to him of four-thousand gold coins." The Buddha said: "your Majesty, first make the offering, then I shall tell you who he is, because if you meet him first, you will not give a single coin." When the king has made his gift, the monk was brought and the king, seeing how short and ugly he was, did indeed regret having given the money. He knelt before the Buddha and said: "Lord, this monk's body is too short and he is exceedingly ugly. By reason of what former good deeds has he come to have such a beautiful voice?"

The Buddha said: "Listen carefully, Your Majesty, and bear it well in mind, and I shall explain it to you. In times long past, when the Buddha Kāśyapa had come to the world to aid beings and had passed into final Nirvana, there was a king by the name of Kalibsi who gathered the Buddha's relics. As the stupa was being constructed for them, four nāga kings came to the king in the form of men and said: "Your Majesty, the stupa for the relics of the Buddha should not be constructed of earth, but of jewels." The king replied: "But I am going to build a stupa twenty-five yojanas high, in the form of a square which will extend for five yojanas in each direction. How can I build such a large stupa out of jewels? No, it will have to be made of earth." The four men said: "We are the four nāga kings. If you consent to build the stupa of jewels, we will supply the jewels." Hearing this, the king rejoiced greatly and said: "Ah, Kings of the Nāgas, if you do give the jewels, it will be excellent indeed." The nāga kings said: "Outside of the city you will find four great springs, each in one of the four directions. If you will draw water out of the spring in the east and make bricks, the bricks will turn into blue lapis-lazuli. If you make bricks with the water from the spring in the south, they will become gold. From the spring in the west—silver, and from the spring in the north-crystal." The king believed this. He then appointed four supervisors, one for each of the four directions, and began work on the stupa. Three of the supervisors worked well and completed the work, but the fourth was lazy and did not. When the king came to inspect the stupa and found the work incomplete, he said to the lazy supervisor: "You have made no effort, have not done your work, and you shall be punished." This angered the man, who retorted: "I do not have the right karma for building this endless stupa." The king said: "Very well, make haste, work hard, and finish it." The man then labored day and night and finally finished the work. When the stupa had been completed and the jewels flashed and sparkled, the artisan who had been lazy saw the beauty of it, he confessed his fault, hung a golden bell to the top of the stupa, and made the vow: "In whatever realm I may be reborn, may I have a melodious voice and may all beings rejoice when they hear it. In future times, may I also meet the Buddha Śākyamuni."

"Your Majesty, it is this monk what at that time was the artisan who built one side of the stupa. Because he did not wish to build it high and because he became angry, he was always been reborn short and ugly. But because he later completed his work with a joyful mind, hung a golden bell on the stupa, and made a vow, he has been born with a melodious voice during five-hundred lifetimes and now has met me and become an arhat."

When the king had heard the Buddha's word and was about to retire, the Buddha asked him where he intended to go. The king said: "Lord, it has come to our attention that there is a wretched criminal in our country by the name of Aṅgulimāla. He is committing vile deeds and going about murdering people. We are going to arrest him." The Buddha said: "Your Majesty, Aṅgulimāla would not now harm a fly, much less murder human beings." The king wondered to himself: "Has the Buddha tamed Aṅgulimāla?" The Buddha, reading his thoughts, said: "Yes, Your Majesty, Aṅ gulimāla is now a monk. His sins have been cleansed, he has become an arhat, and at this very moment is dwelling with me. If you desire to meet him, Your Majesty, I shall introduce you to him." The king proceeded to where Aṅgulimāla was living and just as he reached the door, Aṅgulimāla coughed loudly. Suddenly the king recalled all the people Aṅgulimāla had murdered and fell to the ground in a faint. When he regained consciousness, he got up and went to the Buddha and told what had happened.

The Buddha said: "King, listen carefully. In ancient times, in the land of Benares, there was an extremely poisonous bird that ate deadly insects. The bird's body was so poisonous that when it drew near no one could stand it. Even its shadow passing over a tree would make the tree wither. Upon a certain occasion, this bird flew into the forest and alighted atop a tree and cawed. It so happened that the king of the elephants was standing under that tree, and when it heard the bird's voice it fainted. Your Majesty, Aṅ gulimāla was that bird and you were the elephant." The king said: "Then you, Lord, have turned Aṅgulimāla who, in his madness killed so many people, toward virtue." The Buddha said "This is not the first time that I have tamed that monk. In former times, I also tamed him and turned him toward virtue." When the king asked the Buddha to tell of this, the Lord said:

"In times long past, Your Majesty, aeons ago, aeons beyond counting, there lived in this Jambudvīpa, in the land of Benares, a king by the name of Balamatar. This king and four regiments of his soldiers once went to the forest to divert themselves. Seeing an antelope, they gave chase and the king became separated from his entourage. Weary, he entered a thicket and sat down. In this thicket there lived a female lion who had not yet overcome passion. Seeing the king sitting alone, passion arose in her and approaching the king, she lifted her tail and wagged it. The king, understanding what she wanted, thought: 'If I do not satisfy this lioness, she, being a wild beast, will kill me.' In great fear, he had intercourse with her. When the lioness had gone away, the king's entourage arrived and took him back to the palace. The lioness became pregnant and when the months had passed gave birth to a boy whose body, although human, had striped feet like those of a lion. The lioness knew that this was the king's son and took him to the king, and the king, because this was his own son, raised him. Because his feet were striped, he gave him the name 'Stripefoot.'

"When the boy grew up he became a valiant hero. When his father died he ascended the throne and married two wives, one belonging to the royal caste, the other to the caste of the brahmins. Upon a certain occasion, when King Stripefoot was walking in the park with his wives, he said to them: 'Both of you chase me. With whichever one of you catches me I will spend the day in sport and dalliance,' and ran away. Both queens adorned themselves and gave chase. Along the roadside there was a stone shrine to a god. When the woman of the brahmin caste saw it she stopped and bowed to it and the other queen ran ahead of her, caught up with the king, and when the second queen approached would not let her come near. This angered the wife of the brahmin caste and she told the god of the shrine: 'Deva, while I was bowing to you the other queen won the race. If you actually are a powerful god, why do you not help me?' When nothing happened, the queen gathered many people, knocked down the shrine, and levelled it to the ground. The deva of the shrine, angry and confused, decided to harm the king. He went to the palace, but the deva-guardian of the palace refused to let him enter.

"At that time there lived a rishi on the Mountain of Many Rishis who each day flew through the sky to the palace, where King Stripefoot made offerings to him. One day when he did not come to eat, the deva of the shrine, knowing that he had not come, transformed himself into the form of the rishi and came to the palace. The guardian god immediately recognized him and refused to let him enter. The deva of the shrine then called from outside and when the king heard his voice he commanded that he be allowed to come in. He entered, sat down on the rishi's seat, and when the king had prepared food and offered it to him, refused to touch it and said: 'I do not eat food such as this, I eat meat and fish.' The king said: 'But great rishi, formerly you ate the same food as the servants; how is it that you now wish to eat flesh?' The rishi said: 'In the future I will eat only meat and fish,' and departed. In accordance with the false rishi's words, the king prepared meat and fish and the next day when the true rishi appeared, offered it to him. This angered the rishi, and the king, seeing his anger, said: 'But great rishi, have you forgotten that when you came yesterday you told me to prepare such food?' The rishi said: 'I did not come yesterday, and you are insulting me. Because of this insult may you eat nothing but human flesh for twelve years!' Then he departed.

"Sometime later the king's cook, seeing that there was no meat for the king to eat, went out in search of some but could find nothing. Along the road he spied the body of a dead child and, thinking: 'This will do,' cut of the head, hands and feet, washed the remaining flesh, seasoned it, cooked it, and served it to the king. The king thought it was the most delicious meat he had ever tasted and told the cook: 'This is the best meat you have ever prepared. What is it?' Terrified, the cook prostrated himself and said: 'Your Majesty, if you promise not to punish me, I shall tell you.' When the king had promised that there would be no punishment, the cook told him what had happened. The king said: 'Still, the meat was excellent. In the future prepare only such meat.' The cook protested: 'But king, that meat was from a child that was already dead. Where will I find such meat?' The king then commanded him to kidnap children, and in accordance with the king's order, the cook kidnapped children at night, killed them, and served them to the king the next day.

"Soon there arose in the city a hue and cry because all the children were disappearing and all the ministers came together and took counsel and set to watch at the crossroads. This guard apprehended the king's cook kidnapping a child and took him to the king, saying: 'Your Majesty, many of our children have been disappearing. This is the man who has killed them. We demand that he be punished.' The king remained silent. When this had happened three times and the king did nothing, the ministers told him: 'Your Majesty, we have apprehended a criminal and brought him before you, yet you do nothing. What is the reason for this?' The king said: 'The man is innocent. What he did was at my command.' At this the ministers were enraged and went out to consult among themselves, saying: 'This king who has eaten our children is a monster. To support a king who eats human flesh is not right. The right thing is to do away with him,' and all agreed that the king should be punished.

"Outside the city, there was a pool of clear water where the king went each day to bathe. One day while he was bathing, the ministers and soldiers surrounded the pool and arrested him. Terrified, he asked the soldiers why they were holding him and was told: 'Your subjects will not support a king who eats their children. Because of your evil deeds, you shall die.' The king said: 'It is true that I have done wrong, but I shall refrain from evil deeds in the future. Spare my life!'

The ministers replied: 'If it rains black blood and a black serpent comes and coils itself around your head, we shall spare your life.' King Stripefoot now knew that he would be killed and said: 'Ministers, that you are going to kill me is certain. Give me but a few minutes to reflect, then kill me.' While the ministers waited the king made the following prayer: 'By the power of virtues which I have performed in the past, by having reigned according to the Dharma, and by having honored rishis and holy men, may I now become a dragon and fly up into the sky.' Immediately the king became a dragon and soared up into the firmament. Looking down on the ministers, he said: 'You were going to kill me, but I have been saved through the power of virtue. In the future, may it be you who are killed and may I eat your beloved wives and children.'

"The dragon then flew away to a mountain where he lived. From time to time he came down to that country and ate humans and the people dwelt in great fear. Thereafter many other dragons came to him, became his followers and, upon a certain occasion, they all came before him and said: 'We have become your followers and now we wish you to prepare a great feast for us.' King Stripefoot agreed and told them: 'Very well, we shall capture a thousand princes, kill them, and feast upon them.' Each of the dragons then captured a prince and brought him to the eyrie, but when they counted them there were only nine-hundred and ninety-nine.

"The princes were terrified and said to each other: 'There is no hope for us. If only Sutasomaputra, he of the wise ruses, were to come, he could save us. If only Sutasomaputra were also to be captured!' Then they said to the dragon king: 'Your Majesty since you are going to have a grand feast, you should also capture Sutasomaputra. That would make the feast complete.' The dragon king agreed to this and flew away through the sky to find Sutasomaputra.

At that time Sutasomaputra had gone to the forest with an entourage of many boys and girls and soldiers. When a brahmin teacher appeared, the prince welcomed him, asked him whence he had come, and requested him to instruct them in the Dharma. As the brahmin was teaching, there sounded a terrible noise and all ran away and left the prince alone. Thereupon Stripefoot, king of the dragons, appeared, seized the prince, put him on his back, and flew away. When they had arrived at the eyrie and Sutasomaputra was miserable and weeping, Stripefoot said to him: Holy one, I have heard of your great virtue. You should fear no one. Why are you crying like a baby. Are you afraid of me?" Sutasomaputra said: 'Dragon-King, I do not fear you. I weep because I am infatuated with this body of mine. From the day I was born I have never uttered a falsehood. Just before you appeared, a brahmin came to me and, while he was instructing me in the Dharma, you came, carried me away, and my request could not be fulfilled by the brahmin. That is why I weep. King of the Dragons, kindly allow me to return so that the brahmin may satisfy my longings. Within seven days, I will come back to you and die.' Stripefoot said: 'What you say is not true. If I let you go now, you will escape and never come back. Who would believe you?' Sutasomaputra said: 'You have already said that I cannot escape from you. If I did not return, it would not be hard for you to catch me again.' When Stripefoot heard this, he agreed and let the prince go. Sutasomaputra returned to the palace and rejoiced to find the brahmin. He made great gifts to him and all rejoiced.

When the brahmin learned that the prince would return to the dragon king who would not spare his life, he spoke the following verses:

> 'At the approach of the kalpa's end
> Sky and rivers will burst into flame.

Mount Meru, the seas, and all the rest,
All, all will perish as dust.

The gods, the nāgas, the asuras,
Will be destroyed and disappear.
If sky and earth then come to naught,
How can a kingdom be eternal?

Never exhausted is the Round
Of birth, sickness, old-age and death.
When one's desires are unfulfilled,
Bitter suffering is undergone.

Evil arises from desire.
From nowhere else does it arise.
Since the three worlds consist of suffering,
How can desire's pleasure be eternal?

What arises will disappear.
Effect arises from a cause.
As it develops, there is ill.
The true and certain become false.

People, things, the triple world,
Through ignorance, appear to be.
But all is like a magic show.
How can a kingdom be eternal?

Your mind has no reality,
Although arising from non-knowing,
And dwelling with the serpents four,
It grasps at pleasurable things.

Since form is not eternal,
How can the eternal be in thought?
Since body and mind are separate,
How are you separated from the kingdom?'

'When the brahmin had thus spoken, the prince thought on the meaning of the words and rejoiced greatly. He placed his younger brother on the throne, released his ministers, and explained that he was going to return to the king of the dragons. All the ministers said to him: 'Do not even think of returning to the dragon. Build an iron castle and dwell in it and save yourself. Then Stripefoot can never get you.' The prince said to the ministers and the people: 'After having attained so good a birth would it not be wrong to speak a falsehood? It would be better to die than to lie. I made a promise to Stripefoot and he allowed me to return. Would it be right for me not to return now? You must not create obstacles.'

"The people, in great sorrow, remained silent. When it was time for the prince to go, they accompanied him, wailing. Meanwhile Stripefoot was thinking that it was time for the prince to return and went to the summit of the mountain, watched, and saw him coming in the distance. When the prince drew near the dragon rejoiced as never before and said to him: 'You do not love your own life and it is well that you have come back to me. But what have you done during these seven days that has made you so happy? Tell me this.'

"Sutasomaputra said: 'When I returned home, I heard a brahmin teacher expound the Dharma, which imparts great virtue, and my mind is now pacified. Now it is better for me to die than to live and I rejoice.' Stripefoot asked: 'What was the teaching that you heard?' The prince repeated the verses that the brahmin had taught him. He added that when one abstains from taking life the fruits are exceedingly great, but that to kill was a fearful thing and that it created terrible sins. Stripefoot believed this, rejoiced, arose, and bowed. When the prince said: 'Great King, renounce the terrible sin of taking life and do not commit these evil deeds,' Stripefoot replied: 'Yes, Sutasomaputra, it shall be as you say.' Then the prince said: 'Great King, you should release all the princes that are being held here in your mountain lair.' The dragon king did this and sent all the princes back to their own countries.

"Then Sutasomaputra, having tamed King Stripefoot, taught him the Dharma. He then returned to his own home, gathered together his army, took King Stripefoot, and put him back on his former throne where he ruled justly, no longer eating human flesh as the twelve years of the rishi's curse had now passed."

The Buddha continued: "Your Majesty, at that time it was I who was Sutasomaputra. Añgulimāla was Stripefoot. The people who now want to kill Añgulimāla were those who wanted to kill Stripefoot and, throughout all births, they have always done this. I turned them back from evil deeds and brought them to supreme happiness. Now that I have removed all the obstacles, have perfected all the virtues and attained Buddhahood, I am the tamer of men."

The king bowed to the Buddha and said: "Lord because of what former sins has there been all this killing?'

The Buddha said: "Listen well, Your Majesty, and I shall tell you the reason. Countless aeons ago, there was a great king of Benares by the name of Baladara, who had two sons who were exceedingly strong and comely. Upon a certain occasion, the younger son thought: 'When my father dies, my elder brother will ascend the throne and the kingdom will be his. Once born into the royal line it is not possible to live as a commoner. I shall therefore go to a secluded place and live the life of a hermit.' Going to his father, he told him of his desire, but the king did not approve. The prince insisted, finally the king consented, and the boy went to the mountains.

"When many years had passed, the old king died and his eldest son succeeded him. But he also died soon thereafter and, there now being no heir, the ministers took counsel. They said: 'The youngest son of the old king is now living as a hermit in the mountains. Would it not be well to bring him back and place him on the throne?' The ministers agreed that this would be the proper thing to do. They proceeded to the mountains, found him, and reported that both his father and elder brother were dead and requested him to return and reign. The hermit refused and said in great fear: 'Living in a hermitage such as this I have no suffering. Should I leave and return to ascend the throne, you worldlings, not yet having been tamed, will certainly kill me.' The ministers protested: 'But prince, the royal line has come to an end and you are the only heir. There is now no one to protect the people and we beseech you to have compassion on all beings, come back, and the king.' Reluctantly, the hermit agreed, returned, and became king.

"The hermit had not yet cut off attachment and, after he had become king, a passion for women grew in him. Without his being aware of it, it mastered him. Upon a certain occasion he made the proclamation: 'All maidens in my kingdom must come and have intercourse with me before they are married. After they have done this they may return to their homes.' Thereupon all the beautiful girls in the kingdom went to make love to the king.

"Upon a certain occasion when many people had gathered together, a woman made water in front of everyone. All burst out laughing. The woman turned on them and said: 'What is wrong with a woman making water among other women? When I do this among those who are nothing but women, what is the cause of mirth?' When the people asked her: 'Woman, what kind of talk is this?' she replied: 'In this country only the king is a man. All the rest of you are women. If you were really men, you would do the thing yourself.' The people were ashamed and agreed that the king had departed from correct behavior, and they took counsel as to how to destroy him. Thereupon they agreed to seize him when he went to the park to bathe.

"Then soldiers hid themselves in the park, and when the king came to bathe and had entered the water, the soldiers sprang out and seized him. The king was terrified and asked what was wrong. The ministers told him: 'Your Majesty, you do not follow the Dharma and have become intoxicated with passion. You have insulted all your people and committed improper acts. We are going to do away with you and find a king who is wise and intelligent.' In great fear, the king said to the ministers: 'It is indeed true that I have followed the wrong course and committed disgraceful acts, but I shall do it no more. Spare me!' The ministers said: 'If black snow falls on this country and a poisonous serpent coils itself about your neck, we shall spare you.'. The king, certain that he would be killed, grew angry and said: 'Long ago, when I renounced the things of the world and retired to the mountains, you forced me to return and ascend the throne. I hereby make the vow that if you now murder me, I, in future lifetimes, will again meet and murder you.' Your Majesty, it was because of this vow that all this killing has come about. Aṅgulimāla was that king, and the many people killed by him are those people who took counsel against him. He has killed them in every lifetime."

The king then knelt, pressed his palms together, and said: "Lord, since Aṅgulimāla has killed so many people, will there now be retribution?"

The Buddha said: "Your Majesty, when evil is done, retribution is inevitable. Even now as Aṅgulimāla sits in his dwelling, the fires of hell blaze forth from the hairs of his body." Then, in order to show the retribution for evil deeds, the Buddha said to a monk: "Monk, take the key and open Aṅgulimāla's door a crack and look in." When the monk did this, the key melted. The monk was terrified, rushed back to the Buddha, and told what had happened. Then the Buddha told the great assembly: "This is the fruit of doing evil," and the king and the assembly believed.

Then the Noble Ānanda said to the Buddha: "Lord, I beg you to explain to the great assembly what former good deeds the monk Aṅgulimāla did in order to be borne as powerful as a mighty elephant, as quick as a bird, and has now met the Lord and been liberated from the Round."

The Buddha said: "Listen well, Ānanda. Long ago, at the time of the Buddha Kāśyapa, there was a monk who managed the affairs of the Sangha. One day when he went to weed the fields, a rain storm came up and, when he attempted to get something to protect the crop, he was unable to wade through the water and find anything. He then made a vow: 'In future times may my strength be as great as that of a thousand men and may I move as rapidly as a bird flying. In future times may I meet the Buddha Śākyamuni when he comes to this world and may I be liberated from the Round.' Ānanda, that monk who made the vow was no other than the monk Aṅgulimāla. By having made that vow, by becoming a monk and observing the Precepts, and by doing the work of the Sangha, he has always been reborn comely and with great strength. Now, having met me, he has been delivered from the Cycle of births and deaths."

Then Ānanda, the monks, the king, and the great assembly, having heard the Buddha's exposition of the law of retribution, exerted themselves and thought on the Four Truths. Some became streamwinners, some became once-returners, some became never-returners, and some became arhats. Some brought forth a mind of Supreme Enlightenment. Some entered the realm of no-return. Some directed their body, speech, and mind toward virtue and having faith in the Buddha's word, rejoiced greatly.

38

The Beggar-Woman Named 'Relying on Joy'

◌⋰⋰◌

Thus have I heard at one time: the Enlightenment One was residing in the city of Śrāvastī at the Jetavana monastery in Anāthapiṇḍika's park. At that time, there was in that country a beggar-woman named Relying on Joy who begged her food. When this woman saw the king, the princes, and many other people making offerings to the Buddha and the Sangha, she experienced great remorse and despair and thought: What former evil have I committed that I have been born in this low caste, poverty-stricken, and now if I were to meet the Buddha, have no seed to sow in the field of virtue?"

Upon a certain occasion when she had begged all day and received nothing, she took her only coin and went to an oil merchant. The oil merchant told her: "Woman, you cannot buy oil with a single coin. What are you going to do with oil?" The beggar-woman said: "Householder, I have nothing and am obliged to beg. It was my intention to buy oil with this coin and offer it to the Buddha." The oil merchant pitied the woman and gave her a great deal of oil. The woman then took the oil to the monastery and lighting a lamp, placed it before the Buddha with the following vow: "I have nothing to offer but this tiny lamp, but by virtue of this one offering, may I in future times be endowed with the lamp of wisdom. May I purify the defilements and darkness of all beings and enlighten them."

That night the oil in all the other lamps became exhausted and burned out, but the lamp lighted by the beggar woman Relying On Joy, remained burning until dawn. That day it was Maudgalyāyana's turn to go on the alms-round and when dawn broke he went to take up the lamps. Seeing that a single lamp was still burning, was filled with oil, and still had a new wick, he thought: "There is no reason for this lamp to be burning in the daytime." He tried to blow it out but could not. He then tried to snuff it with his fingers but could not, and finally he tried to extinguish it with his robe, but the lamp kept burning.

The Buddha watched this and said: "Maudgalyāyāna, do you wish to put out the lamp? You cannot. You Śravakas could not even move this lamp, much less extinguish it. If you were to pour all the water from all the oceans over this lamp it still would not go out. The water in all the lakes and rivers of the world would not put it out because this lamp was offered with a mind of firm faith and is of great benefit." When the Buddha had said this the beggar-woman appeared before him, bowed her head at his feet, and the Buddha made the following prophecy: "Woman, in future times, when two entire kalpas shall have passed, you will become a Perfect Buddha called Light of the Lamp." The woman rejoiced and said: "Deva of devas, I beg you to allow me to join the Order." When the Lord had given his permission, the Noble Ānanda and the Noble Maudgalyāyāna, having heard the prophecy and watched the beggar-woman join the Order, knelt, pressed their palms together, and said: "Lord, by reason of what former evil deeds was this woman born a beggar? By reason of what good deeds has she been able to meet the Buddha and attain Liberation?"

The Buddha said: "Ānanda, in times long past when the Buddha Kāśyapa had come to this world, the wife of a prince invited him and the Sangha and, at the same time, a beggar-woman invited him. The Buddha and the Sangha first went to the house of the beggar-woman and she became a once-returner. The prince's wife, being wealthy of a high caste and, was angered at this and she said to the Buddha: 'Lord, why did you not come first to my house instead of going to the beggar-woman?' Nevertheless, she invited the Buddha and the Sangha the next day and made offerings. However, because a thought of anger had arisen in her toward the Buddha and the Sangha, she was reborn in a low caste and as a poverty-stricken beggar throughout five-hundred lifetimes. Because she did invite the Buddha and the Sangha and made offerings, she has now met me, joined the order, and received this prophecy."

When the king, the princes, and the people heard that the beggar-woman, by offering a single lamp, had attained Enlightenment and received a prophecy, they honored the Buddha and made offerings of the four necessities. The boys and girls of the upper and lower castes of that country prepared fragrant, sweet-smelling lamps, brought them to the Jetavana Grove, and offered them to the Buddha. Filling the grove, they appeared like the night sky when it is filled with stars.

Then Ānanda, marveling greatly, praising and lauding the Buddha's virtues which are beyond conception, said to the Buddha: "Lord, I beg you to explain by reason of what former deeds this grove is filled with lamps."

The Buddha said: "Ānanda, in times long past there lived in this Jambudvīpa a king by the name of Vasika who had eighty four thousand minor kings subject to him. To his first wife a son was born whose body was the color of gold and was adorned with the thirty-two signs of a great man and the eighty lesser marks. On the crown of his head there was a transparent jewel. He was so handsome that one never tired of looking at him. When a soothsayer was called to name the child, he was astonished and a exclaimed: 'Excellent! Excellent! This prince has no equal among the gods or humans of this universe. If he marries, he will become a universal monarch. If he becomes a monk, he will become a Perfectly Enlightened One.'

The king was delighted and asked the soothsayer to name the boy. When the soothsayer asked if there had been any unusual signs at the child's birth, and the king said that he had been born with a jewel in his forehead, the boy was named 'Jewel Tuft.' When the boy grew up, he became a monk and through exertion became a Perfect Buddha and aided countless beings.

"Upon a certain occasion the king invited the Buddha and the Sangha and honored them for three months. Among the assembly of monks, there was one called Ārya Upāsika who had made the vow: 'May I become a master of gifts who offers lamps for three months to the Buddha and the Sangha.' Each day he would go into the city and beg oil from the oil merchants and the householders.

"The king had a daughter called Princes Capable who, seeing the monk going to the trouble of visiting the city each day, sent a man to ask the reason for this. The monk told him: 'I have made a vow to offer a lamp to the Buddha and the Sangha for three months. I go to the city to beg oil and the necessities.' When the man reported this to the princess, she was delighted and told the monk: 'Do not go to the city any longer to beg for oil and the necessities. I shall give them to you.' The monk replied: 'So be it,' and departed.

"Thereafter the princess sent lamp oil and the necessities to the monk each day and the monk Ārya Upāsika offered his lamps. When he had brought forth a great mind of compassion, the Buddha made the prophecy: 'Oh monk, in future times, when countless kalpas have passed, you will become the Buddha Dīpaṅkara endowed with the thirty-two signs.' When the princess heard of this prophecy, she thought: 'But it was I who prepared the oil and the necessities. How is it that he obtained the prophecy and I did not?' Going to the Buddha, she asked him concerning this. The Buddha then gave her the following prophecy: 'Princess Capable, in future times, when ninety-one kalpas have passed, you will become the Buddha Śākyamuni and be endowed with the thirty-two signs.' The princess rejoiced, bowed her head at the Buddha's feet, and begged to join the Order. The Buddha approved, ordained her, and she then refrained from taking life, and exerted herself in the Dharma."

The Buddha then said: "Ānanda, at that time the Buddha Dīpaṅkara was that monk Ārya Upāsika. I was the princess. Because in times past I offered a lamp, throughout countless aeons I obtained virtue in the worlds of gods and men. I was born more comely than all others, and now I have become a Perfect Buddha to whom many lamps are offered."

When the Buddha had thus spoken the Noble Ānanda and the entire assembly rejoiced in the Lord's word and believed.

39

Bhāṣicara

❦

Thus have I heard at one time: the Enlightened One was residing on the Vulture's Peak in Rājagṛha. At that time, there was a householder in that country by the name of Saraci who was extremely wealthy and married to a woman of his own caste. When the wife became pregnant and the months had passed, a son was born who was handsome beyond compare. Rejoicing, the parents called a soothsayer, who examined the child and said that he was endowed with the signs of virtue and would be a comfort to his people. Delighted, the parents asked for a name for the child. When the soothsayer asked if anything unusual had occurred before the child was born, he was told that the mother had formerly been unable to talk sensibly, but that when the child had entered her womb she had become more intelligent and could speak clearly, the soothsayer name the child Bhāṣicara.

The child grew up to be intelligent, honest and endowed with great strength. Upon a certain occasion when he went out with the king's son to play, he saw a beautiful girl in the house of a low-caste family, fell in love with her, and wished to marry her. When he returned home and asked his parents to obtain the girl for him, they told him: "Our family belongs to a high caste. How is it possible for us to take a girl from one of the lower castes?" The boy became miserable and said: "What difference does caste make? Obtain the girl for me. If you do not, I shall die." Unhappily, the parents sent a messenger to ask for the girl.

The girl's parents said: "You people are of a high caste; we belong to a low caste and are not your equals. What is the reason that you ask for our daughter?" The messenger told them: "The boy has fallen in love with your daughter. He will not listen to his parents, and they have sent to ask for the girl." The girl's parents said: "If the boy will learn to perform different kinds of acrobatics, dances and tricks, that will please the king; we will give our daughter to him." Thereupon the boy learned different kinds of acrobatics, singing, feats of strength, and so forth.

Upon a certain occasion, the king had brought together many musicians and athletes, people who could climb trees, jump, walk tightropes, etc. The householder's son went there and performed on a tightrope, running back and forth until he was exhausted. The king had been delayed and had not seen him perform and when he arrived told the boy to do something. The boy climbed back up to the tightrope and began to walk across, but when he came to the middle he lost his balance from exhaustion and was about to fall. He cried out for help and immediately Maudgalyāyana appeared, kept him from falling, and said: "Son, would you rather fall to the ground and take a wife?" The boy said: "If you save my life, I shall not take a wife." The monk then took the boy through the sky and lightly placed him on the ground. Rejoicing, the boy followed the monk to the Buddha and, bowing his head at the Lord's feet, honored him. At that moment, the Buddha was explaining that by the giving of gifts, one is born among the highest gods. He also taught that the pleasures arising from desire are defilements, and that when one becomes a monk one experiences great joy. When the boy heard this his mind became freed, he believed with firm faith, and became a streamwinner. Pressing his palms together in reverence, he begged the Buddha to ordain him as a monk and to teach him the Supreme Dharma. When the Lord said: "Welcome," the boy's hair and beard fell away and he was a monk. Exerting himself in the Dharma, his outflows were stopped and he became an arhat.

Thereupon Ānanda said to the Buddha: "I beseech the Lord to explain by means of planting what roots of virtue this boy, who was attached to that girl, was saved by Maudgalyāyana and has now met the Enlightened One and become an arhat."

The Buddha said: "Ānanda, in aeons long past there was a householder in Benares whose wife had born him a son who was handsome beyond compare. One day, the boy found an egg along the seashore and brought it to the householder. The householder accepted it and soon a beautiful bird came out of the egg. He gave the bird to his son, who cared for it. As the boy and the bird both grew, they became inseparable. Whenever the boy wanted to go anywhere, he would get on the bird's back and they would fly through the air.

"Upon a certain occasion, hearing that there was to be a festival in another kingdom, the boy mounted his bird and went to watch it. Arriving in the other kingdom, he put the bird in a tree. Walking on to see the festival, he met the king's daughter, became inflamed with passion, and had intercourse with her. The king immediately heard of this, had the boy arrested, and gave orders for his execution. As he was about to be executed, the boy said: 'Your Majesty, do not kill me with a sword, if I must die, let me commit suicide. I will climb up into a tree and throw myself down.' The king agreed to this, and the boy climbed up into a tree, which was the same tree in which his bird had been placed. The boy mounted the bird, they flew away, and thus the boy's life was saved.

"Ānanda, Bhāsicara was that son of a householder. The girl was the king's daughter, and Maudgalyāyāna was the bird. Because, in a former lifetime, the boy had cared for the bird, it saved the boy's life. Now, when passion arose, Maudgalyāyāna again saved him. The reason why this monk's mind has been calmed and he has attained the fruit that is without the outflows is that in times long past when a Pratyekabuddha had accepted alms from a certain householder in Benares, and the householder requested him to teach the Dharma, the Pratyekabuddha said that he was unable to do this, but threw his alms-bowls up into the sky and it flew away. Thereupon the householder thought: 'Although this holy man has great spiritual powers, he cannot teach the Dharma.' He then made the wish: 'In future times, I meet the Holy Ones and may this Pratyekabuddha teach me the Supreme Dharma.' It is for this reason that his mind has been liberated and he has become an arhat."

When the Buddha had thus spoken, the entire assembly rejoiced. Some became streamwinners, some became once-returners. Some became never-returners, and some became arhats. Some brought forth the roots of virtue of a Pratyekabuddha, and some brought forth a mind of Supreme Enlightenment. All, when they had heard the Buddha's word, rejoiced greatly.

40

The Householder Daṇḍadhara

❧

Thus have I heard at one time: the Enlightened One was residing in the city of Śrāvastī at the Jetavana monastery in Anāthapiṇḍika's park. At that time there was in that country a poverty-stricken brahmin who had an exceedingly ugly wife, no sons, and seven daughters. Although the brahmin had married off the daughters, they and the sons-in-law had come back to live with him. His wife was ill-natured and cursed and mistreated him, the daughters, and their husbands. One day at harvest time, the brahmin borrowed an ox from a neighbor and went out to harvest his grain. He forgot to tie it and it wandered away. The brahmin then thought to himself: "What former sins could I have committed that, when I go to my own house, my wife mistreats me, my daughters and sons-in-law don't even ask me to sit down. Now I've lost my neighbor's ox and won't be able to find it even if I try. What should I do?"

As he sat thus in his misery, he saw the Buddha sitting beside a tree, all his faculties at peace. Leaning on his staff, the brahmin thought: "This monk Gautama is peaceful and happy. He has no wife to abuse him, no ill-mannered daughters or sons-in-law to mistreat him, no ox to borrow when harvest time comes—no troubles at all." The Buddha knew the brahmin's thoughts and said to him: "Elder Sir, that which you have thought is true. I am without troubles. Since I have no wife, how can she mistreat me? I have no seven daughters to come home with their husbands and make my life miserable. I have no worries about a stray ox at harvest time. Would you, too, not like to become a monk?"

The brahmin replied: "Lord, my house is the same as a tomb to me, and my wife and daughters are like enemies. Do allow me, I beg you, to become a monk." When the Buddha had said:

"Welcome," the brahmin's hair and beard fell away and he was a monk. When the Lord had taught him the Dharma, all his defilements were removed and he became an arhat.

Thereupon Ānanda said to the Buddha: "Well it is, Lord, that you have created benefits for all beings without exception. But this brahmin,—what former good deeds did he do that he has now been purified of all the defilements, and has attained to virtue, like a piece of linen that has been bleached?"

The Buddha said: "Ānanda, this is not the only time that I have aided this brahmin and caused him to be happy. In times long past, I delivered him from all his troubles and caused him to rejoice." When Ānanda requested the Lord to explain this, the Buddha said: "Ānanda, listen well and remember, and I shall tell you." When Ānanda replied that he would listen carefully, the Buddha said:

"Ānanda, in times long past, aeons ago, aeons past counting, past reckoning, there lived a king by the name of Beautiful who reigned in accordance with the Dharma. At that time, there was a destitute brahmin in his kingdom by the name of Daṇḍadhara, who had borrowed an ox from a neighbor to do his work. When he returned the ox, the householder was eating, so the brahmin put it in the shed. The ox got out and wandered away. When the householder had finished his meal he went out to the shed to look at the ox, but it was gone. He immediately went to the brahmin's house and asked where the ox was. The brahmin said that he had put it in the shed. The householder said: 'You have lost my ox. I want it returned.' The brahmin replied: 'I did bring your ox back. Where do you want me to look for it?' The brahmin and the householder argued and disputed, and finally decided to take the case to the king. They started on their way and soon they came to a runaway horse. The horse's master shouted to Daṇḍadhara to drive the horse back, and the brahmin threw a stone at it, which crippled its leg. The man said: 'Why did you throw a rock and cripple my horse? You must repay me.' The brahmin said: 'Why should I repay you for the horse? Let us take this to the king and let him decide.'

"The brahmin then became frightened, ran away from the others, and climbed up onto a three-storied shed, inside which a man was weaving. He fell down into the shed, struck the man, and killed him. The weaver's wife caught hold of the brahmin and screamed: 'You have murdered my husband. Now you must bring him back to life!' The brahmin said: 'Who can bring a dead man back to life? Let us go to the king and let him decide this.' As they went along, they came to a large river which crossed the road and saw a woodsman coming down it. He was carrying an axe in his mouth. The brahmin asked the man how deep the water was, and when the woodsman answered that it was very deep, he dropped his axe and lost it in the water. He then told the brahmin that he must pay for the axe. Daṇḍadhara said: 'You, not I, dropped the axe. Why should I repay you? Come, let us ask the king and abide by his decision.'

"As they went on, the brahmin became tired and thirsty. He entered a wineseller's shop and asked for a drink. One of the wineseller's sons was drunk and lying on the floor. The brahmin sat down on him by mistake, the man gasped, swallowed his robe, and choked to death. His mother seized the brahmin and shouted: 'You have murdered my son: You must restore him to life!' The brahmin replied: 'I did not kill your son and I cannot restore the dead to life.' Let us go to the king and let him decide this. 'They went on and came to a śakoṭaka tree upon which a raven was perched. When the raven saw Daṇḍadhara leading all the people, it asked him where he was going. The brahmin said: 'Raven, I have no choice. I have done nothing wrong, but these people are forcing me to go.' The raven said: 'Very well, but I asked you where you were going.' When the brahmin said that they were going to see the king, the raven said: 'In that case, tell the king the following: a raven perches on a śakoṭaka tree. When he perches there, his voice is exquisite, but when he goes to other trees, it becomes unpleasant. Why is this?'

"Going on, they came to serpent who said: 'Brahmin, find out from the king why it is that, when I leave my hole, I am happy, but when I enter it again, I am unhappy.' Soon they met a young woman who said: 'Brahmin, find out from the king why it is that when I am at my parents' house, I want to go to the home of my in-laws, but when I am there, I want to go back to my parents' home.'

"At last they came to the king. When they had bowed to him and sat down, he asked: 'What is the reason for your coming?' All made their complaints. Then the king said to Daṇḍadhara: 'Did you return the ox to the householder's hands or did you simply let it loose?' The brahmin said: 'When I returned the ox the householder was eating, and I didn't tell him that I'd brought it back.' The king commanded: 'Cut off Daṇḍadhara's tongue because he didn't tell, and tear out the householder's eyes because he saw the ox and didn't take care of it.' The householder said: 'This Daṇḍadhara practically stole my ox and I am to have my eyes put out? Surely this is an injustice!'

"The next man said: 'Your Majesty, Daṇḍadhara crippled my mare.' When the brahmin was asked how he did this, he said: 'Your Majesty, as I was going along the road, this man shouted to me to drive back his horse which was running away. I threw a stone at it and cripple it.' The king said: 'In that case, cut out the tongue of the man who shouted to catch the horse and cut off Daṇḍadhara's hands for throwing the stone.' The owner of the horse said: 'My horse has been crippled and now I am to have my tongue cut out? Surely this is an injustice!'

"Then the woodsman spoke: 'Your Majesty, while I was hurrying through the water with my axe in my mouth, this brahmin asked me about the depth of the water. When I answered him, I dropped my axe and lost it.' The king said: 'Normally, people carry things in their hands. When they carry them with their teeth this is the sort of thing that happens. The woodman's front teeth are to be knocked out, and the brahmin, because he asked about the depth of the water, is to have his tongue torn out.' The woodsman said: 'This Daṇḍadhara has made me lose my axe and now I have to lose my teeth? Surely, this is an injustice!'

"Then the woman who sold wine spoke: 'Your Majesty, Daṇḍadhara killed my son.' The brahmin said: 'I was tired and thirsty and asked for wine. When I sat down, I didn't see the boy, who was lying unconscious on the floor. I sat down on him and he died.' The king said: 'It is the fault of the woman for covering up the boy's head. Daṇḍadhara is at fault for killing the boy. The two of you must marry and bring forth another son.' The woman said: 'Daṇḍadhara killed my own son and now I am forced to marry him? Surely this is an injustice!'

"Then the weaver's wife made her complaint. The brahmin said: 'I had many enemies and was afraid and climbed up onto the roof of a shed, lost my footing, and fell down onto the weaver, who died.' The king said: 'In that case you are to become the husband of this woman also.' The woman said: 'How can that be called justice? First this brahmin kills my son, then I have to marry him!'

"There were also there two women who disputed the possession of a young boy. When they petitioned the king for a decision, he wisely said to them: 'Each of you take one of the boy's arms and pull. Whoever is strongest will have the boy.' One woman had no thought for the child's life and pulled hard. The other woman, fearing for the child, was gentle. Seeing this, the king said to the first woman: 'This is not your child. It belongs to the woman who was gentle with him.' The mother then took the child and departed. There were also two women who had a dispute over a bolt of cloth, and the king settled that dispute in the same manner.

"Then Daṇḍadhara spoke to the king: 'Your Majesty, as these people were bringing me here, a snake requested me to ask you why it felt at ease when it left its hole but ill at ease when it came back to it.' The king said: 'Tell the snake that when it comes out of its hole it is hungry and not angry, but when it has eaten and been bothered by the birds, it is ill at ease and exhausted, therefore unhappy when it returns to its hole. Tell it to avoid becoming angry when it digests its food and its coming in and going out will be the same.'

"Daṇḍadhara then told the king what the young woman had asked and the king said: 'Tell the young woman that when she is at her in-laws, she thinks of her parents, and that is why she wants to go home. When she is at her parents' house, she is thinking of her husband and wants to go to him. If she will stay in one place and give up the other, she will be happy and at ease.'

"Then Daṇḍadhara told the king about the raven. The king said: 'Tell the raven that there is gold beneath the śakoṭaka tree and that is why its voice is sweet. Because there is no gold under the other trees, its voice is not good when it perches there.'

"Then the king said: 'Ah, Daṇḍadhara, you have become entangled in many misfortunes, but I pardon you. You are to take the gold that is under the tree, free yourself from poverty, and live out your life doing good deeds.' In accordance with the king's word, Daṇḍadhara took the gold, became wealthy, and lived in happiness throughout his lifetime.

"Ānanda, at that time I was that king. The brahmin about whom you have just asked was Daṇḍadhara. Just as I formerly saved him from misery, gave him wealth and caused him to rejoice, now that I have attained to Perfect Enlightenment, I have again made him glad by giving him the precious treasure of the Dharma."

When the Buddha had thus spoken, the Noble Ānanda and the great assembly believed and rejoiced.

41

Excellent Honey

❦

Thus have I heard at one time: the Enlightened One was residing in the city of Śrāvastī at the Jetavana monastery in Anāthapiṇḍika's park. At that time there lived in that country a wealthy brahmin by the name of Sincir. Being childless, he went to six different gurus and asked whether he would have a son or not. The gurus told him: "It is not your lot in life to have a son." The brahmin returned home, put on an old, soiled robe, and sat in misery, thinking: "I am not fated to have a son. If I were to die, the king would confiscate my property."

The brahmin's wife had made the acquaintance of a Buddhist nun who one day came to the brahmin's house to visit. Seeing the brahmin so miserable, she asked his wife what the trouble was. The wife said: "We have no child and six gurus have told my husband that this is our fate. This is the reason my husband feels so wretched." The nun said: "Those gurus know nothing at all. How could they possibly know such a thing? But the Buddha, the Tathāgata, is now in the world. Since he knows the past and future perfectly, why don't you go ask him whether or not you will have a son?"

When the nun had gone, the brahmin's wife told him what she had said. Putting on a new robe, he went to the Buddha and asked: "Lord, is it my lot in life to have a son or not?" The Buddha said: "Brahmin, you will indeed have a son, and that son will be endowed with virtue. When he grows up, he will wish to become a monk." Hearing this, the brahmin rejoiced greatly and said: "If I have a son, why should he not become a monk? My sorrow is now ended." He then invited the Buddha and the Sangha to his home. The Lord consented by silence.

The next day at mealtime, the Buddha and the Sangha came and sat down on the seats prepared for them. The brahmin and his

wife honored them and served them with various kinds of food.
When they had eaten, they returned, and along the way came to a
meadow with a sparkling, clear spring. The Buddha and the monks
sat down beside it and were dipping up water with their begging
bowls, when a monkey appeared and asked Ānanda for his. Thinking that the monkey would break it, Ānanda, refused to give it to
him. The Buddha said: "Ānanda, give your bowl to the monkey."
When Ānanda gave it to him, the monkey climbed up into a tree
and returned it filled with honey, which he offered to the Buddha.
When the Buddha said: "Take the dirt out of it," the monkey removed the dead insects that were in the honey and again gave it to
the Lord. The Buddha said: "Mix water with the honey and I shall
drink it." The monkey then mixed water with the honey and again
gave it to the Buddha, who tasted it and shared it with the monks
until all were satisfied. The monkey jumped up and down in delight, ran to a ravine, jumped down, and died. When it had died, it
entered the womb of the childless brahmin's wife and when the
months were fulfilled, a handsome and comely boy was born. At
the moment the child appeared in the world, all the vessels in the
brahmin's house were filled with honey. The brahmin and his wife
rejoiced and brought a soothsayer to examine the child. When the
soothsayer asked what signs had appeared when the baby was born
and was told that all the vessels in the house had filled with honey,
the child was given the name of 'Excellent Honey.'

When the boy grew up, he requested permission to become a
monk. The parents refused and the boy told them: "I cannot live in
this place which has no peace. I shall surely die." The brahmin and
his wife discussed this. They recalled that formerly the Buddha
had prophesied that when a son was born to them, he would become a monk. They agreed that if they did not give him permission he would certainly die, and gave their permission. In faith and
gladness the boy went to the Buddha, bowed his head at his feet,
and begged to become a monk. When the Buddha said: "Welcome,
son," his hair and beard fell away and he was a monk. When the
Lord had taught him the Four Truths, his mind became perfectly
liberated, his outflows were stopped, and he became pure. As the
monks went hither and thither for the aid of beings, they noticed

that whenever the new monk became tired and thirsty, he would throw his begging bowl up into the air and it would return to him filled with honey. Thereupon Ānanda said to the Buddha: "Lord, because of what former virtues has this monk Excellent Honey joined the Sangha and quickly become an arhat? What is the reason for this?"

The Buddha said: "Ānanda, do you remember the brahmin named Sincir whom we visited long ago?" Ānanda said: "Yes, Lord, I remember him." The Buddha said: "Ānanda, do you recall how after we had eaten alms-food and were returning, we rested beside a spring in a meadow and a monkey took your alms-bowl? The monkey filled it with honey and offered it to me, and I ate of the honey and shared it with the monks. Then the monkey danced with joy and departed to a ravine and died." Ānanda said: "Yes, Lord, I remember." The Buddha said: "Ānanda, that monkey who offered the honey is this monk, Excellent Honey. Because, when he met the Buddha, he rejoiced and offered honey with a mind of joy, he was reborn as the son of a householder, handsome and comely, has now become a monk, and has stopped the outflows."

Then Ānanda knelt with his right knee on the ground, pressed his palms together, and said: "Lord, what former evil deeds did he to be born as a monkey?" The Buddha said: "Ānanda, in times long past, when the Buddha Kāśyapa had come to this world, a young, newly-ordained monk saw another monk jump across a ditch and said to him: 'Monk, you jump just like a monkey!' The other monk said: 'You do not know me.' The young monk said: 'What do you mean, I don't know you! You are one of the Buddha Kāśyapa's monks.' The second monk replied: 'Do not ridicule me. I am not a monk in name only. I have attained to the four fruits of the monk.' The young monk became terrified and his hair stood on end. He knelt, pressed his palms together, and said: 'Oh monk, I confess the sin of having ridiculed you. Forgive me, I beseech you.' Because he confessed this sin, he was not reborn in hell. But because he ridiculed the monk, he was reborn five-hundred times as a monkey. By keeping an earlier vow, he has now met me, become a monk, and all his sufferings have been brought to an end. Ānanda, this monk Excellent Honey was that young monk who ridiculed the other."

When the Buddha had thus spoken, Ānanda said: "By disregarding acts of body, speech, and mind, the monk failed to guard his speech and had to suffer for this reason." The Buddha said: "Yes, Ānanda, it is just as you say." Then, when the Lord had taught the Four Truths and explained that when the acts of body, speech, and mind are purified the impurities of the mind are cleansed, some became streamwinners, some once-returners, some became never-returners, some arhats, and some brought forth a mind of Supreme Enlightenment. All believed and rejoiced.

42

The Householder Taśila

༄༅

Thus have I heard at one time: the Enlightened One was residing in Rājagṛha in the Bamboo Grove of the Kalandaka Bird. At that time, in the land of Kośala, there lived a high-caste householder by the name of Dalan Masicar who was extremely wealthy. Because he was without child, he made offerings at all the shrines of the devas and nāgas. Because he did this with a mind of firm faith, his wife became pregnant. When the months were fulfilled she gave birth to a son whose beauty was rare in this world. When a soothsayer examined the boy's signs, he named him Taśila. By the time the boy had arrived at maturity, all the householder's buildings were filled with the seven jewels, all his treasure houses were loaded to overflowing, and he lacked nothing.

Upon a certain occasion Vaidurya, son of King Prasenajit, became ill. The physician who attended him said that the boy would recover only if he were treated with white sandalwood. The king thereupon proclaimed throughout his realm: "If anyone has white sandalwood, let him bring it and I shall repay him with a thousand measures of gold." But white sandalwood was not to be found. One day a man came to the king and said: "Your Majesty, in the land of Kośala there is a householder who has a great deal of white sandalwood." The king and his entourage immediately proceeded to Kośala to seek the sandalwood. When they arrived at the householder's residence, the gatekeeper ran to announce to his master that King Prasenajit was at the gates. The householder was overjoyed, went out to welcome the king, and invited him into his house.

As the king passed through the gate he noticed that it was made of silver. As he entered, he saw a woman rare in the world for beauty, who was sitting on a silver seat spinning silver thread, with sixteen young women helping her. The king asked the householder if this was his wife. The householder said: "No, that is the wife of the gatekeeper's servant." When they passed through the next gate the king saw that it was made of lapis-lazuli, and inside he noticed an even more beautiful woman who had eighteen women serving her. The next gate was made of gold. Inside there sat a woman even more beautiful, who had many more serving women, and who wove cloth of gold. When the king asked if this was the householder's wife, he was told that it was not.

When they reached the dwelling of the householder, the king saw that the floor was made of transparent lapis-lazuli. From the roof were suspended forms of animals, sea-monsters, fish, and other sea-animals which, when they swayed in the breeze, were reflected in the floor. Seeing this, the king thought it was water and asked why the palace was flooded. When told that it was transparent lapis-lazuli, the king could not believe it and felt the floor with his hand.

When they entered the palace, which was constructed of the seven jewels, the king was asked to sit down on a seat of lapis-lazuli. He then saw the householder's wife from whose eyes tears were flowing. When the king asked her if his coming had made her unhappy, the woman said: "Your Majesty, I rejoice at your coming. The reason I weep is that your robes smell slightly of smoke." The king asked: "Do you people here not make fires?" When the woman said that they did not, the king asked how they cooked their food. The woman said "When we think of food, delicious food appears by itself." The king then asked what they did for light in the dark of night. The woman said: "We sit by the light of cintamani jewel. Even when we close the doors, the light of the cintamani shines through the cracks and makes everything as light as day."

The householder then bowed and asked the king the purpose of his visit. The king said: "My son, Vaidurya, has been taken ill with fever and we require white sandalwood to heal him. I have come to ask you for some." The householder was delighted and took the king to his treasury, where he showed him his many jewels and treasures. Pointing out countless piles of white sandalwood, said: "Your Majesty, take as much as pleases you." The king asked for two measures and the householder gave them to him.

When the king was ready to return, he said: "Householder, you should go visit the Buddha." The householder said: "Buddha? What does that mean?" The king replied: "Have you not heard? The son of King Śuddhodana of Kapilavastu grew weary of birth, sickness, old-age and death, and became a monk. By dint of exertion, he has become a Perfectly Enlightened One endowed with the thirty-two signs of a great man and the eighty minor marks. He is perfect in Transcendental Wisdom and is the supreme among gods and men. That is why he is called the Buddha—the Awakened." When the householder heard this, he rejoiced greatly and a mind of faith arose in him. He asked where the Buddha was residing and the king told him that the Lord was dwelling in the bamboo grove at Rājagṛha.

When the king had departed, the householder went to see the Buddha. Seeing that the Lord was more magnificent than any king, he had faith and rejoiced, bowed his head, and asked after the Buddha's welfare. When the Enlightened One had taught him the dharma, the householder became a streamwinner. He knelt, pressed his palms together, and asked to become a monk. When the Buddha said: "Welcome," his hair and beard fell away and he was a monk. When the Lord had instructed him in the Four Truths, he became an arhat.

Then Ānanda and the great assembly said to the Buddha: "Lord, what former deeds this monk Taśila do that he has now obtained human birth, has been endowed with the wealth of the gods, and leaving home, has become a monk and attained liberation?"

The Buddha said: "Ānanda, listen carefully, and I shall tell you. In times long past, ninety-one aeons ago, when the Buddha Vipaśyin had come to the world for the weal of beings and had passed into Nirvana, five-hundred monks made the solemn vow: 'We shall seek a deserted place and apply ourselves to the Path of Liberation.' Going to a forest, they took up residence near a pebbly spring, and in one accord said to one of the monks: 'Monk, we are in this hermitage far from a city and it is difficult for us to go out and beg alms. You should go alone, collect alms, and share them with us.' The monk agreed, went to the city each day, taught the Dharma to many householders, collected alms, and shared them with the monks. Among the monks there were four who exerted themselves in meditation and attained the fruit within nineteen days. All the monks then said to the monk who had collected alms: 'Monk, because of you we have been comfortable and attained the samādhi we desired. What you desire now, ask us and we shall fulfill your wish.' With great joy the monk made the following wish: 'In future times may I be born as a man, may I be exceedingly wealthy, and my every wish be fulfilled. May I meet you, holy ones, hear from you more than a hundred-thousand dharmas, may my mind be totally purified, and may I attain Liberation.' Ānanda, because that monk honored the other monks with alms, he was born in a high caste and among gods and men for ninety-one kalpas, never in a poor family. Now he has met me and attained Liberation."

Then Ānanda and the other monks, having heard the word of the Buddha, made great exertions and attained from the first to the fourth fruits. Some brought forth a mind of great compassion. Some reached the realm of no-return. All the great assembly rejoiced and believed.

43

Elephant Helper

❦

Thus have I heard at one time: the Enlightened One was residing in the city of Śrāvastī at the Jetavana monastery in Anāthapiṇḍika's park. At that time, there was born a son to a householder who lived in the country of Magadha. The child was handsome and comely and, when it was born, a golden baby elephant appeared in the householder's treasury. When a soothsayer was called to name the child and asked what signs had appeared at its birth and was told about the golden elephant, it named the boy 'Elephant Helper.'

As the boy grew, the elephant also grew and accompanied him everywhere. One day while Elephant Helper was playing with five other sons of householders who were his friends, the boys began to boast of the wonderful things they had at home. One boy said that in his house the chairs and beds were made of the seven precious jewels. Another said that in his home the pavilions were made of jewels. Still another said that in his house the treasure chests were filled with gold and precious things. Then Elephant Helper told about his elephant: "When I was born a baby elephant of gold appeared. As I grow, it also grows, and even knows my thoughts. I ride it and it goes wherever I want to go. Even its excrement and urine are pure gold. that's the kind of elephant I have." Among the other boys was Prince Ajātaśatru, who, when he heard about the elephant, thought: "When I get to become king I'll take that golden elephant away from that boy."

When Prince Ajātaśatru grew up and had become king, he called Elephant Helper to him and commanded him to give him the golden elephant. When Elephant Helper returned home and reported this to his parents, they told him: "Dear son, Ajātaśatru is cruel, greedy, and quick to anger. He murdered his own father and it would be child's play for him to kill others. He will take your elephant away from you in any case, so it would probably be better if you gave it to him." The son replied: "No one can ever take my elephant away from me," but the father and son mounted the elephant and rode to the king's palace. They mounted, bowed to the king, and wished him well. The king was delighted, asked them to sit down, and offered them food and drink. When they had talked of this and that, the king said he would be glad to accept the elephant and that they might return home.

The boy and his father left the elephant with the king and started out on foot, but they had not gone far before the elephant escaped and appeared before them. The thought then came to Elephant Helper: "King Ajātaśatru does not follow the Dharma, and if he becomes angry because of the elephant, he will cause me trouble. The Buddha is now residing in the world for the joy and benefit of beings. I shall go to him and become a monk." Obtaining the consent of his parents, he mounted the elephant, rode to Anāthapiṇḍika's park, bowed his head at the Buddha's feet, pressed his palms together, and said:

"Lord, I beg to become a monk." When the Buddha said: "Welcome," his hair and beard fell away and he was a monk. When the Lord had taught him the Four Truths, he became an arhat.

Whenever the monk Elephant Helper sat together with the other monks, the elephant would come and sit down beside him. All the people from the city of Śrāvastī would come and gape at the elephant. This made it impossible for the monks to meditate and they complained to the Buddha about it. The Lord called Elephant Helper and told him: "Monk, when all the people come to look at your elephant that is the end of meditation. You must get rid of it quickly." Elephant Helper said: "Lord, when I formerly tried to get rid of it, I could not. What should I do?" The Buddha said: "Monk, say to the elephant three times: 'Elephant, I have left home and become a monk. In the future I shall not need you'—then the elephant will disappear." The monk did this and the elephant disappeared into the earth. When the other monks saw this, they were astonished and said to the Buddha: "Lord, what former good deeds did this monk do that his fruits have so matured? What is the reason for this?"

The Buddha said: "In the field of virtue of the Three Treasures, whatever seeds, no matter how small, a man sows, great indeed will be the harvest. In times long past, the Buddha Kāśyapa had come to the world for the benefit of beings and man's span of life was twenty-thousand years. When the Buddha had aided beings and passed on into Nirvana, many stupas were constructed to house his relics. Within one stupa, there was the image of an elephant, which had been the vehicle of the bodhisattva when he descended from the Tuśita heaven to enter his mothers' womb. This elephant image was slightly broken. When a certain man came to the stupa to honor it and saw the broken image, he thought: 'This is the vehicle of the bodhisattva. I shall repair it.' He then repaired it with clay and painted it. Anointing it, he made the wish: 'In future lives may I always be born in a high caste and possess limitless wealth.' When the man died he was reborn among the highest gods and after that was always reborn as a human-being of high caste and with great wealth. Ānanda, this monk, Elephant Helper, was the man who repaired the elephant image. He has always been reborn possessing great wealth and among gods and men. Because he had faith in the Three Treasures, he has now met me, become a monk, all his impurities of mind have been cleansed, and he has become an arhat."

When the Noble Ānanda and the great assembly heard the Buddha's word they believed and rejoiced greatly.

44

The Brahmin Gives Patches

❧❧❧

Thus have I heard at one time: The Enlightened One was residing in the city of Śrāvastī at the Jetavana monastery in
Anāthapiṇḍika's park. Upon a certain occasion when Ānanda was
accompanying the Lord on the alms-round, he noticed that the
Buddha's robe had become ragged and thought: "This will be for
the taming of beings." When they had completed the almsround
and returned, a brahmin came, bowed to the Buddha, saw his brilliant light and the marks, but also noted that his robe had grown
ragged. Wishing to repair it, he returned home, cut off a piece
from a bolt of white cloth, brought it to the Buddha and requested
him to mend his robe. Out of compassion the Buddha accepted the
cloth and the brahmin was made happy. The Buddha then uttered
the prophecy: "Brahmin, in future times, when a hundred kalpas
shall have passed, you will become the Buddha called 'He With
The Spiritual Powers' and will be endowed with the marks of a
great man." When the Lord had made this prophecy, the brahmin
departed in great joy.

Hearing of this, the high-caste merchants and householders of
that country thought: "Why did the Buddha return such great good
for such a tiny gift?" Immediately they made robes from white
cloth and offered them to the Buddha. Ānanda then said to the
Enlightened One: "Lord, what former good deeds did you do that
everyone now makes gifts of robes to you?"

The Buddha said: "Ānanda, listen well and remember, and I
shall tell you. In times long past, countless aeons ago, when the
Buddha Vipaśyin had come to this world, he resided together with
ninety-thousand followers. Upon a certain occasion, the great minister of the king invited the Buddha and the Sangha to stay with
him for three months so that he might honor them. When the

Buddha had accepted the invitation, the minister returned to his home and began to make preparations. The king then invited the Buddha, but the Lord told him that his great minister had already asked him, and that in accordance with the Dharma he was bound to accept the first invitation. The king returned to the palace, called the great minister, and said: "In this land I, not you, am the head. When I recently invited the Buddha I learned that you had invited him first. You are to invite him later." The minister said: "Sire, my life and limbs are at your command and it will be done as you wish. That the Tathāgata may live long and that Your Majesty's realm may always enjoy peace and prosperity, I shall invite the Buddha later." The king was pleased and said: "Let us invite him together. I shall serve him one day and you will serve him the next." In accordance with the king's word, the two invited the Buddha and the Lord accepted. The minister made a gift of three robes to the Tathāgata and ninety-thousand robes to the monks. Ānanda, I was that minister who gave those robes. Throughout all my many births I have never wearied of creating virtue and the fruit of this has never diminished."

When Ānanda and the great assembly heard this, they exerted themselves in works of virtue. All rejoiced and believed.

45

The First Compassion of the Buddha

◌⳯⳾◌

Thus have I heard at one time: the Enlightened One was residing in the city of Śrāvastī at the Jetavana monastery in
Anāthapiṇḍika's park. Upon a certain occasion when the monks
had come out to summer retreat, they came to the Buddha, bowed,
and enquired after his welfare. When the Buddha, with a mind of
great compassion, asked lovingly and with concern about the
monks' health, Ānanda said: "Lord, how long have you had such
love and compassion for the monks?" The Buddha said: "Ānanda,
if you desire to know this, listen. In times long past, aeons ago, a
sinful man had been born in hell. The guardians of hell, the Yāmas,
harnessed the man to a cart and drove him back and forth without
respite, beating him with an iron hammer. The cart was too heavy
for the man to pull, and they would beat him to death with their
hammers, then bring him back to life. A friend of the man saw him
trying to drag the heavy cart and love and compassion arose in his
mind. He spoke to the Yāmas and told them: "I alone shall liberate
this man whom you have harnessed to the cart." The Yāmas were
infuriated and beat the man to death and he was then reborn among
the gods of the Thirty-Three. Ānanda, I was that man who brought
forth a mind of love and compassion while residing in hell, and I
have been endowed with a mind of compassion for living beings
ever since that time."

When Ānanda and the great assembly heard the Buddha's word,
they rejoiced and believed.

46

King Forehead-Born

❧❧❧

Thus have I heard at one time: the Enlightened One was residing in the city of Śrāvastī at the Jetavana monastery in Anāthapiṇḍika's park, together with a great assembly of twelve-hundred and fifty monks. At one time, the monks were becoming attached to name and fame, were doing unnecessary things and were dissatisfied and accumulating things. The Buddha then taught them concerning those sins which are connected with gain and the attachment to gain.

The Buddha said: "When one is attached to gain and the body disintegrates, one falls into one of the evil births and undergo countless agonies. Therefore you should abandon all non-virtuous deeds. Because of the power of desire, I, also, erred and underwent terrible suffering in former times."

Thereupon Ānanda knelt, pressed his palms together, and said to the Buddha: "Lord, how was it that formerly, because of attachment to the pleasures of desire, you erred?"

The Buddha said: "In times long past, aeons beyond recall, beyond conceiving, beyond reckoning, there lives in this Jambudvīpa a king by the name of Gusali who had subject to him eighty-four thousand minor kings, and had twenty-thousand queens and palaces and ten-thousand ministers. One day, there appeared on his forehead a bump like an egg which was transparent, caused him no pain, and continued to grow until it burst. A boy, golden in color, with black hair, perfect in body, handsome and comely, sprang out. When a soothsayer was called to examine the child, he said: 'This boy bears the signs of amazing virtue and will unquestionably become a cakravartin and be master of the four continents. He then named the boy 'Forehead-Born.' When the child came of age, his father crowned him king over one of his lands. Later the old king became ill and, although all the ministers and minor kings assembled and brought various remedies, they could do nothing and the king died.

"The minor kings all took counsel, proceeded to King Forehead-Born, and said: 'The old king has died and we beg you to take his place.' King Forehead-Born replied: 'If I have the virtue and grace to become the Great King, may the Four Mahārājas, Indra, and the other gods manifest themselves to me and grant me that right.' When he had said this, the Four Mahārājas descended with a vase of perfumed water and anointed him. Indra, Lord of the gods, descended and placed a jeweled diadem on his head and lauded his virtues.

"The minor kings then said: 'Great King, we now request you to proceed to the Middle Country.' King Forehead-Born replied: 'If I have the grace to become king of that country, may the country come to me. I shall not go there.' Immediately the palaces and parks and sparkling waters of the Middle Country appeared before him, as did the golden wheel, the precious elephant, the precious horse, the precious queen, the precious minister, the precious householder, and so forth. He became a universal monarch, master of the four continents. He then ruled in accordance with the Dharma.

"One day when the king saw many people plowing and sowing, he asked his ministers what they were doing. When it was explained to him that the people gained their livelihood in this manner, he said: 'If I have the grace to be king, may a hundred different kinds of delicious food appear and satisfy those who labor and may they never be hungry or thirsty.' Immediately food and drink appeared miraculously.

"Upon another occasion when he was on an outing, the king saw weavers spinning and weaving and asked what they were doing. The ministers explained to him that although food now appeared by itself in abundance, the people had to make clothing to cover their bodies. The king said: 'If I have the grace to be king, may clothing appear to cover all and may the poor and needy have sufficient raiment.' Immediately many kinds of silken garments appeared growing on the trees and all the people had abundance.

"Another time when he was on an outing, the king saw many people playing symbals and other musical instruments. When he asked what they were doing, he was told that the people were all happy because they had an inexhaustible supply of food and clothing and were expressing their joy with music. The king said: 'If I have the grace to be king, may cymbals and musical instruments appear and make music by themselves.' Immediately cymbals and various musical instruments appeared hanging from the branches of the trees and made music by themselves.

"Then, by virtue of the king, a rain of the seven jewels came down and filled the entire land. The king asked his ministers why this had taken place and they told him: 'Your Majesty, this is due to your own virtue and the virtues of many living beings.' The king said: 'If it is by virtue of many living beings, may the jewels fill the entire country, but if by my virtue alone, may they fill my palace only.' Immediately the rain of jewels ceased to fall on the country and descended into the king's palace for seven days and seven nights.

"For eighty-four thousand years King Forehead-Born lived in this Jambudvīpa enjoying the pleasures of the senses. One day a yakśa appeared at the gate of his palace and cried out in a loud voice: 'Great king, in the east there is a continent called Pūrvavideha which is joyful beyond compare. Why does Your Majesty not go there to enjoy himself?' As soon as the king desired to go there, a golden wheel appeared in the sky. The king and his ministers and the seven precious possessions soared away through the firmament to the great continent in the east. All the minor kings who had not yet paid homage to him now proceeded to Pūrvavideha where they honored him and delighted in the pleasures of the senses for eighty-thousand years.

"Once again the yakśa appeared and said: 'Great King, in the west there is a continent called Aparagodānīya which is exceedingly delightful. Why do you not go there?' The king agreed, went there and remained for four-thousand years enjoying himself. Then the yakśa advised him to go to the northern continent of Uttarakuru where the exceedingly wealthy live. The king and his entourage went there and for eighteen-thousand years enjoyed the pleasures of the five senses. Again the yakśa appeared and told the king that in the heaven of the Four Mahārājas he would find delights beyond compare. The king took his four armies and his ministers and departed through the sky. When the Four Mahārājas saw them approach, they were terrified, called out their armies and went forth, but were unable to overcome the king and returned home. The king and his entourage then remained in the realm of the Mahārājas for ten-thousand years, living in delight.

"The king then wished to go to the realm of the gods of the Thirty-Three and flew through the air in that direction. At that time there were five-hundred rishis residing on the slopes of Mount Meru. As the king's elephants and horses flew over them, their droppings fell on the rishis, who wondered what they could be. One of the rishis, more learned than the rest, said: 'The King Forehead-Born is proceeding to the realm of the gods of the Thirty-Three. These are the droppings from his horses and elephants.' This so enraged the rishis that they pronounced magic formulas to paralyse the king and his entourage in the sky, and they were unable to move. The king then proclaimed: 'If I have the virtue to be king, may the rishis appear before me and pay homage.' The rishis immediately came before him and paid homage. The king proceeded to the realm of the gods of the Thirty-Three and beheld their alabaster palaces gleaming with light. The gods felt great fear and closed and bolted the twelve-hundred great gates, but when the king blew his trumpet and twanged his bowstring, the gates opened automatically. Indra came out to greet the king, took him to his palace, and he and the king sat down together on a great throne. Both appeared so alike that unless one looked carefully it was impossible to distinguish one from the other. For six long world-periods, the king and his entourage remained in the realm of the gods enjoying the pleasures of the five senses. At that time Indra, lord of the gods, was the incarnation of the bodhisattva Kāśyapa.

"Upon a certain occasion, the king of the asuras came with his army to make war with Indra. Indra's army was defeated and his soldiers took refuge in the palace. Then King Forehead-Born blew his trumpet and twanged his bowstring, and the army of the asuras retreated in fear. The thought then came to the king: 'Since I am invincible and no one can compare with me, why should I share the rule with Indra? I shall kill him and rule alone.' The moment he thought this evil thought he fell from the realm of the gods and found himself in his own palace. As his hour of death approached, he was asked: 'If people come and ask why King Forehead-Born fell, what should we tell them?' The king replied: 'If that question is asked, tell them that it was because of the power of desire. And you may also say that King Forehead-Born, although master of the four continents, and although he lived for many thousands of years, brought down showers of jewels, and even went to the realm of the gods, fell from his high estate because he did not abandon the pleasures arising from desires.'

"Oh monks, gain and fame are great evils. They must be rejected and one must exert oneself in the direction of Enlightenment."

Then Ānanda asked: "Lord, what former good deeds did that king do to reap such fruit?"

The Buddha said: "Ānanda, in times long past, countless aeons ago, when the Buddha Pūrna had come to the world to aid beings, a certain brahmin decided to marry. In accordance with the customs of the world he was obliged to offer a handful of grain at the marriage ceremony. As he went out to plant the grain for this, he met the Buddha. The man's mind became clear and he attained to faith and he sprinkled the grain he was going to plant over the Buddha. Four grains fell into the Buddha's begging bowl, but one of them struck the Buddha's uṣṇīṣa on his head. Because of the four grains that dropped into the begging bowl, he became master of the four continents. Because one grain touched the Buddha's uṣṇīṣa, great merit arose, he was born from the king's forehead and became endowed with the riches of gods and men."

When the assembly had heard the Buddha's word, some attained the first fruits, some the second, some the third. Some attained the fruits of an arhat. All had faith in the Lord's word and rejoiced.

47

The Ten Sons of Sumana

Thus have I heard at one time: the Enlightened One was resid
ing in the city of Śrāvastī at the Jetavana monastery in
Anāthapiṇḍika's park. The householder Anāthapiṇḍika had a beautiful daughter by the name of Sumana whom because he loved her
more than all his other daughters, he took her wherever he went.
Upon a certain occasion, the householder went to pay homage to
the Buddha and took his daughter with him. When she saw the
Enlightened One, a mind of great joy arose in her and she wished
to perfume his dwelling with incense. As she stood before the Lord
holding a mango in her hand, the Lord asked her for it. When the
girl had placed it in his hand he tasted it, the Buddha wrote down
the names of the best kind of incense and gave the names to the
girl. When the father and daughter returned home, they went to the
market and bought the various kinds of incense that would please
the Buddha. Later, the girl returned to the Jetavana grove and sat
there each day grinding incense.

One day the king of Tikcaśrī sent one of his sons to Rājagṛha.
Arriving in the city, he went to the Jetavana grove where he saw
the girl grinding incense, fell in love with her, and decided to marry
her. He went to King Prasenajit to ask permission, and when the
king asked who her father was, the boy told him it was
Anāthapiṇḍika. The king said: "There is no need to ask me, you
will have to ask the girl's father." The boy said: "Your Majesty, if
you will not reprimand me, I'll kidnap the girl." When the king
said: "Do so," the boy assembled his entourage, mounted an elephant and rode to the Jetavana grove. He seized the girl, put her
on his elephant, and rode away. Anāthapiṇḍika gave chase but was
unable to overtake them, and the prince took the girl to his own
country and married her.

Soon the princess became pregnant, and when the months had passed gave birth to ten eggs. When the eggs broke open, a handsome boy came out of each. When the boys grew up they became mighty hunters. One day their mother said to them: "Sons, you must not kill wild animals." The boys replied that there was nothing they enjoyed doing more and that if their mother prevented them, it meant that she didn't love them. Their mother told them: "It is not because I don't love you, but rather because I do love you that I wish to prevent you from committing evil deeds. Because of the sin of taking life, one falls into hell and is reborn there as a deer, a sheep, a rabbit or some other kind of animal. One suffers death over and over again at the hands of the lords of death and goes through unbearable suffering. If you wish to be spared this terrible suffering, you should refrain from your evil deeds. This is the reason I am trying to prevent you from killing." The boys said: "What you have just told us; did you hear it, or did you simply make it up?" The mother said: "I heard it from the Buddha." The boys asked: "Buddha? What does that mean?" The mother said: "Sons, have you not heard? The handsome son of King Śuddhodana, although a world-monarch, found no pleasure in sickness, old-age, or death. He became a monk, meditated on the Way, and attained the longed-for Supreme Enlightenment. His body of sixteen cubits is endowed with the signs, he is perfect in the three knowledges and the six spiritual powers. He clearly knows the three times: the past, the present, and the future, like a myrobalan fruit in the palm of his hand."

When the boys heard this, they rejoiced and asked where the Buddha was. When their mother told them that he was residing in the city of Śrāvastī, they asked her permission to go there. Then went to their grandfather in Śrāvastī, who took them to the Buddha in the Jetavana grove. When the boys saw the Buddha's signs, which appeared to them even more splendid than they had imagined, they rejoiced greatly. When the Lord had taught them the Dharma they attained the eye of the Dharma and asked to become monks. The Buddha asked: "Sons, do you have your parents' permission?" When they said that they did not, the Buddha said: "Without obtaining the permission of one's parents it is not possible to become a monk." Anāthapiṇḍika said: "Lord, I am these boys' grandfather and I beg you to ordain them." When the Buddha said: "They may become monks," their hair and beards fell away and they were monks. By exerting themselves in the Way, they soon became arhats. The ten monks were never separated from each other, lived and went everywhere together, and the people of that country, seeing them, had faith.

Then Ānanda said to the Buddha: "Lord, these ten monks—what former good deeds did they do to be born in a high caste, to meet you, and to attain the state of an arhat? What is the reason for this?"

The Buddha said: "Ānanda, in former times, ninety-one aeons ago, the Buddha Viśvabhuj had come to this world, aided beings, and passed into Nirvana. Countless stupas were built to enshrine his many relics. It so happened that upon a certain occasion when an old woman was repairing one of the stupas that had fallen into disrepair, ten travellers passed that way. Seeing the old woman, they asked what she was doing. She told them: 'This stupa is a place of offerings. If I repair it, I shall attain the fruit of great virtue.' Hearing this, the men rejoiced greatly and helped her repair the stupa. When the work was completed, they made a vow to be reborn as the old woman's sons. From that time throughout ninety-one kalpas, they have always been reborn as gods or men and have always been happy and blessed in the three ways. What are the three? First, they were handsome and comely; second, they have been honored by all; and third, they have always had long lives and never fallen into the hells. Now they have met me, all their impurities have been cleansed, and they have attained the bliss of arhats. Ānanda, this girl Sumana was that old woman and these ten arhats were those ten men."

When the Buddha had thus spoken, all believed and rejoiced.

48

Upagupta

☙❦❧

Thus have I heard at one time: The Enlightened One was residing in the city of Śrāvastī at the Jetavana monastery in Anāthapiṇḍika's park. At that time, there lived in that country a brahmin-mendicant by the name of Upagupta who was of keen intellect and could foretell the past and future. This brahmin went to the Buddha and asked to be ordained into the Sangha saying: "If in wisdom and vigor I will be equal to Śāriputra, ordain me. If not, I shall return home." When the Buddha said that this would not be, the brahmin did not become a monk and went back to his home. Sometime later, the Buddha said to the monks: "A hundred years after I have passed into Nirvana, if this brahmin becomes a monk, he will be endowed with wisdom, possess the six spiritual powers and benefit countless beings."

At the time of his final Nirvana, the Buddha said to Ānanda: "Ānanda, I have entrusted all the sutras to you. Memorize them and disseminate them widely." In accordance with the Buddha's word, Ānanda memorized the sutras. At his Nirvana, he said to the disciple Yaśa: "Yaśa, I shall pass into Nirvana and I entrust the sutras to you to be preserved and propagated. In Benares, there is a householder by the name of Gupta who has a son called Upagupta. Ask him to become a monk, ordain him, and at the time of your Nirvana, entrust all the sutras to him."

When Ānanda had attained Nirvana, Yaśa memorized the Supreme Dharma and greatly benefitted beings in the world. Upon a certain occasion, he went to Benares and became acquainted with a householder, became friends with him, and visited him often. When a son was born to the householder, he was named Upagupta and before he had come of age, Yaśa requested that he become a monk. The householder said: "This, my beloved son, must carry on my line. He cannot become a monk. But if another son is born, I shall give him to you." Later, another son was born and was called Nandagupta. When Yaśa asked for this boy, the householder said: "My elder son does the outside work and the younger son does the work inside. He cannot become a monk. But if another son is born, you may have him."

Yaśa was endowed with the three knowledges of an arhat and knew the abilities of beings. He searched to see whether it was the fate of either of these boys to become a monk, and seeing that it was not, ceased to ask for them.

Later, another son, handsome and comely, was born to the householder and Yaśa again went to ask for him. The householder said: "The child is too young now, but when he grows up I shall give him to you." When the boy grew up he was endowed with great intellect. His parents gave him money and established him in business. Upon a certain occasion Yaśa visited him, taught him the Dharma, and establishing in him one-pointedness of mind, told him: "When evil thoughts arise, place a black pebble on the table. When good thoughts arise, place a white one there. Then see which outnumbers the other." The man, whose name was Upagupta, did this, and at first there were many more of the black pebbles. Then the black and white pebbles gradually became equal, and finally, through effort and meditation, only white pebbles remained. Bringing forth thoughts of virtue, he attained to the first fruits.

At that time there lived in that city a certain courtesan. One day, she gave money to one of her servant girls and sent her to Upagupta to buy flowers. Upagupta gave her more than she paid for. When the girl took the flowers to her mistress, the woman was astonished and said: "This is twice as many flowers as you used to obtain for the same price. How did you get so many?" The girl said: "The man who sold me the flowers was very unusual and gave me more without the usual haggling. He is very handsome and you would enjoy meeting him." The courtesan then sent an invitation to Upagupta to visit her home, but he refused. Again and again she invited him, but he never went.

At one time, the courtesan had intimacies with a certain prince and, coveting his jewels, she murdered him and hid his body in her house. The king had all the houses searched. When the prince's body was found in her house, the king had her hands, feet, nose and ears cut off and impaled her on a stake. While she was still alive, Upagupta came to her. The courtesan said: "Formerly, when I was beautiful, you never came to see me. Why do you bother now?" Upagupta said: "It was because I was attached to your form that I never came. Now I have come out of compassion.

"He then taught her the Dharma concerning the four kinds of impermanence:

> "This body is foul and filthy.
> Its true nature is suffering.
> It is empty and without a self.
> Even if one searches,
> One finds no refuge there.
> The body is insentient.
> Only the stupid are attached to it."

He then told her: "Woman, you should not be attached to this filthy body." When the courtesan heard this, she attained to the totally pure eye of the Dharma and Upagupta attained the fruit of no-return.

Yaśa again requested the householder to allow his son to become a monk. When permission was granted, the son was taken to the temple and given the monastic vow. When he was twenty years old he took the vow of the arhat. Through practicing introspection and the four works, he became a conqueror of enemies, perfect in the three knowledges and the six spiritual powers. Attaining unequalled ability of speech, he attracted many people and taught them the Dharma.

Upon a certain occasion, the evil Māra showered a rain of gold coins among the assembly. All seized the coins and forgot to listen to the Dharma. The next day when Upagupta was again teaching the Dharma, Māra sent down a shower of flowers and again all the assembly fell into disorder. The next day, when many people had again assembled and the Dharma was being taught, Māra took on the form of a blue elephant with six tusks from which flowed sparkling water. In each stream of water, there was a beautiful girl made of crystal singing. And as the elephant walked softly back and forth, the assembly was amazed, stopped listening to the Teaching, and watched the elephant. The next day Māra transformed himself into a beautiful woman, came to the assembly, and when the people saw her they forgot to listen to the Dharma. Thereupon Yaśa transformed the woman into a skeleton of dry, white bones. When the assembly saw this, they were horrified, listened to the Dharma with concentrated minds, and there were many who attained to the first fruits.

At that time there was a dog who came daily to the monks, would sit with its ears cocked and listen as the Dharma was being taught. When it died, it was reborn as a deva and sat on the same seat as the evil Māra. Māra thought: "How has this virtuous one come here and become my equal? I must find out about this!" Investigating, he found out that the deva had formerly been a dog and thought: "The monks are humiliating me." Seeing from afar the monk Upagupta sitting in samādhi, he placed a jeweled diadem on his head. When Upagupta arose from samādhi and felt the diadem on his head, he investigated and learned that it was Māra who had placed it there. By means of his spiritual powers, he called Māra and placed a hat made of the dog's dead body on Māra's head, saying: "This is in return for the diadem which you presented to me." Māra returned to his own realm, saw that his hat was the body of a dead dog and tried to remove it, but could not. Going to Indra, he said: "Indra, take this terrible thing off my head." Indra said: "Impossible. Only the person who put it on can take it off. I cannot." Then Māra went to all the kings of the gods and the asuras and asked them to remove the vile thing from his head but, like Indra, they could do nothing. Discouraged, Māra went back to Upagupta and said: "The Buddha was endowed with great virtue and great compassion, but you Śrāvakas are terrible people. It is true, I did surround the bodhisattva with eighty-thousand hosts of Māra, attempted to obstruct him from attaining Enlightenment and tried to confuse him, but he never held it against me and was always compassionate. Why do you do something so terrible to me in return for a little joke I wanted to play?"

Upagupta said: "Māra, you are right. How can anyone compare with the Buddha? How can a pile of sand compare with Mount Meru? How can a cow-hoof puddle compare with the great ocean? How can the timid fox compare with the lion, the king of beasts? I was born too late to see the Lord, but I have heard that with your magic powers you can create the Buddha's body. Do this now and let me see it." Māra said: "I will create the imitation of the Buddha's body, but you must not worship it." Then Māra magically transformed himself into the body of the Buddha, golden in color, sixteen cubits in height, endowed with the thirty-two signs and eighty lesser marks, shining with light, more brilliant than the sun and moon. When Upagupta saw this he said: "I worship the Buddha, not you, Māra." Māra said: "Oh, venerable Upagupta, out of compassion remove this dead dog from my head." Upagupta said: "King Māra, if you will bring forth a mind of compassion and love and become a refuge to beings, the dead dog will become a jewelled necklace. But if you bring forth a mind of sin and evil, it will remain a dead dog." In great terror, Māra gave up his evil deeds and brought forth a mind of virtue. Then the monk Upagupta tamed innumerable beings. They attained the fruit and all praised him, saying: "Because of your great virtue, beings without number and beyond conceiving have been tamed." Upagupta said: "Even when I was born as an animal, I tamed beings and attained the fruits of the Holy Ones. Why is it so unusual that I tame beings now?" The great assembly said: "Tell us, we beg you, how you formerly tamed beings."

Upagupta said: "In times long past, there were once five hundred Pratyekabuddhas who resided on a mountain called Many Rishis in the land of Benares. Each day, a monkey would come and honor them and make offerings. Later the Pratyekabuddhas moved to another place and five-hundred mendicants took their place. Some of these mendicants worshipped the sun and moon, others were fire worshippers. One day when the sun worshippers were holding their legs in their hands and the fire worshippers had kindled their fire, the monkey pushed the sun worshippers over and extinguished the fireworshippers' fire. Then he sat upright in meditation. As he had formerly imitated them, this surprised the mendicants and they said: "The monkey no longer follows our way of practice. Let us follow his way." Gradually they began to imitate the monkey, to think like the monkey did, and their minds were tamed and they understood the true nature of things and became Pratyekabuddhas. At that time, I was that monkey." The assembly then asked: "Holy One, why did you take birth as a monkey?"

Upagupta said: "Long ago, ninety-one aeons ago, when the Buddha Vipaśyin had come to the world, the monks resided on the mountain called Many Rishis. One day when a monk who had obtained the fruit was running up the mountain, another monk said: "Hey, monk, you run like a monkey!" For that reason he was reborn as a monkey five-hundred times."

Thereupon the four classes of hearers abandoned coarse talk and employed proper speech. Some of them became stream-winners, some became never-returners, some became arhats. Some brought forth the roots of virtue of a Pratyekabuddha, while some brought forth a mind of Enlightenment and became fearless. All the assembly believed and rejoiced.

49

The Five-Hundred Swans Who Were Born As Gods

∞⊱✦⊰∞

Thus have I heard at one time: upon a certain occasion when the Enlightened One was residing in Benares, teaching gods, men and the four classes of hearers in a meadow in a forest, five-hundred swans flew overhead. Hearing the Buddha's word, they were delighted, turned about in the sky, and flew down near the Buddha. But they were caught in a net which a hunter had set and the hunter killed them. They were immediately reborn in the realms of the gods as sixteen-year old boys who were exceedingly beautiful and shone with a brilliant light like the Golden Mountain. They asked themselves by the power of what virtue they had taken this birth. Searching former births, came to know that it was because they had listened to the Dharma taught by the Buddha. Taking celestial flowers and incense, they proceeded to Benares in Jambudvīpa and, with their divine light, illuminated the place where the Buddha was residing. They bowed at his feet, pressed their palms together, and said: "Lord, by hearing the teaching of the Buddha we have been reborn as gods. We now beseech the Lord to teach us the Supreme Dharma."

When the Buddha had taught them the Four Truths and they had understood their meaning, they became streamwinners and would never again be reborn in the three evil births. Returning to the realm of the gods, they stopped all the outflows.

Then Ānanda said to the Buddha: "Lord who were those gods who came here tonight, illuminated the entire area with the light of the gods and bowed at the Lord's feet?"

The Buddha said: "Ānanda, listen carefully, bear it well in mind and I shall tell you. One day while I was teaching the Dharma to gods, men, and the four classes of hearers, five hundred swans heard the voice of the Dharma. When they alighted near me a hunter caught and killed them. Because, when the swans heard the voice of the Dharma, a mind of firm faith arose in them, they were reborn in the realm of the gods of the Thirty-Three. Learning that they had been reborn there because they had heard the Dharma from me, they came to pay me homage."

When Ānanda heard the Buddha's word, he rejoiced greatly and believed. He said: "It is marvelous, Lord, marvelous, that the Enlightened One has come into this world. The rain of the Dharma nourishes us. If beings born as animals are able to attain the highest fruits by hearing the Dharma, what can be said of men? The virtue of those who believe with firm faith is beyond measure."

The Buddha said: "Excellent, Ānanda, excellent! It is as you say. The Buddha has come to the world to give aid and joy to all beings. He brings down the rains of the nectar of Dharma everywhere and nourishes all beings. Therefore, Ānanda, exert yourself in the Dharma of the Buddha with onepointedness of mind."

When the Lord had thus spoken all believed and rejoiced.

50

The Lion With the Firm Mind

❧

Thus have I heard at one time: the Enlightened One was residing in the city of Rājagṛha on the Vulture's Peak. At that time Devadatta who constantly harbored evil thought toward the Buddha, was thinking: "I shall do away with the Tathagata and set myself up as the Enlightened One." He spoke to Prince Ajātaśatru as follows: "Prince, it would be well if you were to kill your father and ascend the throne yourself. It would be well if a new Buddha and a new king were to rule the country properly." Thereupon Prince Ajātaśatru murdered his father and usurped the throne. Among the people of that country, this created an ill feeling toward the monks. When the disciples came to the city to beg, they were given nothing and returned with empty alms-bowls.

The monks then went to the Vulture's Peak and reported to the Buddha. "Lord, Devadatta has led the masters of gifts into sin. They now dislike the monks and refuse to give alms." The Lord then said to Ānanda: "Ānanda, when beings bring forth evil thoughts toward the monks who have donned the red robe, they also bring forth evil thoughts concerning the Buddhas, the Pratyekabuddhas, and the arhats of the past, present, and future. When they bring forth evil thoughts concerning the Holy Ones of the three times, the fruits of this sin are inconceivable and inexhaustible. Why is this? It is because the religious robe is the badge of the Conquerors of the three times. Those who shave their hair and beard and put on the dyed religious robe will quickly become liberated from suffering, will stop the outflows, will attain to Transcendental Wisdom, and will become a refuge, a protector and a savior to all sentient beings. He who brings forth a mind of faith toward those who have become monks and put on the dyed robe will obtain countless virtues. Formerly, Ānanda, through reverently honoring the monks who had donned the dyed religious robes, I became a

Perfect Buddha." Ānanda said: "Lord, I beg you to relate how you formerly honored the monks who wore the dyed robe."

The Buddha said: "Ānanda, listen carefully and bear it well in mind. In times long past, countless aeons ago, there was a king in this Jambudvīpa by the name of Śaṅkara who ruled over eighty-four thousand lesser kings. At that time there was no Buddha teaching in the world, and the Pratyekabuddhas who lived in the mountains and forests would fly through the air to aid beings and were often cared for by wild animals. At one time, there lived in the mountains a resplendent, golden-haired lion called Firm Mind who ate only herbs and fruits and harmed no living creature. A certain hunter, seeing this lion, rejoiced and thought: 'I am indeed fortunate. I shall kill this lion and take its golden pelt to the king, who will reward me and I shall be rich.' Shaving his hair and beard, he put on the religious robe, concealed his bow and arrows under his arm, and went to where the lion was. Finding it asleep, he shot it a poisoned arrow. The lion awoke and sprang to attack, but seeing the religious robe, thought: 'This man will not be long in the world. He will soon be liberated from all suffering. Why is this? It is because this robe is the badge of all the Holy Ones of the past, present, and future. If I were to harm him this would harm the Holy Ones of the three times.' Putting aside all thoughts of killing, he said as he was parting from this life: 'A-lā-la, ba-sā-sa, svāhā!' Immediately the sky and the earth trembled, and although there were no clouds, rain fell. The gods searched for the cause of this and when they saw with their divine eye that a hunter had killed a bodhisattva living in the forest in the form of a lion, they let fall a shower of flowers of the gods and honored the lion's body.

"The hunter skinned the lion and took the pelt to King Śaṅkara and asked for a gift in return. The king thought: 'In the scriptures it is written that an animal with golden hair is either a bodhisattva or one of the great Holy Ones. It would not be right to give this man a gift. If I were to do this, I would be as guilty as he.' He gave the man a trifling present and asked: 'When you killed the lion were there any unusual signs?' The hunter said: 'When the lion lay dying it said eight words, the heavens and earth trembled and rain came down out of a cloudless sky. The gods also sent down a shower of flowers.' When the king heard this he was deeply grieved and faith and reverence arose in his mind. He called together his ministers and ancient wisemen and inquired concerning the lion's words, but no one could explain them. The king then invited a certain wise rishi by the name of Śyāma who lived in a remote hermitage. When the rishi had come, he asked him the meaning of the lion's words. The rishi said: 'A-lā-la means that only the person who has shaved his hair and beard and puts on the dyed religious robe will be quickly liberated from birth and death. Ba-sā-sa means that those who shave their hair and beards and put on the religious robe have drawn near to the wisdom of the Holy Ones and the bliss of Nirvana. Svāhā means that those who shave their hair and beards and have put on the religious robes are honored by gods and men throughout the three worlds.' When the rishi had explained this, the king rejoiced greatly and called together his eighty-four thousand minor kings. He then constructed a carriage of the seven precious jewels, placed the lion's skin on it, and ordered that it be exhibited to all and honored with flowers and incense. He made a golden casket, placed the lion's skin in it, and enclosed it in a stupa. All those who pondered on these virtues were reborn among the gods when they died.

"Ānanda, because that lion brought forth a mind of virtue toward the man who wore the religious robe, he was born as a cakravartin monarch for a hundred-thousand kalpas. Because he gave happiness to all beings and performed acts of virtue, he became a Buddha. You must not think that that lion was anyone else. I myself was that lion. The king who honored the lion's skin, was reborn as a leader of gods and men throughout ten long kalpas, and who created perfect virtue is now the bodhisattva Maitreya. Śāriputra was the rishi. The hunter who killed the lion was Devadatta."

When the Buddha had thus spoken, the great assembly rejoiced greatly and said: "Lord, not understanding the Buddha's great virtues, we do evil deeds, even before him. But we repent and confess these evil deeds." In great compassion, the Buddha then taught the Four Truths in accordance with the former causes of each. Some became streamwinners, some once-returners, some never-returners, some became arhats. Some brought forth a mind of Supreme Enlightenment. Then Ānanda and the four classes of hearers had faith in the Buddha's word and rejoiced.

51

The History of the Lizard

❦

Thus have I heard at one time: the Enlightened One was residing on the Vulture's Peak in the city of Rājagṛha. At that time, there was a large pond near the city into which the people threw their waste. In the pond there lived a large, four-footed lizard which was similar to a snake. The lizard had lived in this pond for countless years and undergone endless misery. Sometimes it stayed in the water, sometimes it came out on the banks. Upon a certain occasion the Buddha and his followers came to the pond and when the Lord saw the lizard, he asked the monks whether they knew by reason of what former causes the lizard was there. None of them knew, and they requested the Buddha to explain it to them.

The Buddha said: "Monks, listen well and bear it well in mind. In times long past, when the Buddha Vipaśyin had come to the world to aid beings and had passed into final Nirvana, there were four-thousand monks who followed the pure course. They dwelt in a hermitage on the side of a mountain. To the east and west of the hermitage there were fruit trees and herbs in abundance, and among the trees there was a delightful site with a spring of sparkling water. At that time, by dint of great exertion, all the monks had attained from the first to the fourth fruits.

Upon a certain occasion, five-hundred merchants who were going to sea in search of precious gems. They lost their way and by chance arrived at the mountain where the monks lived. Seeing the monks' great exertion in coursing, they wished to make offerings and vowed that if they returned without mishap from their sea-voyage, they would make gifts to the Sangha. This the monks approved in silence. The merchants went to sea, found great treasure, and returning safe and sound, offered great treasure to the monks. The Noble Sangha accepted it and put it in charge of the monk who managed the Sangha's affairs. Some time later, when the alms-supplies had become exhausted, they thought of using the treasure and told the custodian: 'Monk, take the treasure given us by the merchants and sell it in order to obtain supplies.' The monk said: 'The treasure was given to me alone, not to you.' The Sangha replied: 'The treasure was not given to you at all. It was given to the entire assembly and merely entrusted to you for safekeeping.' The monk then became angry and said: 'Don't you eat until you vomit? And don't claim the treasure as yours. It isn't. It belongs to me.' When the Sangha saw that the monk was of an evil mind and had given way to anger, they dispersed, each monk going to his own place.

"Because of that monk's evil intentions toward the Noble Sangha, when he died he fell into hell and underwent inconceivable suffering, in unspeakable filth, for ninety-one kalpas. Liberated from hell, he was reborn in this filthy pond and has suffered here for aeons. The former Buddha Sikhin came to this pond with his monks, saw the lizard, and explained its former deeds, and so did the Buddhas Viśvabhuj, Kanakamuni, and Kāśyapa. And now I, the Buddha Śākyamuni, tell you the history of this lizard and the thousand Buddhas of the future good aeon will also come to the banks of this pond and tell the history of this lizard."

When the monks had heard this teaching of the Buddha, they were so exceedingly terrified that their hair stood on end. Thereafter each monk guarded the workings of his body, speech, and mind. All believed and rejoiced in the Buddha's word.

52

The Monk Kyunte

❦

Thus have I heard at one time: the Enlightened One was residing in the city of Śrāvastī at the Jetavana monastery in
Anāthapiṇḍika's park. At that time, the Noble Śāriputra would look
with his deva eyes three times during the day and three times during the night to see which beings were ready to be tamed. If he saw
that any were ready, he would go to tame them.

It so happened that, one day, a dog had followed a group of
merchants who were going to a far country to trade, stole a piece
of meat from one of the merchants, and ate it. Enraged, the merchant broke the dog's legs and left it in the desert to die. When
Śāriputra saw with his deva eye that the dog was in misery and
starving, he donned his religious robes, took his alms-bowl, and
flew through the air to where the dog was and compassionately fed
it. The dog gratefully ate the food, then Śāriputra taught it the Supreme Dharma, and it soon died. It was immediately reborn as the
son of a brahmin in the city of Śrāvastī.

Some time later when Śāriputra was begging alms and came
to that brahmin's door, the brahmin asked why he was alone and
had no companion. Śāriputra said that he had no companion and
that, if the brahmin had a son, he would be glad if he gave him to
him. The brahmin said: "I do have a son by the name of Kyunte.
Now he is too young to become a monk, but when he grows older
I shall give him to you."

Śāriputra returned to the Jetavana grove, but remembered the
brahmin's words. Seven years later again went to the brahmin's
house and asked for the boy. The brahmin gave his son to him,
Śāriputra took the boy to the Jetavana grove, ordained him, and
when he had taught him the supreme Dharma the boy's mind was
liberated and he attained to the bliss of an arhat. He then became

endowed with the five powers and grew perfect in wisdom. Later, when he investigated what deeds he had done in a former lifetime to be able to meet the holy Śāriputra and become a monk, he saw, through the power of knowledge, that he had been a dog. He saw that his present teacher, Śāriputra, had taught him the Dharma and because of this, he had now obtained a human body and attained bliss. Seeing this, he rejoiced and thought: "I have been liberated from suffering through this teacher's grace. Out of respect for the teacher and in gratitude, I shall never leave him or cease to honor him in this lifetime."

Then Ānanda said to the Buddha: "Lord, what evil deeds did this monk do in a former lifetime to be reborn as a dog?" The Buddha said: "Ānanda, in times long past, during the time of the Buddha Kāśyapa, there was a young monk who had a beautiful voice and all rejoiced when he chanted the hymns of praise. There was also an old monk who was an arhat, but he had a poor voice and chanted badly. One day the young monk with the beautiful voice insulated the old man saying: 'Oh monk, your voice sounds like a dog barking!' The old monk said: "Monk, do you know who I am?" The young monk said: 'Yes, you are a sthavira under the Buddha Kāśyapa.' When the elder monk said: 'I am an arhat endowed with all the virtues of a monk,' the younger monk was afraid, regretted what he had said, and asked forgiveness. Although the old monk wished him well and said: 'May your faults be purified,' that young monk was reborn as a dog for five-hundred lifetimes. Then, because he became a monk and kept the Precepts, he has met me and become totally liberated."

When the Buddha had thus spoken, Ānanda and the great Assembly believed and rejoiced.